S0-DVG-778

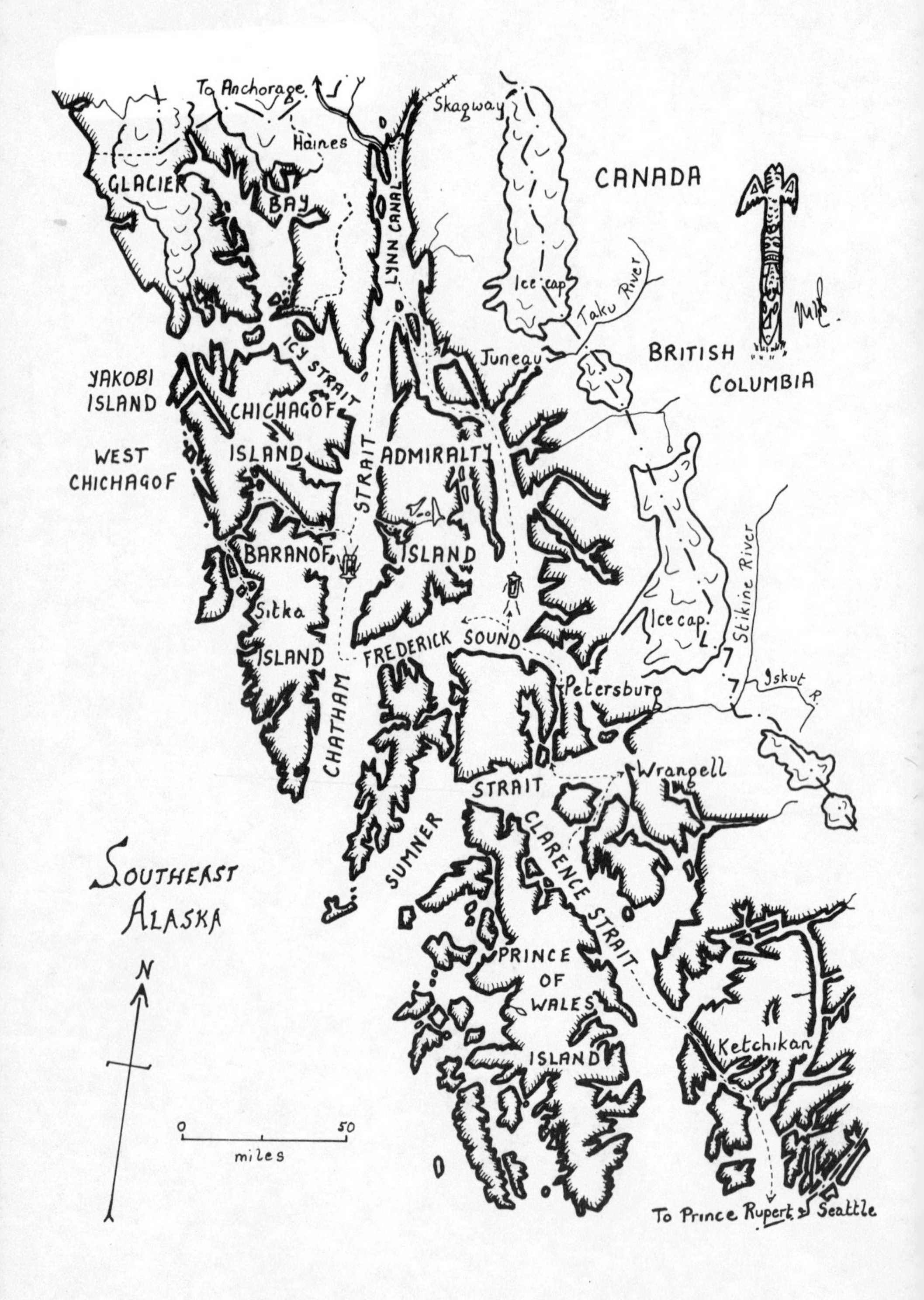

To Anchorage
Skagway
Haines
GLACIER
BAY
LYNN CANAL
CANADA
Ice cap
Taku River
Juneau
BRITISH
COLUMBIA
ICY STRAIT
YAKOBI
ISLAND
CHICHAGOF
ISLAND
WEST
CHICHAGOF
STRAIT
ADMIRALTY
ISLAND
BARANOF
Sitka
ISLAND
Ice cap.
Stikine River
FREDERICK SOUND
CHATHAM
Petersburg
Iskut R.
Wrangell
STRAIT
SUMNER
CLARENCE
STRAIT
SOUTHEAST
ALASKA
N
PRINCE
OF
WALES
ISLAND
Ketchikan
0
50
miles
To Prince Rupert & Seattle

Discover Southeast Alaska

WITH PACK AND PADDLE

Margaret H. Piggott

The Mountaineers SEATTLE

SOUTHEAST ALASKA MOUNTAINEERING ASSOCIATION

Organized 1965

To promote an interest in wilderness recreation in Southeastern Alaska.
To study the topography, history, and ecology of the Southeastern Alaska region.
To preserve by the encouragement of protective legislation or otherwise the natural beauty of the Southeastern Alaska region.
To bring together people mutually interested in wilderness recreation.

THE MOUNTAINEERS

Organized 1906

To explore and study the mountains, forests, and watercourses of the Northwest;
To gather into permanent form the history and traditions of this region;
To preserve by the encouragement of protective legislation or otherwise the natural beauty of Northwest America;
To make expeditions into these regions in fulfillment of the above purposes;
To encourage a spirit of good fellowship among all lovers of outdoor life.

Library of Congress Catalog Number: 74-81954

719 Pike Street
Seattle, Washington 98101
Manufactured in the United States of America
Second printing November 1978

Published simultaneously in Canada by
Douglas & McIntyre Ltd.
1875 Welch Street
North Vancouver, British Columbia V7P 1B7

ISBN 0-916890-35-X

Cover Photo: View of Skagway from A. B. Mountain
All maps are by the author.

To the Tongass Conservation Society,
To Polly Dyer,
And to all others who look up to the hills with love and respect.

Twin peaks from Mahoney Mountain

CONTENTS

FOREWORD

Like so many of the world's remaining wildernesses, Alaska is suffering from the heavy hand of mankind. The sentiments expressed by the regional contributors to this book reflect concern either directly or indirectly with man's alienation from his environment. The towns in Southeast Alaska, whose frontier charm is a great asset visitors travel thousands of miles to savor, are bowing to the overpowering forces of this frantic modern age and are subject to rapid changes.

While writing this guide I was able to stay one step ahead of the chain saw and bulldozer, but in the interval between writing and publication changes may have occurred. My apologies, therefore, if a route is difficult to find or follow because of recent upheaval.

Please bear with me; go into this sublimely beautiful land while it still beckons. Enjoy yourself but tread softly, do not wantonly hurt any living being, go silently and listen, leave no permanent marks of your coming or going, and return many times blessed because you entered Nature's halls with humility and trod her high places with love.

Margaret H. Piggott
Ketchikan, Alaska

ACKNOWLEDGEMENTS

Even though I wandered alone through Southeast Alaska for a summer to research most of the trails included in this volume, I could not have managed without the help of friends, both in Seattle and Southeast Alaska.

Barbara Kalen of Skagway is, in essence, my Skagway editor. She has offered criticism and advice, given support and encouragement. She is also the only person who works consistently on Skagway trails with trimmers to keep them visible within encroaching brush. My thanks to her grandson, Dale Albecher, for proving it is possible for a six-year-old youngster to reach Devil's Punchbowl in a day and enjoy the summer snows up there! Thanks also to the White Pass and Yukon Railroad for their help toward a late-season recheck of Laughton Glacier and Chilkoot trails.

The encouragement and criticism of Ray and Vivian Menaker, in whose house this book was born, is much appreciated. Credit should also be given to Paul Swift and other Haines citizens who worked to reopen the old trail up Mount Ripinski.

Chuck and Alice Johnstone and Jack Calvin, of Sitka, made my inclusion of West Chichagof possible. Chuck Johnstone also worked to render my kayak unsinkable. This, I am ashamed to say, was after two months spent in Glacier Bay with questionable flotation. (If anyone wishes to emulate my mistakes, he should be sure to have been born under a lucky star! It is an experience I never wish to repeat.) Thanks also to Dr. George and Dee Longenbaugh for their support.

Robert Howe, Superintendent, Glacier Bay National Monument, Greg and Barbara Streveller, Bruce Paige, Charles Janda, Dennis and Manya Wik, and Penny and Mike Ruks helped to make my trip to Glacier Bay not only possible but enjoyable.

In Juneau, Joe and Kay Greenough, Tom and Carol McCabe, Jackie and Elmer Landingham, and Michael and Terri Ellis helped with support, advice, and transportation. Richard Powers, Chatham Ranger District, U.S. Forest Service, kept me up to date with information on Forest Service trails.

Bob and Edith Nelson of Thayer Lake Lodge encouraged me to visit Admiralty Island, a decision never to be regretted. The time spent on the island was the highlight of a glorious summer. Thanks are also due to Jon and Lesley Lyman for their hospitality in Angoon and for showing me Kootznahoo Inlet shortly after the tide had turned. The sight of those tidal falls, rapids, rips, and white wall of water was unforgettable.

Petersburg trail possibilities were discussed and trails examined with

Virginia Colp, to whom my thanks are due for her interest and help. Orvel and Carmen Holum, Jay Snodderly, and Ed K. Browne were instrumental in making possible the Ketchikan section of the book. Pete Martin of Anchorage rescued my Glacier Bay photographs, regrettably overexposed, from complete failure.

In Seattle, Ira Spring's advice and blunt criticism were invaluable and instrumental in upgrading my photographic efforts. Al Robinson consistently took care of the small but important details I tried to avoid! Many thanks also to Sherry Filbin, who helped with the final drafts on the maps; Ward Irwin, who checked the canoe section; and John and Polly Dyer, ex-Alaskans, in whose house the bulk of the manuscript was written.

The poem "Break Up" originally appeared in *Cultus Coulee* by Charles Lillard (Sono Nis Press, Surrey, British Columbia, 1971) and is reprinted here by permission of the author.

Margaret H. Piggott
Haines, Alaska

BREAK UP

Snow country.
Glaciers calve in this goose-weather
And these excesses of God leach the warm.

A white landscape lurking in the angles
Of a barbiturate calm.
A black frontier, keening ground beyond
The rood's shadow.
Too quick for the camera,
You linger in myth and rune.
The inanimate Basilisk.

The blind hand reaches out.
Wolves howl from their pulpit of bones,
A million years old tonight.

Charles Lillard

INTRODUCTION

Southeast Alaska Panhandle has one of the finest coastlines in the world, and even in this mercenary age it retains unsurpassed wilderness. On its north and east boundaries mountain ranges shoot up from tidewater, relentlessly scored and ravaged by the forces of wind and water and ice. Long, probing fingers of the sea penetrate the coastline in sheer-walled fjords and, in the more northerly latitudes, meet head-on the glaciers which carve their path to the sea under the tremendous pressure of the icecaps above. The mountains range in altitude from 6000 feet in the south to 18,000 feet east of Yakutat, 500 miles northwest of Ketchikan.

Islands float offshore, their snow-covered peaks and rock spires, 4000 to 6000 feet high, guarded by a blue-green mantle of rain forests. Threading its way between the islands and the mainland is a "Marine Highway," or "Inside Passage," that connects the towns within the Panhandle, which, with the exception of Haines and Skagway, have no other surface communication with the Outside.

The virgin forests of Sitka spruce, yellow and red cedar, mountain and western hemlock, and lodgepole pine that blanket the mainland and the islands are the soul of the Panhandle. Their perfume pervades the atmosphere and they march in wave after wave over the foothills, to be stopped only by the highest peaks and the tidewaters — or by the chain saw. These great rain forests, and the wildlife and plant life they support, enter inevitably into the soul of this book, since most trails start and end in tall trees or gain access to glaciers or alpine meadows through the forests.

The trails described in this book are practically all on public land, most of it administered by the U.S. Forest Service. Some trails are long — the 35-mile Chilkoot takes two to four days, for instance; some are short, like the trail to the petroglyphs in Wrangell, which is only a few yards; and some are reached only by canoe or kayak. All are interesting and have something unique to offer, whether it is a close-up of the forest floor, a breathtaking view, a sight of wildlife, or a glimpse into gold rush history. All the trails that are worthwhile and reasonably accessible are recorded. Most outlying U.S. Forest Service trails, reached only by plane or boat, are excluded.

The book's organization is based on the towns linked by the Marine Highway ferry system. The regions described follow a logical sequence from south to north, following the northbound ferry route. In addition, three exceptional wilderness areas are described which require bush flights or special boat charter to gain access to their inner recesses. All three are threatened in one way or another: Glacier Bay by mining, West Chichagof and Admiralty Island by logging and subsequent intrusion of roads into wilderness.

ACCESS

The Alaska Panhandle is barely visible on most maps and few people realize it exists until they read the cruise ship and Marine Highway literature. To many, Alaska is a land of permafrost and igloos. In fact it has a temperate coastline almost half the length of California's, and the major industries are fishing, tourism, and the export of wood products to Japan. Size is the forgotten factor. Anchorage is two time zones northwest of Southeast Alaska and 1100 miles from Ketchikan, situated at the southern end of the Panhandle. The closest major U.S. city is Seattle, Washington, 700 air miles from Ketchikan and 930 air miles from Juneau.

The State of Alaska has a Marine Highway System — a ferry service connecting Seattle and Prince Rupert, B.C., with the ports of Ketchikan, Wrangell, Petersburg, Sitka, Juneau, Haines, and Skagway. A smaller ferry runs between Juneau and Hoonah on the south shore of Icy Strait on Chichagof Island. Ferries are planned to other small towns.

During the summer season the ferries are crowded; reservations must be made well in advance for car space and limited stateroom accommodation. At no extra cost airplane-type seating is available on all ferries for those who choose to sit up all night. At present, the least crowded times to travel northbound are from late August to the end of May, and southbound from October to late June. For information on schedules and prices write to the Alaska Marine Highway System, Pouch R, Juneau, Alaska 99801.

The present policy of the Alaska Marine Highway allows kayaks and canoes to be carried aboard free by fare-paying passengers during slack periods when deck space is readily available, but this policy may change in the future with a change in demand. Large groups should arrange their schedules beforehand with the Traffic Manager, Pouch R, Juneau. The same policy at present applies to bicycles (nonmotor).

The three major cities of Southeast Alaska, Ketchikan, Sitka, and Juneau, have direct jet airline connections with Seattle and Anchorage. All the other towns have regular flights and floatplane or amphibious bush flight operations. Haines is linked by road with the Alaska Highway, and Skagway is linked by railroad with Whitehorse, Yukon Territory.

Many trails start within walking distance of ferry terminals and cruise ship tie-up points, and they have been described with this in mind. However, transportation is needed to most other trails starting beyond city boundaries, and this may present a problem to some visitors from Outside. A bus service connects Juneau, Douglas, and Auke Bay; Ketchikan has bus service between the center of town and the ferry terminal 1.5 miles north. Taxis are available in all towns. Bicycles are a suggested alternative form of transportation in rural areas for impecunious outdoorsmen. Those wishing to park their cars at the roadhead in Haines may do so for a small charge at most garages.

Flights into back country (e.g., West Chichagof and Admiralty Islands) are floatplane, bush operations limited by current weather conditions. Since poor weather can delay flights for one or two days, parties relying on a plane rendezvous should take more food than necessary for the expected length of stay. Alaska Discovery Wilderness Adventures, P.O. Box 41, Haines, Alaska 99827, runs kayak tours to Glacier Bay and Admiralty Island for those who would prefer to have their itineraries planned for them and/or do not have their own boats.

WEATHER

Good weather is a gamble. Some summers are consistently sunny, others notorious for the frequency of rainstorms. But bad weather has its advantages, too — the greatest clarity and, it seems, the greatest beauty, come after a rainstorm. The mountains glisten, and at times appear to have taken two steps forward.

Rainfall is heavy in the Southeast Alaska Panhandle, and raingear and waterproof boots are important for most trails. Ketchikan has an annual average of 154 inches, Juneau 86 inches, Sitka 96 inches; Haines and

Skagway have only 60 and 26 inches, respectively. There is less precipitation in summer than winter, the wettest month being October. Fresh water is usually available, especially at alpine levels, except on small tidal islands and during late dry summers after the snow melt has gone.

A warm current parallels the coastline, resulting in a generally temperate climate. Haines and Skagway have a greater variation between summer and winter temperatures than other areas because they are more inland, sheltered by the St. Elias Range from open Pacific Ocean.

The following are normal daily maximum temperatures, summer and winter:

	May to September	*November to March*
Ketchikan	62°F	38°F
Sitka	57°F	35°F
Juneau	59°F	29°F
Haines	62°F	27°F
Skagway	63°F	27°F

Winter lows in Haines and Skagway may occasionally reach −20°F, with strong winds adding a chill factor of slightly more than 1° for every mile per hour of wind speed. Juneau also suffers from strong Taku winds, with winter temperatures occasionally below zero. A clear, sunny, summer day in the Panhandle may have temperatures as high as 80 or 85°F. but when rain clouds obscure the sun, temperatures will probably remain around 50°F.

If ice in any quantity is encountered in coastal waters, both air and water temperatures drop dramatically. It is often 20° colder before the face of a glacier than it is in town (or even just around the corner). Always take plenty of warm clothing in such tidal inlets.

ADMINISTRATIVE AGENCIES

About 70 percent of Southeast Alaska is administered by the U.S. Forest Service as the Tongass National Forest. Areas around the cities are administered by boroughs and the State, and other small areas are under the U.S. Bureau of Land Management. Alaska Natives own areas adjacent to their villages, and Annette Island is a reservation. Glacier Bay became a National Monument in 1925 and is a candidate for National Park status with restrictions on motor vehicle use in the back country. Some jurisdiction may change whenever the State of Alaska selects additional federal lands as provided in the Statehood Act of 1959.

Most trails in Southeast Alaska are under U.S. Forest Service management. Only a selection of them are included in this guide as many are not readily accessible to roadheads, and others (especially South Tongass) have not been maintained for many years. Almost all trails close to cities will be taken over by State or local borough authorities in the wake of the recent State land selections.

Recently the North Tongass Forest Service resurrected most old miners' trails in the neighborhood of Juneau and Skagway, and C. C. C. trails on Admiralty Island. Some trails in the vicinity of Ketchikan and West Chichagof need rehabilitation; some have been affected (and others will be) by the building of access roads and extensive logging activities. South Tongass Forest Service has experimented with continuous boardwalk on some old trails, for example, Naha (not included in this guide) and Perseverance Lake. This has proved effective in areas of poor drainage, muskeg, or bogholes, but it is not aesthetically pleasing through the forests and on well-drained hill slopes. Continuous boardwalk with stairways has the added disadvantage of making winter travel difficult and unpleasant.

The map of the Tongass National Forest available from the U.S. Forest Service, Tongass National Forest, Juneau, Alaska 99801, is an excellent quick reference and also gives addresses of ranger districts and information on Forest Service cabins where available (e.g., West Chichagof, Admiralty Island, and Laughton Glacier). A fee of $5.00 a night, to help cover the cost of maintenance, is charged parties for the use of cabins. Length of stay is limited to 7 days.

Trails managed by the State of Alaska are, for the most part, in good condition. The State has assumed responsibility for the Chilkoot Trail (U.S. portion) for many years and continues to do so, although since 1972 it has been managed jointly with the National Park Service. Legislation is expected to be introduced shortly in Congress for a Klondike Gold Rush National Historical Park incorporating the Chilkoot Trail, part of the city of Skagway, White Pass, and an interpretive center in Seattle. There is a possibility that Canada also will give special status to its portion of trail.

However, plans have been tossed around for years for an international Yukon-Taiya hydroelectric power project, which, if allowed to materialize, would raise the level of Lake Lindeman 20–35 feet (the experts are not sure of the actual figure), flooding Lindeman City and Bennett townsites and forcing relocation of the historic Chilkoot Trail and the White Pass and Yukon Railroad.

WILDLIFE

Wildlife is prolific and varied in Southeast Alaska, ranging from mice to Alaska brown bear (known also as the grizzly). Douglas squirrels, martens, and mice are diminutive but bewitching creatures whose liquid eyes, twitching noses, and playful tricks enchant the onlooker. But do not be fooled. They will happily steal unattended food from the careless

Sitka black-tailed deer (R. T. Wallen)

camper and leave him to starve in the wilderness. Those who use backwoods shelters and toilets will discover that porcupine dearly love to nibble such structures (see S9, Laughton Glacier). Their penchant for chewing through old tires on abandoned cars is not so well known, but could become a source of embarrassment to anyone who leaves a parked vehicle unattended for a few days in the neighborhood of a rubber-addicted porcupine.

Wolves and black bears are found only on the islands south of Frederick Sound and on the mainland, whereas brown bears are found only on the islands north of Frederick Sound and on the mainland. Otters, beavers, minks, and Sitka black-tailed deer are fairly widespread; moose range in the Stikine, Taku, and Chilkat River flats. Coyotes, mountain goats, wolverines, and lynx are present on the mainland, although the latter two species are rarely seen.

In tidal waters, harbor seals, killer whales, harbor and Dall porpoises, and humpback whales are commonly seen. Killer whales are readily recognized by their prominent dorsal fin which cuts the water like a knife. Dall porpoises are sedate and quiet, surfacing with a sigh, apparently oblivious to the presence of a canoe. Their cousins, the harbor porpoises, by contrast, are playful and pit swimming skills against the oncoming prows of motor vessels.

Steelhead, Dolly Varden, cutthroat, rainbow trout, and the five varieties of anadromous Pacific salmon may be seen in the streams and rivers, depending on the season. A fishing pole is a definite asset on short walks as well as long overnight hikes. Some of the trails near Juneau offer winter fishing through the ice (e.g., Windfall Lake). A State fishing license must be obtained before fishing anywhere within the State of Alaska, including Glacier Bay National Monument. Applications may be made through the Department of Commerce, Juneau, or any sporting goods store in Southeast Alaska.

Wolves

The wolf is an embattled species. Driven out of Europe and the southern part of the North American continent by superstitious fear and hatred, the wolf has found his last frontier. His wild, mournful cries are still heard across the unspoiled wilderness of Alaska and northern Canada. Yet even here the wolf is a villain; his subsistence is those game animals coveted by man, and he is relentlessly persecuted.

Men blame the wolf for their own lack of hunting success. In Southeast Alaska, prime game in the forests are deer, but the deer's main limiting factor is winter, not wolves. Deer seek forage along the beaches in winter and are dependent on forest trails, avoiding deep snow in open areas, to lead them to the littoral zone. In severe winters, the availability of forage is limited to a thin strip along the beaches, and many deer do not survive whether they are in wolf range or not. Even so, the wolf is blamed for both real and apparent lack of deer, and a hue and cry has been raised to reinitiate a poisoning program.

Packs of dogs, allowed to run at will by their owners, roam the villages and towns of Southeast Alaska and are more likely to be responsible for deer maulings and other mischief than are wolves. Why do so many fear wolves? My meetings have been ones of wonder and respect. The obvious distress of two wolves, close to what must have been a denning area, gave me the sense of intruding into a private home. When I finally retreated in response to their desolate howling, the wolves politely followed me to the invisible line that marked the edge of their territory, and in unison howled a farewell. Their soaring song was deeply moving. Let's hope my generation is not the last to hear it.

Brown and Black Bears

Alaska brown bears are synonymous with the grizzly indigenous to the western states and Canada. Black bears have many color phases, from cinnamon to the rare blue glacial bear, and lack the massive size and hump of the brown bear.

Both species demand respect from those who hike in the woods, as their behavior is unpredictable and potentially dangerous. If common sense and care are exercised, however, most direct confrontation with bears can be avoided. A shrill whistle will deter bears which are merely curious and not already annoyed or cornered. A bell with a high frequency sound, attached to boots or pack, will warn most bears of a person's presence and — most important — will give a mother bear a chance to retreat with her cubs to a safe distance. Mothballs are sometimes carried by hikers, especially those planning to camp, because of their reputation for discouraging bears; if nothing else, they mask the odor of food.

Campers should keep their food well away from tents and canoes; it is best hung in a tree at least 100 feet away. Cans should be washed immediately after being emptied. Since fish probably has the greatest attraction for bears, be sure no fish odor persists around boats or camp.

Although some people (including those in the U.S. Forest Service and the State of Alaska's Division of Parks) advocate guns, their effectiveness is debatable. Confrontations with bears are rare, and a high ratio of gun-toting individuals in the woods creates its own hazards. Besides, the marksman must be a good enough shot to kill the bear with the first bullet, as a second chance is rarely available. Bears do not die easily and when wounded are doubly dangerous, at that time or in the future. Carrying a gun is an individual decision, but it includes responsibilities toward others who are in the woods.

Birds

No wilderness experience is complete without the howling of red-throated loons. Their evening dirge slides down the atonal scale like the wail of banshees before a funeral. Their second theme, a bloodcurdling, burbling, rising laughter, evokes scenes from Macbeth. Once heard and identified, these cries will never be confused with the falsetto-tremolo whistle of the common loon.

Despite their spine-tingling lament, red-throated loons are wary birds

Bald eagle in flight (R. T. Wallen)

that flush off the water when approached, their ululations changing to querulous quacks as soon as they become airborne. By contrast, common loons yodel with resonant voices on the wing and in the water. When disturbed they will dive, but they are often curious and will swim toward a canoe singing softly. Arctic loons are less numerous and rarely heard.

These beautiful birds form a triad with coyotes and wolves as eloquent, self-appointed spokesmen for wilderness. When they are gone, wilderness as we know it is also gone.

This nation's emblem, the bald eagle, is common throughout the coastal islands and is seen especially over tidal waters and salmon streams. In fact, the ubiquity of this magnificent raptor is a source of pride to Southeast Alaska, and many Alaskans share the pleasure of watching its intimate life habits and battles through the kitchen window while washing the dishes. Sightings are made frequently from ferries and tour ships, much to the joy of visitors, and even those who never ordinarily notice a fluff of feathers in flight (unless destined for the dinner table) are impressed by the bald eagle's majesty and mastery of the sky.

The Panhandle would lose its sparkle without ravens — gregarious, noisy, and unkempt clowns seen within the confines of most towns and villages. They turn somersaults in the air, then make the onlooker gulp by dropping like a stone out of sight. They banter and cajole. Their rich repertoire of liquid bell-like tones, honkings, gurglings, and clickings fills the air with staccato sound. They mob birds twice their size and hurl obscenities at each other and at passing ships. The raven has been deified and endowed with mystical powers by the Tlingit Indians and other Northwest Coast tribes. A bird so personable, possessing a sense of humor so appealing to man, is worthy of such an honor.

In spring when the cottonwood pervades the atmosphere with its sweet fragrance, varied thrushes sketch a sound profile mornings and evenings, with single, quavering, flute-like whistles repeated in different keys. Other thrushes repeat their songs, and small birds such as warblers enliven the bushes with a flash of color and their own inimitable ditties. Sparrows give plaintive calls, grouse boom in hill slopes, and willow ptarmigans, Alaska's State bird, sharply warn hikers to "go-baaakk go-baaakk." The ptarmigan also enjoys sliding down tent flies at 5:00 A.M.!

The Panhandle is rich in water birds (trumpeter swans winter in undisturbed back country on some islands) and predators (merlins, sparrowhawks, and golden eagles are occasionally seen above alpine meadows). Other birds such as kingfishers, creepers, woodpeckers, and dippers add their personalities to the forests and shores.

Those wishing a more comprehensive checklist for Southeast Alaska should write to the Alaska Department of Fish and Game, Subport Building, Juneau 99801.

Devil's club

FLORA

Rain Forests

Virgin rain forests have a spacious, cathedral-like quality with light shafting among huge trees, and moss-covered floors sometimes smothered with Canadian dogwood. Selectively logged areas leave much the same effect since damage is minimal, but old clear-cuts are not pleasant for hiking through since thick undergrowth and logging debris bar the way. Logging activity is extensive on the islands and mainland around Haines and much of it can be seen from the ferry. The forests surrounding many of the cities have seen logging at one time or another: Sitka by the Russians over 100 years ago, and Juneau by miners at the turn of the century. Skagway and Haines lost part of their virgin forests to fires, shortly after the gold rush.

The forests of the Alaska Panhandle are composed mainly of western hemlock and Sitka spruce. Mountain hemlock is found especially at higher elevations, and lodgepole pine is found in mixed stands above Skagway but otherwise on the edges of the forest in open areas. There are red and yellow cedar stands in the southern half of the Panhandle and isolated groves farther north.

Learn to recognize the devil's club (a member of the ginseng family) as soon as possible. It is a ubiquitous plant whose large, umbrella-like leaves grow on long, spiny stalks that sometimes reach a height of 10 feet. In fall, vertical clusters of red berries ripen in the center of the plant and the leaves turn a radiant golden-brown. Although devil's club is highly photogenic and beautiful, avoid contact at all costs. Fine barbs penetrate the skin and will stay for a week or more. It is advisable to wear leather gloves on hikes, especially when descending steep slopes, as invariably the devil's club is the only solid plant within reach when a slip occurs!

Skunk cabbage is found in muddy places and often in the middle of wet trails. In spring the plant is pale yellow, but it is noted for its coarse green leaves later in the year and is used as forage by bears and deer. Various mosses, ferns, lichens, and mushrooms add to the kaleidoscope of colors and patterns on the forest floor.

Muskeg

Every now and again, usually on poorly drained soils, the flow of forest falters and the trees part. Stunted pines and cedars hover nervously around the edge of the clearing and advance tentatively into the opening, seeking a delicate balance between a desire for light and a dislike for waterlogged soils. These clearings may be a few yards in diameter or several miles long in a series of meadows, and are generally referred to as "muskeg." They are frequently found on ridge tops or extended over large flat stretches and are characterized by brackish peat pools, beaver ponds, and bog.

Both muskeg and forest are lush with cranberries, blueberries, huckleberries, etc., and flowers are found in profuse growth, ranging from blue asters, forget-me-nots (Alaska's State flower), and monkshood to white pyrolus, Grass of Parnassus, swamp gentian, mauve columbines, and fireweed.

When crossing muskeg, do not miss the minuscule kingdom found at foot level. Tiny, red, insectivorous plants, standing an inch or so tall and shaped very like pincushions, thrive in bog. They are commonly called sundew; particularly fine examples of two types, *Drosera rotundifolia*,

Skunk cabbage

with racket-shaped leaves, and *Drosera angelica*, with spatulate leaves, are found in abundance on the White Sulphur Springs trail, West Chichagof. Sundew are also found in the Spaulding Meadows, Juneau and almost any other muskeg. The leaves are covered with sticky barbs to entrap small flies, and on dew-laden mornings they sparkle like jewels. Bog violet or butterwort (*Pinguicula vulgaris*) is another insectivorous plant found in muskeg. The blue flower is violet-like, but it can be distinguished by its pale green, waxy leaves. As soon as a fly alights, the leaves curl up and digestive juices are secreted over the hapless victim.

Alpine Regions

At tree line trees diminish in size and then disappear altogether as heather, heath, grass, moss, and lichen gain the ascendency. The upper limit of tree growth is almost 2500 feet above Ketchikan, 2000 feet above Sitka, and 3200 feet above Haines and Skagway, which is situated at the head of a protected, landlocked inlet. Above the tree line is the alpine zone, and after snow melt in late summer it is often smothered with flowers such as lupine, cranesbill, columbine, gentian, moss campion, and various saxifrages.

Beaches

Some robust plants have the awkward habit of growing in areas of periodic tidal inundations. ("Awkward" because lush, innocent-appearing growths in the intertidal zone can encourage campers to set their tents below the high tide mark.) Examples include various saltwater grasses, plantains (goose tongue), and cinquefoil, a pretty yellow flower belonging to the rose family.

Goose tongue and sea-beach sandwort (seapurslane) are edible, succulent beach greens found in patches throughout the Panhandle within the littoral zone. Attractive white flowers of strawberry carpet many beaches, and the blue-green leaves and small, bell-like flowers of *Mertensia* (lungwort) hug the ground, radiating outward like the spokes of a wheel. Purple fields of fireweed give a blaze of color to the stream banks, and dwarf fireweed and coltsfoot add color to the rocks above the tidal zone.

Glacier Bay is a distinct entity. Because of recent, rapid glacial recession and continual uplift, vegetation in the upper reaches of the bay is sparse. Early pioneers are two species of mountain avens, *Dryas drummondii* and *Dryas octopetala*, with yellow and white flowers respectively; moss campion in robust mats of tiny pink flowers; and equisetum, a brilliant green horsetail frequently found close to streams. Mountain avens excels as a soil binder, *D. octopetala* forming dense mats over the ground. Its toehold in sedimentary gravels is fragile, although tenacious, and encourages growth of secondary soil binders such as alder, cottonwood, and willow. Spruce then gradually takes over and attains supremacy, with park-like forests similar to those around Bartlett Cove becoming established after about 150 years.

For a small charge, booklets entitled *Wild, Edible and Poisonous Plants of Alaska* and *Know Alaska's Mushrooms* may be obtained from the University of Alaska, Co-operative Extension Service, Box 109, Juneau 99801.

EQUIPMENT

STOP! Think before going out! Ask yourself whether you could survive a night in the open with the clothes you have with you and whatever extras may happen to be in your pocket. Even those going for a short walk should ask this question, as the temptation is to go farther than originally intended or to wander off the trail.

The Mountaineers have compiled a list of Ten Essentials — items that they consider essential for survival. These are: (1) extra food, (2) extra clothing, (3) map, (4) compass, (5) matches, (6) firestarter, (7) knife, (8) first aid kit, (9) flashlight, and (10) sunglasses.

Extra Food

This can consist of chocolate, candy, nuts, or other high-energy food stuffed into a pocket or rucksack.

Extra Clothing

Walk in shorts and short-sleeved shirt if you prefer, but always take long pants and a long-sleeved *wool* sweater, with rain- or windproof outer jacket. Woolen socks should be worn, and warm hat and gloves taken.

The importance of wool to maintain body heat (especially when clothing is wet) cannot be overemphasized. The chances of getting wet in Southeast Alaska are higher than in most other places, so wool plays an even more important role here in holding off the insidious onset of hypothermia. Wet down is practically useless, since it loses almost all its insulating properties; down should only be used as an alternative to wool when temperatures are likely to be well below freezing. Similarly, cotton does not maintain body warmth when wet through.

Raingear is a valuable asset for all lowland trails in Southeast Alaska, and rainproof pants and jacket are indispensable for hiking through wet brush. On high, exposed mountain slopes and ridges windproof clothing over wool is a good combination for summer rainstorms and wet snow. Rainproof material allows condensation on the inside during heavy exertion and may cause as thorough a soaking as would a good dose of rain. All raingear used for hiking should be well ventilated to allow the escape of moisture.

Map and Compass

These items really go together and all people who stray from roads or beaches should understand how to use both (see page 26, Orientation). Even Alaskans supposedly familiar with their local terrain have become lost in the woods when walking, mushrooming, berry-picking, or hunting, because they did not have these essential items. The best alpine trails can be lost when fog creeps up from below or settles down from above. A sudden weather change of this sort can catch the uninitiated or unobservant hiker unawares and radically alter his chances of safety unless map and compass are available. (Fog can also drastically lower air temperatures; thus, the need for warm clothing.)

Maps may be obtained in person from the U.S. Geological Survey on the fourth floor of the Federal Building, Juneau; or by writing to the U.S.G.S., Fairbanks, Alaska 99701 or U.S.G.S., Federal Center, Denver, Colorado 80225. The maps referred to in this guide are the U.S.G.S. series 1:63,360 (scale of 1 inch to 1 mile) unless otherwise indicated. These maps are topographic and adequate for most uses. Note that the scale is slightly different from that of the U.S.G.S. 15 minute series (1:62,500 or approximately 1 inch to 1 mile) in common usage in most of the States.

Matches and Firestarter

Extra warmth from a fire may be a life-saving factor if you are lost, wet, or cold. Smoke signals are often the only way to attract attention in Southeast Alaska's heavily forested terrain, where most searching is done from the air. Even on the beach, a fire is still the best way to attract attention when in distress.

Matches should be waterproofed. This can be done by dipping them individually into melted household wax, then letting them dry. They can then be wrapped in a wax-soaked rag to hold them together, if preferred. (The rag is useful as a firestarter.) The best matches to use are the large kitchen kind — not book matches. Do not take cigarette lighters instead of matches, although they can be used as an additional source of fire.

A candle makes a good firestarter. In an emergency, pitch from pine trees may be used. During or after a heavy rainstorm, look for red cedar bark on the underside of leaning or fallen trees, and low dead spruce branches for kindling.

Knife, First Aid Kit and Flashlight

These items are self-explanatory. The flashlight may not seem necessary, but it can become a desperate necessity when the return has been delayed by unforeseen circumstances. Extra batteries should also be taken.

Sunglasses

These are essential in the winter, on summer snows (usually found above tree line), and on open water.

Other Equipment

Sturdy hiking or climbing boots are needed for alpine trips, although rubber boots with lug soles and tops extending to mid-calf are just as necessary for low, wet hikes through the forests.

In bear country tie a bell to boot or pack. A whistle may also be a deterrent to bears in the vicinity (see page 17).

Strong twine, rope, and a signal mirror are useful. Nylon cord should always be taken when snowshoeing, in case of trouble with the bindings. Cord may also be used to wrap around the snowshoe frame for greater traction on steep slopes. Brush trimmers (small garden shears) are helpful on poorly maintained trails, and insect repellent becomes a necessity during the summer months.

A waterproof fly-sheet is recommended for all tents. A porous inner tent will then allow the escape of moisture and discourage condensation. It is advisable to have a mosquito net fitted into the doorway.

RIVER CROSSINGS

All rivers should be treated with respect; their dangers are not always apparent at first sight. But if common sense is used, many of the potential hazards of river crossings can be avoided. When planning to cross:

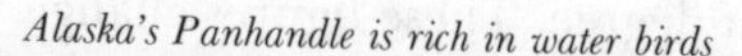
Alaska's Panhandle is rich in water birds

1. Look for the widest place, where current speed and depth are diminished. If the river runs into a lake or bay, cross as close to the mouth as possible since (a) volume is sometimes less, due to seepage into the gravel beds, and (b) braided channels often occur, each easier to cross individually.
2. Take socks off but leave boots on to allow for firmer footing.
3. Undo pack waistband.
4. Use a long stick for counterbalance, or link hands. Sometimes a handline or a belay with a rope is necessary.
5. Keep feet apart, and face upcurrent if difficulty occurs.
6. Measure the party's ability to cross by its weakest member.

On warm, sunny days, a stream that presents no difficulties in the early morning can become a raging torrent by afternoon at times of snow melt or when glaciers are its source. Be prepared for large chunks of floating ice in glacial rivers and rolling rocks in all streams; the impact of such missiles can knock a person off balance. In murky waters, a common characteristic of glacial torrents, the leader should probe the bottom with his stick to eliminate the possibility of deep holes in the crossing area.

If in doubt, *do not cross*.

ORIENTATION

Finding North

The difference between true north and magnetic north is known as "declination." Each U.S.G.S. topographic map shows the declination of the area it represents at the bottom of the sheet, and the maps in this guide show the declination to the nearest degree. These figures change imperceptibly from year to year.

The compass needle points to magnetic north, which is between 28° and 31° east of true north in Southeast Alaska. When the compass is being used in the field, set the map out on a flat spot and note the declination for the area marked on the map. Set the compass needle (usually the red end) on *magnetic* north (*x* number of degrees east of the "north" marked on the compass). The map can then be turned to correspond with true north and south. Next, identify the surrounding natural features such as peaks and valleys. This should always be done before bad weather obscures distant landmarks.

To avoid confusion, never allow the compass needle to point to the north marked on the compass when taking readings. Make sure it always points to magnetic north; if unsure of yourself, mark magnetic north on the compass for future reference. The compass north will then indicate the direction of true north. Practice lining up map and compass in familiar surroundings before going off into new terrain.

It is important to know that some metals deflect a compass needle. Be sure, when using the compass, that such things as ice axes, knives, and belt buckles remain outside the zone of influence, and be alert to the possibility of local underground ore deposits.

Learn to recognize the North Star; it is the one star which remains in a fixed position over the north axis of the earth.

Time of Day

The sun is south at noon at the center of each time zone. (The reading refers to *geographic* or "true" south, *not magnetic* south.) Also, as a general rule, the sun is east at 6:00 A.M., west at 6:00 P.M., southeast at 9:00 A.M., southwest at 3:00 P.M., northwest at 9:00 P.M, etc. The center of the Pacific time zone is 120° longitude. Ketchikan is approximately 131° 50′ longitude (11½° west of the center of the Pacific time zone), and Haines is approximately 135° longitude (15° west of the center of the Pacific time zone). The sun takes 4 minutes to travel 1° westward. Thus it is 46 minutes behind Pacific standard time in Ketchikan, and 50 minutes behind PST in Haines; therefore it is due south at 12:46 P.M. in Ketchikan, and due south at 1:00 P.M. in Haines. When daylight saving time is in effect, allowance must be made for the extra hour by subtracting 1 hour. Watches can be set by sunrise and sunset — if known — and canoeists can check theirs by high and low tides if they have an up-to-date, local tidetable. In fair weather, when a watch is not available and time is not a factor, place a stick vertically in the ground. The sun is due south when the stick shadow reaches its shortest length.

GARBAGE AND VANDALISM

Carry out all garbage, including plastic tarps; it is unsightly and unpleasant for those who follow. Never bury cans or other garbage. Bears will be attracted to the area — a serious potential problem to future hikers and campers — and the buried cache will be dug up and scattered around, inviting rodents to the scene. For convenience, take a spare plastic bag along and flatten the cans to reduce their bulk.

Please respect all private and public property found in the back country. Do not forget that any damage done to U.S. Forest Service, State, or National Park Service property is taking money out of your own pocket. Private cabins exist in almost all the areas described in this book, but their locations have been purposely omitted to discourage vandalism. Yes, even Alaska with its sparse population is afflicted with the curse of vandalism to trails, trail signs, boats, and cabins. Those within easy reach of towns, powerboats, trail bikes, snowmobiles, and roads are especially vulnerable. The cabins should be left as found — or in slightly better condition — and the firewood restocked. In the past, some cabins have been instrumental in saving the lives of lost hunters, hikers, and light plane pilots. The next life saved may be yours.

ALL TERRAIN VEHICLES

Motorized and foot traffic on the same trail are just not compatible. Trail bikes are a hazard to less agile walkers, such as older tourists and families, and the noise pollution caused by bikes and snowmobiles is an assault on the ears and the quiet dignity of forest and mountain wilderness.

The Chilkoot Pass, for instance, has no part in our contemporary, convenient, clockwork world. It belongs to the past. Its history is of man's struggle with primitive tools against a hostile environment, and snowmobiles have no place here. The winter wilderness beyond is a world of tangible silence, broken only occasionally by the howling of wolves. The snowmobile has no place here either.

Some of the better trails, built and maintained at considerable public expense, have been damaged by trail bikes. The improvements to the trails in themselves increase accessibility to bikes, so that many of the trails on which money is spent incur heavy damage (e.g., Indian River and Lower Dewey Lakes). Policy is needed on ways and means to stop motorized traffic on foot trails. Signs are ignored, pushed over, or used for target practice. Physical barriers are probably the best answer to the problem.

TROUBLE

Plan ahead for possible emergencies. Always let someone know where you are going and what time to expect you back. Roughly divide the day in half and turn around at half time unless the terrain is well known and the return is downhill.

Alaska's weather is unpredictable and can change for the worse, in summer as well as winter. To avoid trouble one must set off on a hike with this in mind. Clouds come seemingly from nowhere and suddenly envelop the hiker, causing marked temperature drop and visual difficulties on alpine ridges.

The Coast Range mountains appear diminutive to some persons from Outside, accustomed to the Sierra and Rockies. But do not be misled by their lack of height. The weather slams into these mountains ferociously and unpredictably, and their ridges fall away into sudden precipices. Way back yonder, ice fields and sheer-walled nunataks glimmer wickedly in a trackless, trailless wilderness.

Snow arrives on the tops by September and often stays until late June or July. By April it has consolidated, and steps are kicked by climbers on hard snow slopes at alpine levels. Avalanche danger is high after heavy snowfalls from November to February and during spring snow melts in April and May. Always be wary of avalanche dangers in steep-sided valleys or on alpine slopes at these times of year, for example, at Chilkoot Pass, Mount Juneau, the ridge to Mount Gastineau (Mount Roberts), Perseverance, and Sheep Creek.

Ridges tend to develop cornices and are highly unstable at any time. (A cornice is windblown snow which overhangs beyond the sharp edge of a ridge.) Eventually cornices collapse, causing avalanches. Cracks often appear shortly before collapse, so do not stray over cracks on a snow-covered ridge, and stay away altogether from the edge.

The word "exposure," as used in this book, means a situation of potential danger without adequate protection. An exposed slope is one which offers no protection to the hiker, is open to a prolonged fall (e.g., over a cliff), and on which a slip can be fatal. Examples are steep slopes above tree line covered with hard spring snow; these should not be attempted by hikers inexperienced in handling ice axes. Specific examples are Mount Juneau, Twin Peaks, and A. B. Mountain. In unskilled hands an ice ax is a drawback rather than an asset.

Sudden weather and temperature changes can bring on hypothermia, and everyone should know its symptoms and treatment before embarking on serious high-level camping and hiking expeditions, winter low-level expeditions, and canoeing in glacial-fed inlets. Briefly, hypothermia is a drop in body temperature due to cold or wet conditions and/or fatigue. It can be recognized by slowing of pace, clumsiness, disorientation, apathy, and irrational behavior. The victim must be made as warm and comfortable as possible and given food and a hot drink, if conscious. (Do not give alcohol!) Do not put a hypothermia victim directly into a down sleeping bag — it insulates only and does not necessarily raise the body temperature. Get into the bag with the patient, or warm it first with your own body heat. *Do not leave the patient alone.*

Never try shortcuts off a mountain, especially in poor weather or gathering darkness. It is, in the long run, quicker and safer to return by the trail or route of access. In emergencies, fires and movement will increase the chances of being spotted from the air. Do not stand still and expect to be seen. If uninjured, run (in circles if necessary) and wave a brightly colored or white jacket to attract attention from passing aircraft. (Do not wave to aircraft otherwise. If seen, your wave may be misinterpreted as a distress signal.)

These warnings are not meant to intimidate the potential hiker but to help him enjoy these glorious rain forests and mountains by having prior knowledge and understanding. A good hiker is one who knows and understands his limitations. He will know when to turn back and when to sit tight; and he will never be caught without the Ten Essentials stuffed into his pocket or pack.

Hiking on high ridges or kayaking in tidal inlets can be a humbling but ennobling experience, as one is confronted with the true insignificance of man in the face of nature, stripped of his mechanical trappings.

CANOEING

The term "canoe" is used in this book to mean either a canoe or a kayak, and "canoeist" either a canoeist or kayaker, unless "kayak" and "kayaker" are specifically mentioned for the purpose of distinguishing between the two different types of craft. At those times, for the purpose of clarity, the term "open canoe" is also used.

Canoes can be transported by the Alaska State Marine Highway (see Access, page 12). Foldboats are less expensive and more convenient for air charter, since few planes are equipped to handle the nonfolding type.

The paddling times given in this guide are adaptations of my actual times, based whenever possible on neutral conditions, that is, those without the influence of winds, tidal currents, etc. In special areas, such as Mitchell Bay to Angoon, it is assumed that the canoeist will be paddling with the current as advised in the text, and times are adjusted accordingly.

Canoeists who use this guide should take the following precautions:

1. All craft should have adequate flotation. Styrofoam wedged fore and aft will keep kayaks afloat under most conditions, right side up or upside down. Otherwise use inflated floats (e.g., beach balls or air bags

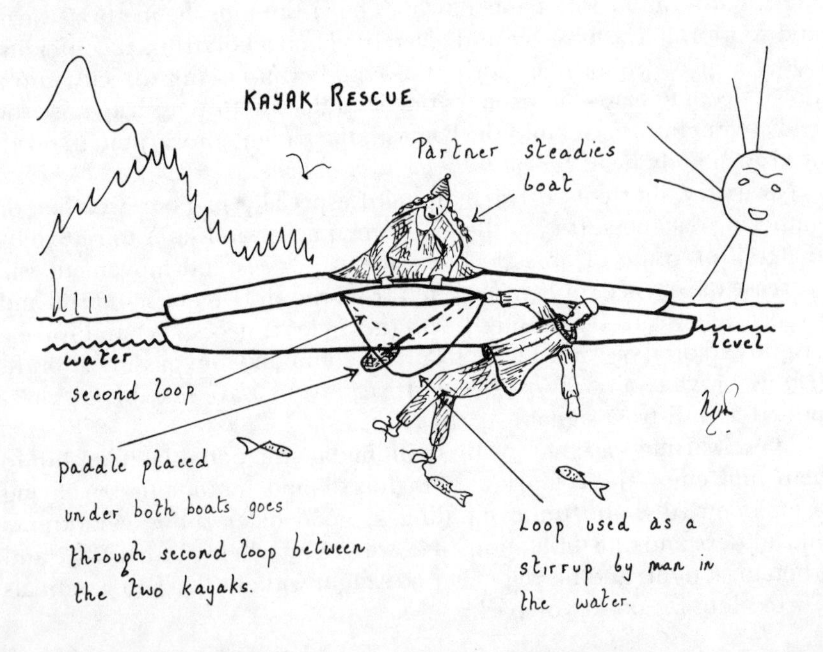

designed for kayaks).

2. Coast Guard-approved life jackets should always be worn.

3. All boats should have the following equipment: canoe repair kit, painter fore and aft (for towing, tying up, and rescue), large bailer, spray cover (kayak), extra paddle. All equipment should be tied down and stowed in waterproof bags (rubberized cotton bags or well-sealed plastic bags inside a stuff bag).

4. *Practice adequate rescue techniques in familiar waters with other members of the party before beginning a trip.* A simple method is to take a prepared looped line, long enough to go across the cockpit and dangle in the water (a foot or more on the stirrup side — about 10 feet altogether). When rescue is necessary, place a paddle through one end of the loop between the rescuer's boat and the victim's righted boat. The paddle should go crosswise under both boats. The loop then crosses the cockpit of the victim's boat and acts as a stirrup for the victim to step back into his kayak. The paddle acts as a stabilizer (see diagrams).

If a long loop is not available, the lines fore and aft can be tied together to make a stirrup in the water. The rescuer then has to stabilize the boat himself from the opposite side. This requires some strength and skill.

If an upset kayak has to be towed to shore, or if flotation is inadequate to keep the kayak afloat when full of water, leave the boat upside down. It is easier to tow and will not sink since air is trapped underneath.

Unskilled kayakers and those in open canoes are warned not to ven-

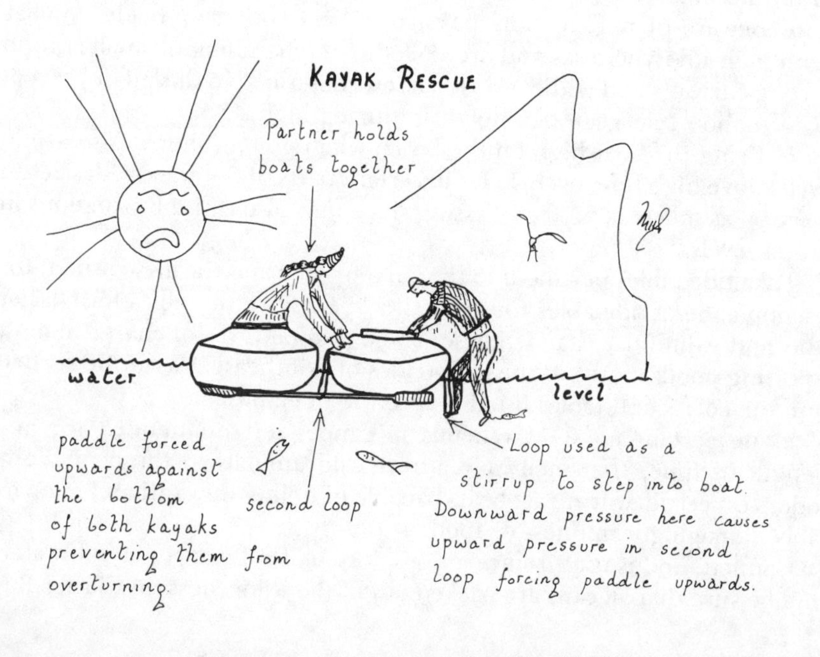

ture into coastal waters exposed to ocean swell, poor weather conditions, or floating ice hazards, e.g., West Chichagof from Dry Pass northward; Glacier Bay — Muir Inlet and Johns Hopkins Inlet, open shoreline north of the Beardslee Islands, and exposed shoreline in the West Arm.

Be sure waterproof matches, firestarter, and extra food that won't be spoiled by immersion in salt water (e.g., chocolate) are on one's person at all times.

5. Those paddling extensively in tidal and ice-covered waters should wear clothing consistent with the conditions. The best is a full-length wet suit, but this is uncomfortable if worn continually. A water-ski suit with short sleeves and pants is insurance against freezing during a short-term immersion; on cool days this can be worn under woolen clothing. Otherwise, a long-sleeved woolen sweater and woolen pants should be worn. Air temperatures before a glacier are often 20° lower than temperatures a mile away, and ice-covered waters are barely above freezing.

Of all these alternatives, only a full-length, cold-water wet suit is sufficient protection against prolonged exposure in icy waters. A wet suit made for cold waters gives from 4 to 6 hours' protection. A ski jacket with woolen sweater and pants gives from 30 to 60 minutes under the same conditions. (Times cannot be given accurately because of the great disparity between people and their reaction to cold.)

Determine how long cold water can be withstood in the clothes to be worn by immersing yourself in icy waters before embarking. Do not stray too far from land, and be sure rescue skills assure prompt extrication from the water.

6. Beware of narrow tidal passages unless you are already familiar with their idiosyncrasies and are skilled in the handling of small craft in strong currents and eddies. Most narrows described in this guide (except Kootznahoo Inlet) can be safely run during high slack.

7. Bring the boat high on the beach when going ashore. Also, camp well above high tide level. Tides in certain parts of Southeast Alaska can vary by as much as 20 feet. Passing ships may also cause fluctuations in water levels.

Take tide tables pertinent to the current year and the area visited; for example, Sitka tidetables for West Chichagof, Juneau tables for Glacier Bay and Admiralty Island. These can be obtained free of charge in most sporting goods stores in the main cities of Southeast Alaska. Be sure to use the correction tables listed before the tidetables.

8. Be certain no food remains in canoes left unattended for any length of time; the smell may attract wild animals to the boat. Fishy odors especially will attract bears capable of holing the craft and irreparably damaging it in quest of food.

Canned food is useful since it doesn't spoil if submerged in salt water, but be sure that all cans are packed out of the wilderness (in Glacier Bay they can be taken either to Goose Cove or Bartlett Cove). Wash cans so that bears and rodents are not attracted to the camp, then flatten them for carrying out.

TRAIL TIMES AND CONDITIONS

Mileages and hiking times given with each trail description are one way unless otherwise stated. If return times are not given, estimate the same length of time for the return. The times quoted are an adaptation of my times and should, therefore, be fairly consistent. Your times may differ from mine, so find your mean and adapt this to the travel times given. Mode of travel and motivation make a difference in times. Overnight backpackers will be considerably slower than those without campgear; those determined to reach alpine heights will be faster than those stopping to study the flora or bird life en route.

Rather than giving a blow-by-blow account of every hill and corner, trail descriptions dwell more on the highlights and on the problems encountered. This allows the hiker some leeway for discovery without encountering serious difficulty. Do not expect the trails to be exactly as described, as they change depending on maintenance, or the lack of it. Underbrush grows back rapidly after clearing; recent windfalls sometimes change the picture enough to cause temporary loss of the trail.

Camping is usually mentioned only when outstanding camping spots are on or close to the trail described.

KEY TO MAPS

All maps in this guide are close to the given scale but have been drawn freehand. On most forest trails and all alpine trails, the hiker should carry the correct topographic quadrangle.

I was asked by a small child what the vertical "arrows" were. The "arrows" are supposed to represent trees.

The animals, houses, cabins, people, and such are not, by any stretch of the imagination, drawn to scale. I hope they bear sufficient likeness to the real thing that a key is not necessary!

Do not correlate the number of switchbacks encountered with those shown on the map. Those shown (except for the trail to Lower Dewey Lake, S2) are only an indication, and are not necessarily accurate.

Most symbols are explained on each map or become self-explanatory with descriptive terms (e.g., "Mendenhall Flats" and "tidal flats" within stippled, shoreline zones).

Coastlines are shown with a heavy line and sometimes hachuring to give a three-dimensional effect.

When more than one trail is seen, the main trail described in the text is drawn with long, dark dashes. Spur trails or other routes are shown with shorter dashes and are lighter in texture.

Skull and crossbones mean danger!

DEFINITIONS

Black ice: Ice laden with dirt, debris, and glacial moraine, found close to the periphery of receding glaciers. Potentially hazardous, black ice is deceptive in appearance, with glacial ice under a veneer of dirt, and is sometimes honeycombed with hidden ice caves.

Cirque: A steep-walled mountain basin, usually open at one end.

Crevasse: A crevice or crack appearing on the surface of a glacier; often both deep and wide and can be hidden under a thin crust of snow.

Cwm: A Welsh word (pronounced "coom") meaning a hollow or valley. In mountain terminology cwm is synonymous with cirque.

Deadfalls, windfalls: Fallen trees, usually windblown.

Icefall: A heavily crevassed, steep part of a glacier; or an ice avalanche.

Moraine: An accumulation of material, such as gravel and rocks, deposited by a glacier. Sometimes it is difficult to see where the moraine ends and the glacier starts (see "black ice" above).

Nun: A small, unlighted buoy with a circular middle and tapering to the ends.

Nunatak: A sharp rock spire or a steep-sided rocky knoll, found within an ice field or glacier or left after glacial shrinkage.

Outside: An Alaskan term for the contiguous United States.

Quick mud: (My term) Soft mud found during the spring-summer thaw (May or June), especially in Glacier Bay. It is possible to lose a boot in the worst patches.

Serac: A vertical tower of ice, often unstable, found on the terminus or in the icefall of a glacier.

Shingle: English term for pebbles or small, rounded stones, like those found on a beach.

Terminus: The end of a glacier; often sheer-walled and highly unstable in tidal inlets.

Tides

Ebb: Outgoing tide.

Flood: Incoming tide.

Slack: A short period of time at high and low tides when movement or flow of the water ceases.

Trail Gradings

Sightseeing: Anyone, old and young alike, should be able to enjoy the walk. No special equipment is required except a raincoat and the usual pocket stuffed with nuts or candy, etc., but sturdy shoes or boots should be worn (almost all trails are wet and sloppy after heavy rains).

Forest or low level: The going is rougher, sometimes with considerable elevation gain, though the trail generally stays within the forest (except Glacier Bay). The trail may be wet, requiring rubber boots, and may not be found as readily. The Ten Essentials should be taken.

Alpine: Usually strenuous. The Ten Essentials should be taken and good boots worn. At certain times of year an ice ax is necessary on steep slopes. These trails — or routes — are for experienced hikers who understand their limitations in unfamiliar territory. All these trails go above the tree line and are subject to the vagaries of Alaska weather at high levels.

ROADSIDE CAMPGROUNDS

Ketchikan

Ward Lake, 8 miles north of town
Settlers Cove, 20 miles north of town

Wrangell

Pat's Creek, 11 miles south of town
City campground, 1 mile south of town

Petersburg

Ohmer Creek, 23 miles south of town
Sumner Straits, 27 miles south of town

Sitka

Starrigavan, 7 miles north of town (close to the ferry terminal)
Sawmill Creek, 7 miles south of town

Juneau

Mendenhall Lake, 13 miles north of town (4 miles northeast of Auke Bay ferry terminal)
Auke Village, 16 miles north of town (on the beach, 2.5 miles north of Auke Bay ferry terminal)

Haines

Portage Cove, 1 mile south of town (outskirts of Port Chilkoot)
Chilkoot Lake, 10 miles north of town (head of Lutak Inlet)
Downtown

Skagway

City Park, 1 mile north of the ferry terminal (in town, off Broadway)
Liarsville, 3.5 miles north of town

CONSERVATION ORGANIZATIONS

Ketchikan

Tongass Conservation Society
(a chapter of the Alaska Conservation Society)
P.O. Box 2282, Ketchikan 99901

Southeast Alaska Mountaineering Association (SEAMA)
(member, Federation of Western Outdoor Clubs)
P.O. Box 1314, Ketchikan 99901

Wrangell

Stikine Conservation Society
Wrangell 99929

Petersburg

Petersburg Conservation Society
(a chapter of the Alaska Conservation Society)
P.O. Box 992, Petersburg 99833

Sitka

Sitka Group, Alaska Chapter, Sierra Club
Sitka 99835

Sitka Conservation Society
(a chapter of the Alaska Conservation Society)
P.O. Box 97, Sitka 99835

Juneau

Juneau Group, Alaska Chapter, Sierra Club
Juneau 99801

Haines and Skagway

Lynn Canal Conservation, Inc.
Haines 99827

Alaska Conservation Society
P.O. Box 80192, College 99701

Sierra Club, Alaska Chapter
P.O. Box 2025, Anchorage 99501

Friends of the Earth
719 7th Avenue
Fairbanks 99701

Sitka Spruce

K1 Deer Mountain (alpine)
K2 Blue Lake (alpine)
K3 Twin Peaks (alpine)
K4 Ward Lake (sightseeing)
K5 Perseverance Lake (sightseeing)

Southeast Alaska: a blending of sea and land into a magnificent wilderness of islands, bays, fjord-like inlets, mountains, and rain forest — a wilderness at this very moment being plundered in the name of progress. Now, before it is too late, portions of this treasure should be formally classified "wilderness" to give them the protection they deserve and need, to preserve a treasure that is far more valuable in its pristine state than if it is used for short-term monetary gain.

Tongass Conservation Society
Ketchikan

KETCHIKAN

The city of Ketchikan still remains an interesting fishing town, despite the influence of the pulp industry during recent years. The town is long and narrow, with its frontage along the partially protected waters of the Tongass Narrows. Its width is composed of houses and wooden-slatted streets perched precariously on steep, wooded hillsides, lending a unique charm to the place.

The city is situated on Revillagigedo Island (shortened to "Revilla" by the local populace) in the Alexander Archipelago, at the southern end of the Southeast Alaska Panhandle. At present, its main road extends north of town approximately 20 miles, and south of town it runs about 14 miles to Beaver Falls. Ketchikan can be reached by the Alaska Marine Highway ferry system from Prince Rupert, B.C., or Seattle, Washington, or by jet air service from Seattle with a short ferry crossing to Ketchikan. The Alaska State ferry terminal, 1.5 miles north of the downtown district, is linked to town by a city bus service about every half-hour.

The low-level trails in the Ketchikan area give the visitor an insight into the magnificence of the Alaskan rain forests. On both Ward Lake and Perseverance Lake trails, Sitka spruce, western hemlock, and cedar arch high over one's head; at eye level, devil's club predominates.

The trees start to thin and become more stunted at about 2000 feet. Views open up between the trees, and as one reaches the alpine realm, panoramas of the larger islands of the archipelago — Gravina, Annette, and Prince of Wales — and sweeping views inland to the interior of Revilla surround the viewer. In good weather, extensive views of snow-capped peaks in the mainland range are visible, as well as many miles of the Inside Passage north and south of Tongass Narrows. Sometimes bald eagles and often ravens soar on thermals rising from the peaks, and deer and black bears occasionally wander over the ridges.

Raingear is essential for almost any walking in the Ketchikan area, since the rainfall is heavy. Thus, drinking water is rarely a problem except after an unusually dry spell. Most of the alpine areas have good overnight campsites as long as a spot is carefully selected. Wood will be scarce above tree line and a small stove would be a useful item to take along.

Maps required are Ketchikan quadrangles B-5 and B-6.

K1 DEER MOUNTAIN

The 3000-foot pointed peak of Deer Mountain dominates the city of Ketchikan. A well marked trail to the summit provides an excellent opportunity for anyone in Ketchikan with just a few hours to spend to experience a walk in an Alaskan rain forest. It is also good for those who plan to make a one-day or overnight trip to the summit. The trail starts from the edge of town.

First find the Post Office (in the Federal Building) in the downtown district of Ketchikan. Proceed past this across Ketchikan Creek and by the Thomas Basin small-boat harbor. At the top of a small rise turn left

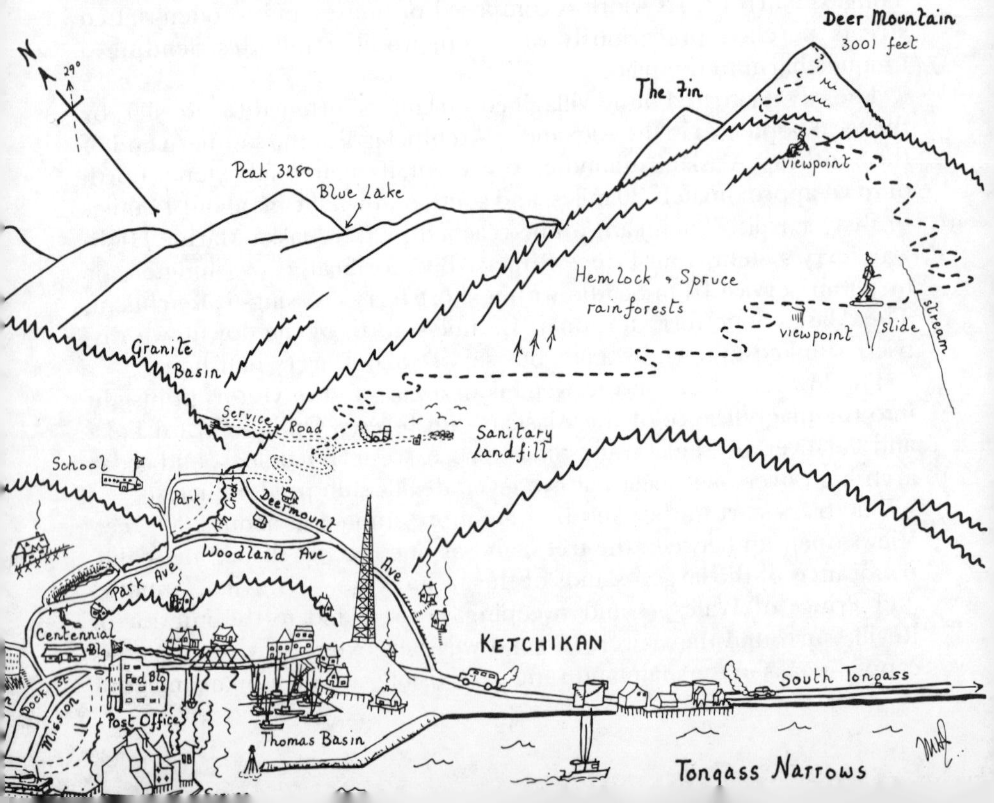

Sunset over Prince of Wales Island, from Deer Mountain

up Deermount Avenue and walk to the end of the road. At the last house turn right up a gated dirt road signposted for the Ketchikan Sanitary Landfill.

The road climbs steeply uphill in a series of sharp curves (watch for traffic) for about half a mile and has open views of Ketchikan behind. If an early departure from the road is preferred, SEAMA has recently rehabilitated the old trail, starting about 900 feet below the final rise in the road and the road division.

If this turn is missed, climb the last hill to a division in the road. To the right is the Sanitary Landfill and to the left Ketchikan Lakes. Turn left, and within a few yards the Deer Mountain trail strikes off to the right across open muskeg toward the base of the peak. Despite repeated vandalism, SEAMA manages to keep a signpost upright at this point for most of the summer.

The trail is boardwalk across the muskeg before it goes into the trees. It then gains altitude by a series of zigzags through forest, and is easily followed as long as care is taken when detouring around windfalls. At about 1500 feet elevation a viewpoint is reached with an overlook of Annette Island and the south entrance of Tongass Narrows. Strong hikers will reach this point within an hour, though most will need 2 hours or more. In late summer, the last stream found along the trail is crossed a short way beyond the viewpoint. The trees become considerably shorter and sparser as the 2000-foot level is reached, where views open up to the south and west. Keep a sharp lookout for a glimpse of the

Tlingit village of Saxman below. As the steepness of the trail diminishes, the platform of an old cabin site is reached to the left of the main trail. From here Ketchikan is spread out below, as well as extensive views north and west of Gravina Island, Prince of Wales Island, and the Marine Highway running north.

The trail climbs steeply once more through the remaining trees, tending to favor the northern, open aspect of the peak. A trail, traversing beneath the final summit and signposted to Blue Lake, leads to the left. The right fork is preferable as a direct route to the summit. The last 400 feet are steep but not difficult. About 300 feet below the summit on the east side is a U.S. Forest Service Cabin.

Grade forest, alpine
Distance 3 miles one way
Time 3 hours up, 1.5 hours down
Elevation gain 3001 feet
Trail condition good
Trail characteristics rain forest and alpine
Limitations weather and steep snow slopes under summit until June
Access by foot from cruise ships and center of town
Administrative agency: within State Selection; maintained by SEAMA

K2 BLUE LAKE

Blue Lake, 2650 feet above sea level, is 2 miles farther along a gradually rising ridge running north-northeast from Deer Mountain. (The ridge can be found in foul weather by following magnetic north from

Blue Lake

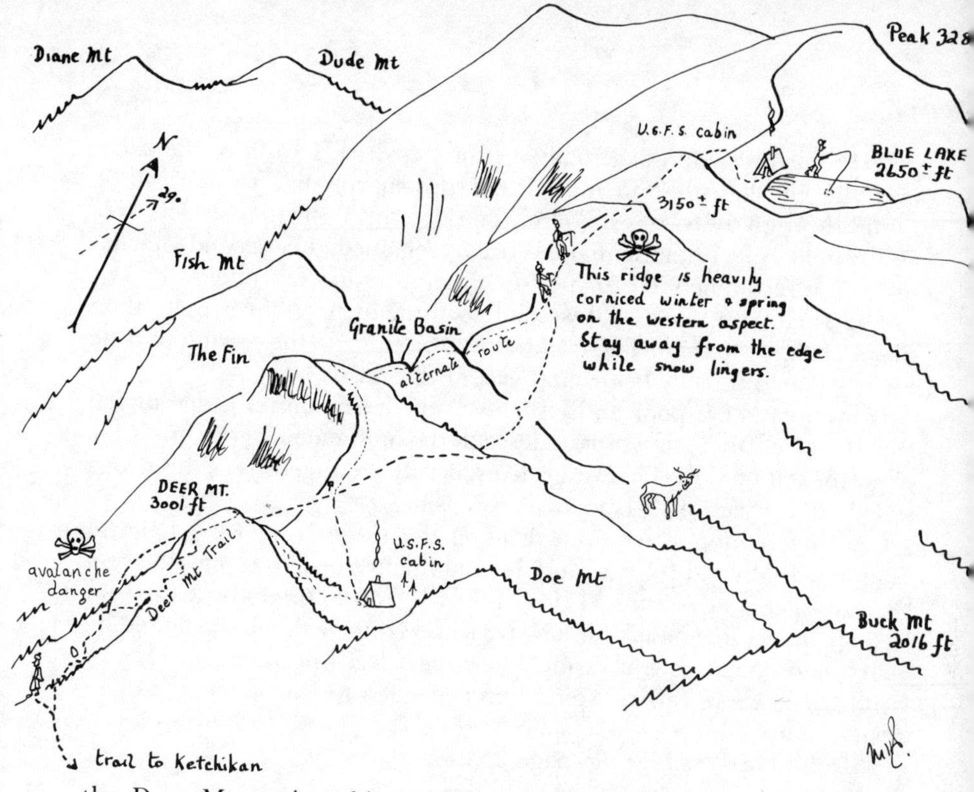

the Deer Mountain cabin.) It is a worthwhile extension of the Deer Mountain trail; the ridge is open most of the way with extensive views of mountains all around and the sea to the south, west, and north. Stay off the west edge of the ridge during the spring in case lingering snows are still corniced. A U.S. Forest Service cabin at Blue Lake may be used with prior permission. The lake, usually free of ice after July 1, is stocked with grayling.

See the Deer Mountain trail description (K1) for access to this trail. One may either go over the summit of Deer Mountain and descend to the cabin behind the peak or take the left fork about 400 feet below the summit. The fork traverses the peak on the north side to the saddle between Deer Mountain and the Fin, the second peak along the ridge. In winter and early spring this path crosses avalanche slopes and should not be attempted. Later, when the snow consolidates, the slope is exposed and an ice ax is needed. In summer it is a pleasant, simple traverse.

From the saddle between Deer Mountain and the Fin, there are two alternatives:

1. Take the trail that starts at a small Forest Service signpost on the saddle and goes east, then northeast, and traverses the east slope of the Fin. It descends about 100-150 feet at first, then ascends gradually to regain the ridge about three-quarters of a mile farther on. Tall metal Forest Service markers may be located under cloudy conditions if they stay upright after perennial storms.

2. From the signpost (actually a trail "crossroads") follow the ridge over the Fin. Past the Fin summit it drops sharply but a route can be found through dwarf trees. Follow the ridge through another cleft over an exposed gully until the marked trail is regained. The second alternative is not recommended for non-mountaineers in the winter.

The ridge rises for the next half to three-quarters of a mile, then drops abruptly to a col. The trail follows the ridge to the col and to Blue Lake, situated directly below and east of the col.

If the weather is poor and visibility limited, stay on the ridge or the trail traverse. Do not attempt to descend the mountain directly, however great the temptation. The west side especially is dangerous as this drops steeply in a series of cliffs to Granite Basin.

One may continue northward along the ridge from Blue Lake to Mahoney Basin and John Mountain, and finally down to White River on George Inlet. The continued ridge hike is a two- to three-day trek from Ketchikan; arrangements for a boat pickup from White River should be made beforehand. A trail from White River leads northeast to Harriet Hunt Lake, where car transportation is needed for the journey back to town.

See additional trail listing, page 254.

Grade alpine
Distance 2 miles one way from Deer Mountain
Time 1.5 hours from Deer Mountain (from Ketchikan, 5 hours one way; 8 hours round trip)
Elevation gain 700 feet northbound from Deer Mountain col; 800 feet southbound; 3400 feet from Ketchikan
Trail condition fair
Trail characteristics alpine
Limitations: snow cornices on ridge in winter and spring, and weather
Access by foot from Ketchikan via Deer Mountain trail
Facilities: cabin available; check with U.S. Forest Service
Administrative agency: within State Selection; presently maintained by U.S. Forest Service

K3 TWIN PEAKS

Two graceful, shapely peaks are visible from the starboard side of the northbound ferry as it steams across the entrance to Carroll Inlet toward Mountain Point. (Mountain Point is recognized by the first sighting of houses and a road on Revilla Island.) The peaks, called Twin Peaks, make a pleasant day's outing for experienced hikers if a ride can be found to Beaver Falls, at the present end of the South Tongass Highway.

From the ferry terminal turn right through town and follow the shore road to the end (about 14 miles). Beyond Herring Cove the last 4–5 miles of road are gravel. Parking is available just before reaching Beaver Falls power station.

Lower Silvis Lake is reached by a dirt service road that leads to the left and up a hill beyond the power station. The road climbs steeply at first, following an old pipeline trail, then more gradually to Lower Silvis Lake dam, about 2 miles from Beaver Falls power station. Do not go beyond the Forest Service picnic grounds at the dam. In 1969 a slide removed part of the road to Upper Silvis Lake and buried a powerhouse on the south shore of Lower Silvis Lake. The area remains unstable and further slippage is possible.

Twin Peaks rise above the road on the southwestern skyline. At the top of a rise, immediately before descending to the picnic grounds, turn left off the road and climb the bank directly above. Brightly colored flags may be evident at the edge of the trees, indicating the beginning of the route. If not, find the best route up a series of steep banks, requiring scrambling and some easy tree climbing! As soon as the initial steep climb eases, many ways open up, but follow the ridge south. Shortly afterward, a thick patch of devil's club is encountered at the base of another steep slope. Go to the left up a steep gully — avoid the use of devil's club for handholds! Not far above, the trees become scattered and then disappear. Keep left once more to stay clear of brush; alpine meadows are finally reached, carpeted with flowers and rising steeply to the cragbound north peak directly above.

The shoulder on the west flank of the lower, north peak is reached by

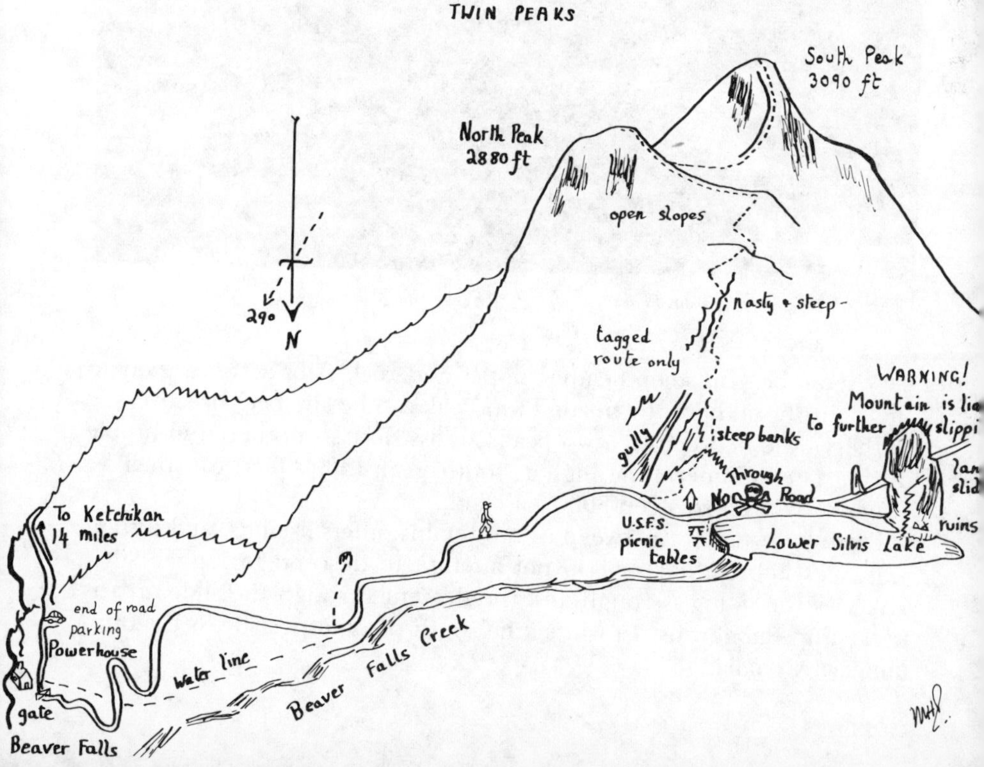

TWIN PEAKS

Upper Silvis Lake from Twin Peaks

easy scrambles on steep heather slopes and rock slabs across a gully to the right. From here the north Twin Peak can be climbed, or traversed to the saddle between the two peaks across slopes smothered in lupine during late summer. The higher, south peak (3090 feet) can then be reached by a short, steep 300-foot climb.

From both peaks the sweep of mountains, inlets, islands, and distant seascapes is breathtaking. Do not attempt to descend to Upper Silvis Lake, as the going is rough and the descent through the slide area is tricky and dangerous. In winter the south peak, especially, is a mountaineering challenge.

On the return trip a steep gully (seen from the road shortly before you turn off to climb the ridge at the beginning of the hike) provides glissading to the road during spring when the snow level is low enough.

Grade alpine
Distance 3 miles one way
Time 4 hours up, 2 hours down
Elevation gain 3090 feet (south peak)
Trail condition tagged route only
Route characteristic mountain
Access by car from Ketchikan to Beaver Falls (14 miles)
Administrative agency: within State selection; currently under U.S. Forest Service management

K4 WARD LAKE

Ward Lake has a pleasant 30–50 minute walk — depending on how much sauntering is enjoyed — around three sides of the lake. Both north and south shores of the lake have picnic sites, and there are some off the road on the east side. The lake can be reached by car or bicycle from Ketchikan.

Turn left from the Ketchikan ferry terminal and take the North Tongass Highway to Ward Cove about 7 miles away. Ward Cove is unmistakable because of a pulp mill located on the north shore. At the head of Ward Cove turn right onto a gravel road immediately before the main road crosses Ward Creek. About a mile up the gravel road Ward Lake is reached, but continue to the main campgrounds situated on the northern end of the lake, 1.5 miles beyond the turn. A large parking area and two covered picnic areas are provided.

The trail is not difficult to find — go through the picnic grounds and follow the lake shore. Watch for huge Sitka spruce and western hemlock, some "woven" into odd and interesting growth patterns, lining the lake shore. Also note the evidence of past selective cutting along the west shoreline above the footpath. Tree seedlings have taken root in some old stumps, and many other stumps are covered with bracket fungi. Count the annular rings on windfalls, recently sawn through to clear the trail, and discover the age of the smaller trees.

Continue along the pathway to the west end of the lake, where a bridge crosses Ward Creek. On the far side of the bridge a williwaw (a sudden, strong, circular gust of wind) uprooted a number of trees, probably during the 1968 Thanksgiving storm. A short way beyond this, there are more picnic tables and a spur road leading into the main gravel road.

Follow the lake shore along the road to the original starting point. Magnificent spruce, hemlock, and red and yellow cedar stands in this section are worth a leisurely study. Bald eagles and ravens are common

Ward Lake trail

birds in the vicinity of Ward Lake, and raven antics are a source of delight to the initiated as well as the casual visitor.

Grade sightseeing
Distance 1.6 miles complete circuit
Time 30–50 minutes
Elevation gain none
Trail condition good
Trail characteristic nature walk
Access by car or bicycle from Ketchikan (8.5 miles)
Administrative agency U.S. Forest Service

K5 PERSEVERANCE LAKE

A short, pleasant walk leads to Perseverance Lake through forest and muskeg. Take along a fishing pole since there are trout in the lake. Unfortunately, most of the trail is boardwalk. This helps with the short areas of muskeg but makes walking on the old forest floor somewhat artificial. In winter, the boardwalk is dangerous, as the snow conceals holes and stairways. The stairways and the tendency for snow to form a ridge in the center of the boardwalk preclude the use of snowshoes and skis.

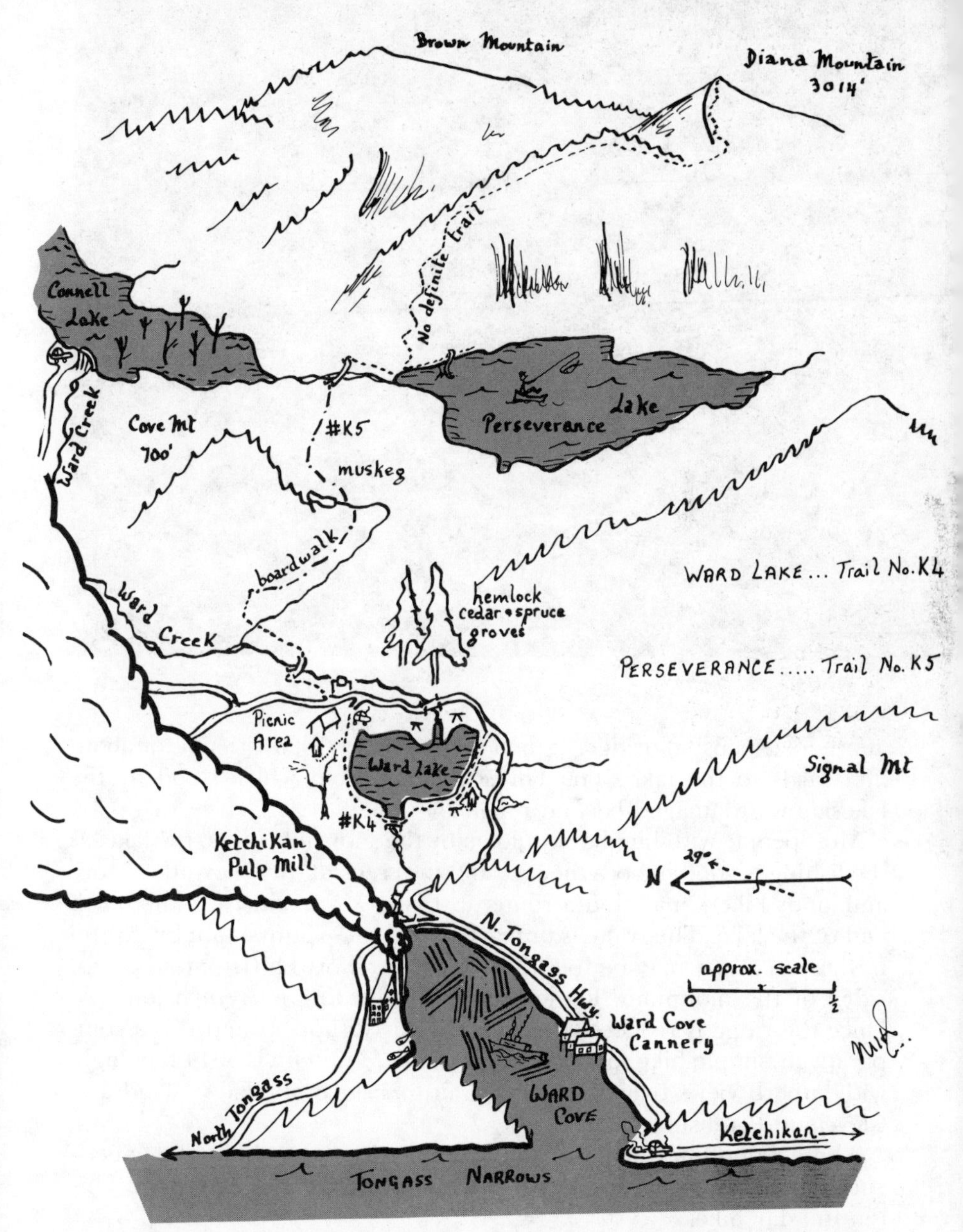

See the Ward Lake trail (K4) for directions to reach the Ward Lake Recreational Area. A few yards past the Ward Lake parking area, there is a parking spot with a U.S. Forest Service sign for Perseverance Lake on the right. The trail is very easy to follow, down some steps and across a suspension bridge over Ward Creek. Within about a quarter of a mile, the trail becomes boardwalk. It climbs steadily through the trees for half a mile before emerging briefly into muskeg. It travels through trees once more until it finally crosses the outflow from Perseverance Lake by

On Perseverance Lake trail

another suspension bridge. It then follows the creek upstream for about 200 yards to the lake. The Forest Service cabin which stood by the lakeside was damaged beyond repair by vandals.

Most people with families would enjoy the short hike up to the lake, as the fishing is good in both the lake and the creek at the lake outlet. More ambitious hikers may find a route up Diana Mountain from the north end of the lake. The route is unmarked and steep at first, but by careful navigation a way may be found through the short bluffs onto the west ridge of the mountain. Remember the route for the return journey. Once the ridge is reached, the trees quickly disappear and it is a comparatively simple hike to the summit. Diana Mountain is 3014 feet high, with superb views over Clarence Strait to Prince of Wales Island and Cleveland Peninsula.

Those extending their walk onto Diana Mountain should be experienced in mountain travel and should take along the Ten Essentials. This is a full-day hike.

Grade sightseeing (Diana Mountain alpine)
Distance 1.7 miles one way (Diana Mountain 3 miles)
Time 1 hour each way (Diana Mountain 3 hours up, 1.5 hours down)
Elevation gain 560 feet (Diana Mountain 3100 feet)
Trail condition too good, boardwalk (Diana Mountain no trail)
Trail characteristics forest and muskeg (Diana Mountain alpine)
Access by car or bicycle from Ketchikan (8.5 miles)
Administrative agency U.S. Forest Service

The Wrangell area of the South Tongass National Forest, like other areas of Southeast Alaska, is managed by the U.S. Forest Service for one dominant single use — logging. Values other than timber harvesting are given little or no consideration despite directives to the contrary in the Forest Service's "Multiple Use Management Guide."

One of Wrangell's areas of outstanding beauty is the Stikine River Valley, which winds its way from coastal coniferous forests, through glaciers to the comparatively arid interior of British Columbia. Much of the river is navigable and as yet untouched. However, the Forest Service includes the timber in the Stikine River Valley in its inventory of marketable timber. Consequently, there is little doubt about the fate of the scenic, wildlife, and recreational values of the river in the not too distant future. Unless drastic changes occur soon in the U.S. Forest Service policy, this and other recreational and wilderness assets in the Wrangell area will soon have been destroyed.

Dale Pihlman, Chairman
Stikine Conservation Society
Wrangell

WRANGELL

Wrangell has an enviable position at the mouth of the Stikine River, fronted by rain-washed islands and the tidal waters on which the light is constantly changing. The Stikine was successfully used by a few gold seekers in 1898 as the gateway to their Eldorado, and the river has been a source of communication both before and since. Thus, Wrangell has been an important town since Russian days, and she still retains her air of bustle with a sawmill downtown half hidden behind huge Japanese lumber ships.

The days of scheduled amphibian air access — once the delight of tourists — ended when an airstrip was built behind town, but one can still come in through the front door by ferry, tour ship, or charter floatplane. The Alaska State ferry system makes regular stops at Wrangell, northbound from Ketchikan and southbound from Juneau and Petersburg. Ketchikan is 100 miles south and Petersburg 35 miles north.

There are two trails of interest, one only a few yards long, the other a short walk through the forest.

W1 **Petroglyphs (sightseeing)**
W2 **Rainbow Falls (forest)**

P1 **Petersburg Creek (forest)**
P2 **Petersburg Mountain (alpine)**

Not formally described as a trail, but worth a visit nonetheless for those with 40 minutes or so to spare, is Shakes Island. Marked on the W1 map as a small island within the boat harbor toward the south end of town, it has a fine collection of totems and a community house. To reach Shakes Island from the ferry or tour ship, turn right and walk through town to the Japanese mill and small-boat harbor. The totems on Shakes Island will be seen across a high, wooden bridge-walkway.

The topographical maps for Wrangell are Petersburg B-2 (with the city) and B-1 quadrangles.

W1 PETROGLYPHS

A short walk can be taken from town or the ferry terminal to the beach to see some ancient Indian carvings called petroglyphs. The walk is no more than 0.8 mile from the ferry terminal, 0.9 from the tour ship tie-up point downtown, or a few yards from the road if a car is used.

From the ferry terminal turn left immediately, or from the center of town walk along the front to the ferry terminal, and continue along the beach road going north. The road climbs a small hill past a trailer court on the right and many private houses on the beach side below the road. A small stream is crossed and within 300 yards a long, straight boardwalk heading for the beach will be seen on the left. This walk is public access to the beach and should be followed until within a few yards of its end. Step off to the left on a trail which runs behind a private house to the beach. The whole boardwalk is only about 250 feet long, but care must be taken if the boards are wet, as they become very slippery.

The beach, if searched in both directions, will yield fine examples of petroglyphs on rocks embedded in the shingle. Better luck may be had if one goes north along the beach, but carvings will be found both ways.

Petroglyph rubbing, Wrangell

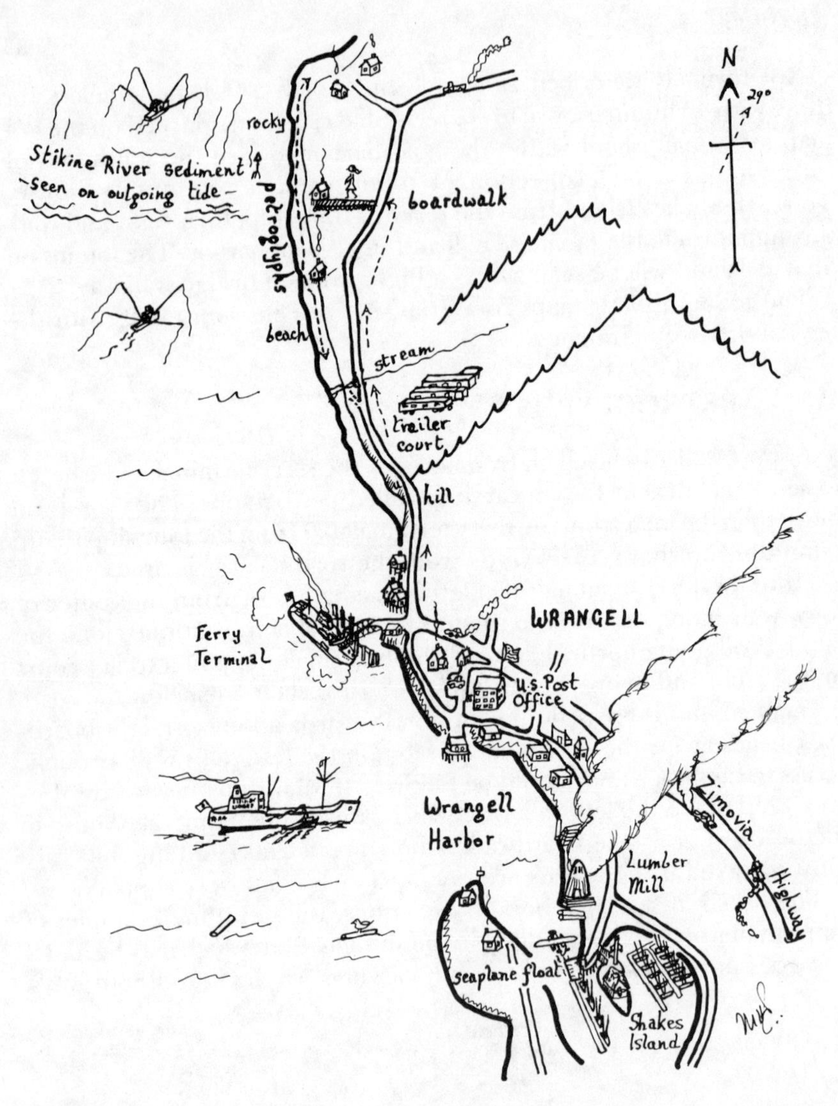

They can be successfully photographed wet or dry. Do not use chalk to highlight the carved lines; not only is it illegal to deface monuments of this order, but the end result is less authentic. Much better results are obtained by putting the camera away altogether, placing a blank sheet of paper over the carving, and rubbing it with pencil, charcoal, or crayon. A good reproduction can be taken away as a momento without damaging the carving.

Most of the petroglyphs are under water at high tide, so consideration should be given to tidal fluctuations. Allow at least an hour from the ferry terminal, or an hour and 15 minutes from town, to view the petroglyphs and return.

Grade sightseeing
Distance 0.8 mile from ferry terminal
Time 1 hour round trip minimum
Elevation gain 50 feet
Route characteristics historical, beach
Access by foot from Wrangell
Limitation high tide

W2 RAINBOW FALLS

Rainbow Falls are situated in the woods south of Wrangell. The approach through forest from the road is about 1 mile; the trail is somewhat wet, requiring waterproof boots. There is also a short, sharp climb of about 500 feet before reaching the falls.

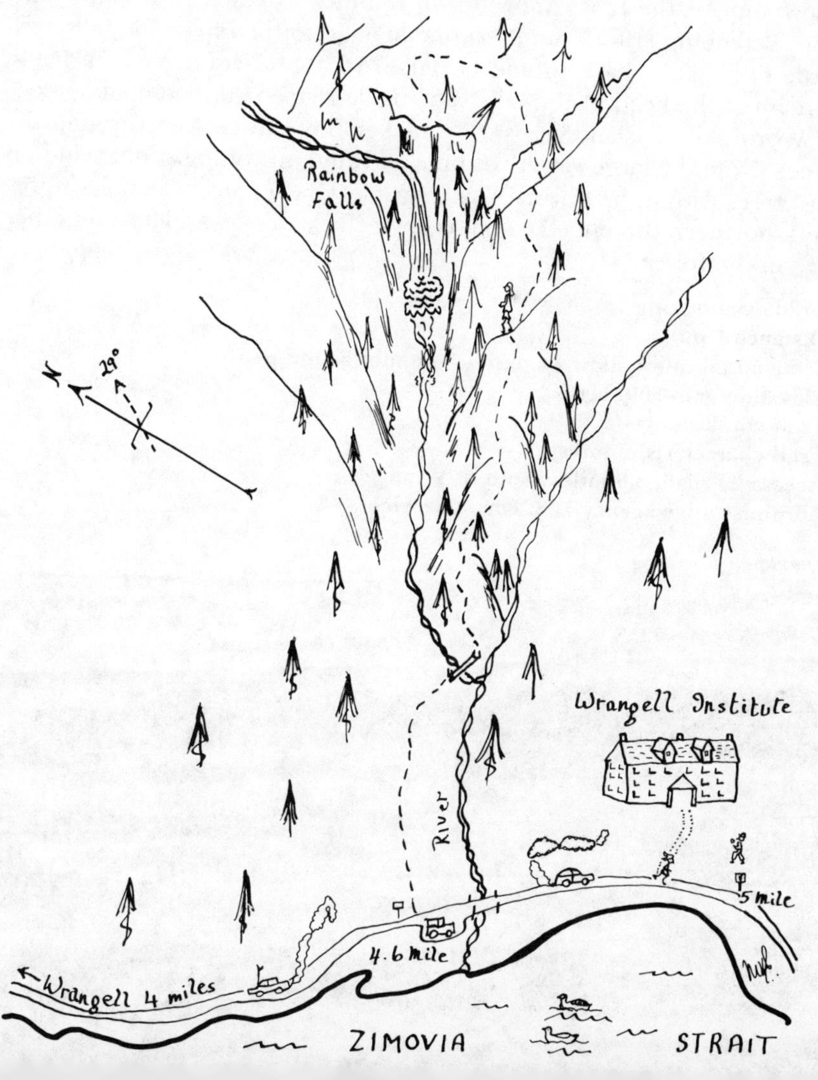

Those not averse to making this into a long day can walk along Zimovia Highway to the beginning of the trail. The road is fairly free of traffic and closely follows the shore, which retains some of its primitive beauty. Shore birds, herons, phalaropes, bay ducks, porpoises, seals, or an occasional whale may be observed in the tidal waters.

From Wrangell take the shore road 4.6 miles south to a U.S. Forest Service trail sign that stands at the edge of the forest to the left of the road, shortly before reaching the Wrangell Institute. Cars can be parked on the right side; do not park on the road.

The trail starts on the north side of a small river close to the Institute and follows it upstream through some short boggy patches. It then crosses the river and climbs steeply up a ridge separating two stream courses. Eventually it relents, climbing more gradually through the forest to a viewpoint of the falls. Allow 30–40 minutes to reach this point. With more climbing (10–15 minutes) one may go to the top of the falls on a little-used path. Care should be taken by those wishing to reach the stream at the head of the falls. The bank is steep and loose and risky.

Woronkofski Island across Shoemaker Bay can be seen through the trees. Note the large variety of bracket fungi on rotting stumps and on live trees within the forest. Watch for black bears, deer, Douglas squirrels, northern three-toed woodpeckers, chickadees, warblers, and other life in the forest.

Grade sightseeing
Distance 1 mile
Time 50 minutes; allow 1 hour, 45 minutes round trip
Elevation gain 500 feet
Trail condition good
Trail characteristic forest
Access by road, 4.6 miles south of Wrangell
Administrative agency U.S. Forest Service

Ducks near Petersburg

Miss Piggott's book is not just a trail guide, it is also an expression of deep feeling from one who recognizes the real greatness of this land. To be profoundly honest, I would prefer her impressions not be recorded on the printed page, as it will make more people want to come to this area and people ultimately destroy that which is most valuable. In this age, the best for Southeast Alaska would be to close all access. Perhaps in the future humanity will appreciate this wild area for its true values, but unfortunately we are not yet at that point in time. The cries of progress and development are too loud and greed too strong a motive.

Much of my life has been devoted to the study of wild animal populations. I have just returned from a forced visit to the concrete jungles of the south, and in the mass human hysteria that I witnessed there I see a stress syndrome similar to that which triggers animal population fluctuations. On returning to this land, I realize how important the quiet places are to man's sanity. If, in this age, one can still find peace of mind, it is in areas like Southeast Alaska where the forests, the water, and the mountains are still largely unchanged and where, above all, there are few people. There is still the feeling of space and you can still live by your own resources.

I share Miss Piggott's feeling for the beautiful, lonely places where man realizes how insignificant he is. Some of these can be reached by the trails herein described. I hope they are not paved before you have the opportunity to walk them. "Nonconsumptive use" is a term we often hear today. For Southeast Alaska it must become reality if the things we cherish most are to survive. Come and share, but please do not take away.

Harry Merriam
Petersburg

PETERSBURG

Petersburg is a thriving, bustling, Scandinavian fishing town situated on Mitkof Island about halfway between Juneau and Ketchikan. It is separated from Kupreanof Island by some long and extremely narrow, navigable straits. These straits, the Wrangell Narrows, are a major shipping lane within the Inside Passage into Petersburg.

In clear weather the mainland mountain range, about 25 miles away, makes a splendid backdrop to the many wood-frame buildings spread around a fishing harbor and along the shoreline. The ferry makes regular stops in Petersburg, both north- and southbound, by running through the Narrows — an experience in itself. In winter, deer can often be seen on the beaches. Bird life is extremely varied and interesting because, in both summer and winter, the Narrows are a sheltered backwater. Watch for murrelets running, then rising off the water in front of the ferry, and hundreds of Bonaparte's gulls playing on or above the water. Old squaws, harlequins, loons, goldeneyes, cormorants, mergansers, scaups, buffleheads, teals, hundreds of scoters, and others shelter and feed in these waters, depending on the season.

Two trails are worth a visit, though both are across the bay and require transportation arrangements. The first is a low level hike with plenty of good fishing. The second route goes just above the tree line, giving sensational views of the Wrangell Narrows and the town.

Maps required for both trails are Petersburg quadrangles D-4 and D-3.

P1 PETERSBURG CREEK

Petersburg Creek is an estuarine creek on Kupreanof Island. It drains Petersburg Lake about 9.5 miles from Petersburg and empties into Wrangell Narrows across from town. It is a favorite fishing and hunting haunt of local residents and visitors from Outside, now presented for study as wilderness by the U.S. Forest Service. Logging in the side valleys with the building of an access road up the creek was first proposed, but such an outcry was raised by local citizens that plans had to be shelved. The controversy over Petersburg Creek became a catalyst in the formation of a Petersburg chapter of the Alaska Conservation Society.

A trail runs from tidewater to Petersburg Lake, giving hikers access up the creek. During the salmon run in August and September, black bears often fish in the creek. Hikers with a license and a fishing pole can try their own luck on Dolly Varden, steelhead, and cutthroat trout, plus silver, pink, chum, and sockeye salmon (anglers are advised not to compete too closely with bears). Bald eagles often soar over the bluffs, and ducks and geese usually feed on the lake during the fall. Even an occasional trumpeter swan may wing his way overhead.

Prospective hikers may have to arrange transportation through Blue Star Cruises, King Salmon Motel, or Tides Motel to reach the creek. A charter flight can also be made into Petersburg Lake; arrangements would then have to be made for a boat pickup at the tidal end of the creek. If the visitor has his own small boat, there are two choices:

1. Ride on a high tide to the "Third Cabin" (about 4.5 miles from Petersburg), where the trail is good. This choice is limited by tides; either

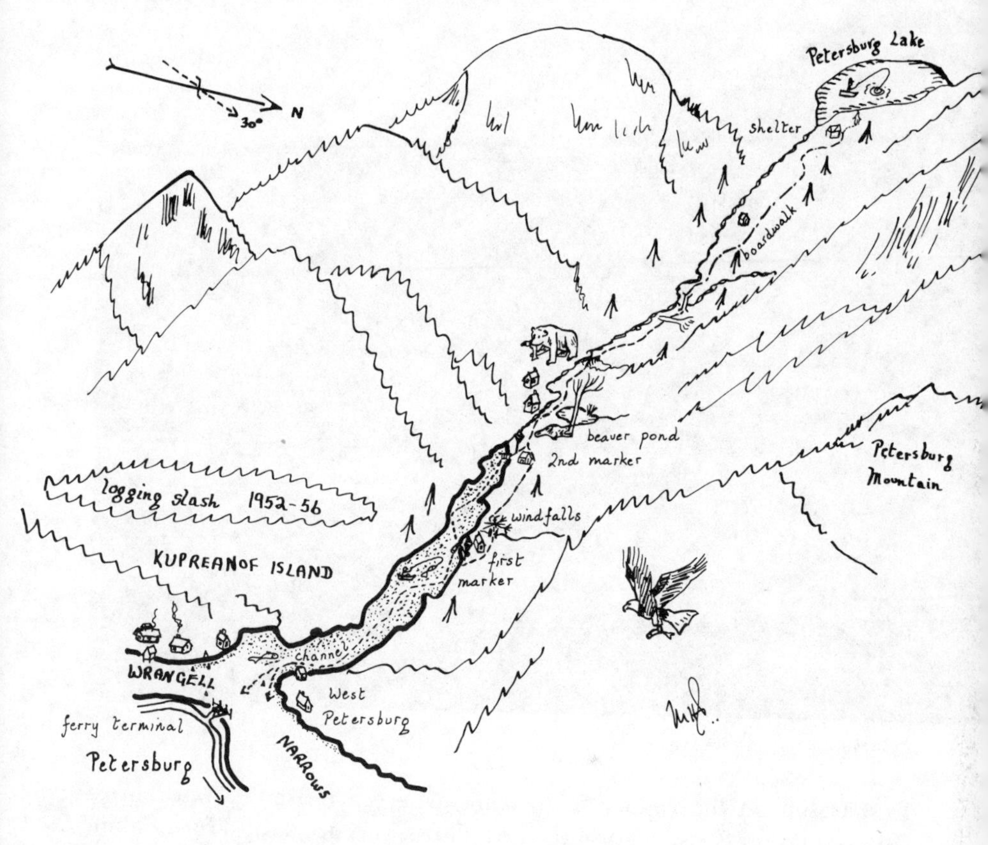

plan to return for the next high tide or go for a short 15- to 20-minute walk.

2. Go with the boat only as far as the "First Cabin," about 3.5 miles from town. This alternative allows greater leeway with tides, and there will be less trouble refloating the boat if the return does not synchronize with high water. The best time to go is between high and low tides.

Take raingear and warm clothing also; it is surprising how cold one gets during the crossing in a small boat, even though it takes only 20–30 minutes from town. Take sandwiches in a day pack, as well as a fishing pole — the round trip is long. Also, those with their own boats should be sure lighting is within U.S. Coast Guard specifications, in case a return crossing has to be made after dark.

Run the boat across Wrangell Narrows to the mouth of Petersburg Creek, located west of the center of town and almost directly across from the ferry terminal. Warning: This is a busy crossing and *large vessels must be given right of way*. A strong tidal race runs through the Narrows at certain stages of the tide.

The creek lies northwest. Proceed upstream for about 2.7 miles to the

Petersburg Creek (Jerold Deppa)

First Cabin on the right (north) bank, where a red and white Forest Service marker is visible; or if the tide allows, run up to the Third Cabin, where a similar marker is located on the right bank.

If the decision is to land at the first marker, securely fasten the boat at the high tide water mark, then look for the trail behind the cabin, visible from the beach. The trail crosses a creek close by and almost immediately disappears into a massive tangle of windfalls. Gravitate to the left, but if the trail is lost head for the nearby beach. Once across the windfalls, the old path is fairly easily followed to the second marker (Third Cabin).

From the second marker, the trail is good and follows Petersburg Creek upstream past a beaver pond and over a long boardwalk that forms a bridge over another large pond. The trail needs brushing in places but is not hard to find. A big windfall is encountered shortly before arriving at "The Fork," a tributary running into Petersburg Creek. Muskeg is next and is crossed on a long section of planking, past a small warming hut on the left. Shortly after the trail goes back into the trees, the lake is reached. There is a cabin near the lake, but vandalism and carelessness have rendered it no better than an open shelter. It is possible that another cabin will be put in its place.

The trail is wet and boggy in patches, and good boots should be worn.

Grade forest
Distance 6.5 miles from the first Forest Service marker (First Cabin); 5.5 miles from the second Forest Service marker (Third Cabin)
Time 3.5 hours one way, plus a 30-minute small-boat crossing from Petersburg. Allow a full day or overnight stay. Time is dependent on tides
Elevation gain 200 feet
Trail condition poor from First Cabin, good from Third Cabin
Trail characteristics valley, muskeg, rain forest
Limitations access and time dependent on tides
Access by small boat from Petersburg, 3.7 miles from small-boat harbor or by charter plane
Administrative agency U.S. Forest Service

P2 PETERSBURG MOUNTAIN

Petersburg Mountain (elevation 2750± feet) is the dominant peak north of town across Wrangell Narrows. The walk to the summit is well worthwhile for strong hikers because of the views obtained. The trail is rough and sporadically marked, with water only after recent rain, about three-quarters of the way to the ridge. Otherwise the route is dry in late summer. Camping sites are poor to nonexistent on the peak.

See the Petersburg Creek trail (P1) for boat arrangements across the

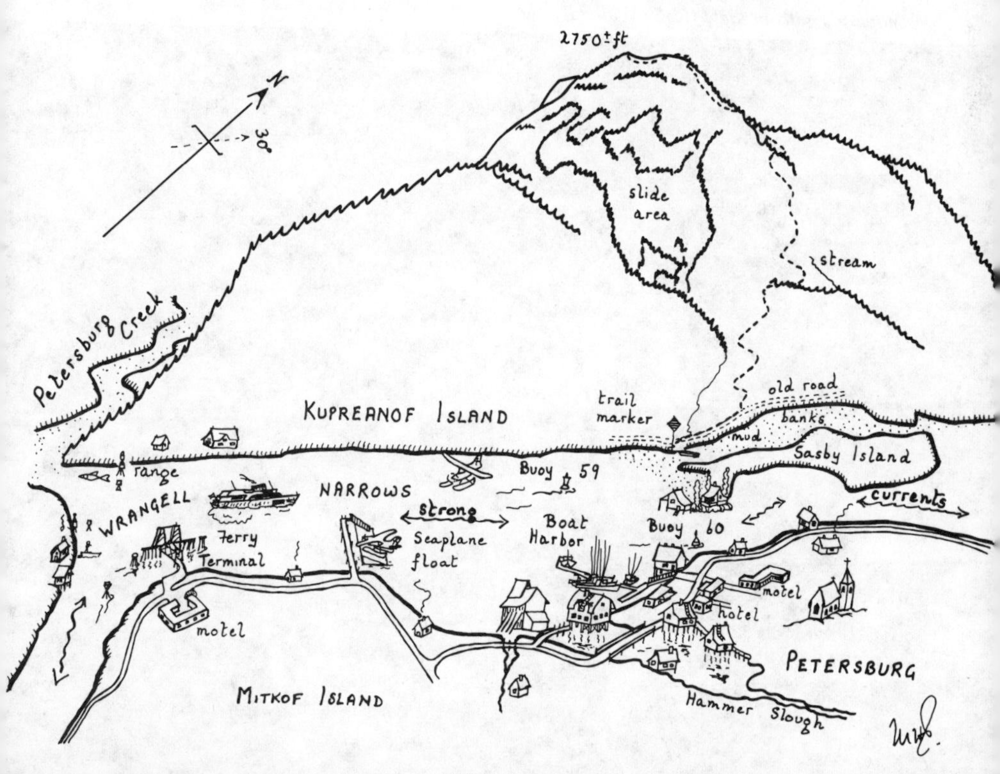

Narrows. Run the boat due north from the city boat harbor (past black channel marker buoy, number 59) to the tidal flats behind Sasby Island, where a red and white Forest Service marker will be seen. Beware of tidal race through the Narrows and watch for shipping. Be sure larger ships are given right of way in these narrow waters. Also be sure that lighting for the boat is within U.S. Coast Guard specifications in case of return after dark.

The state of the tide is not quite as important here as in Petersburg Creek but is still worth consideration since large mud flats may leave the boat high and dry at low tide. It is best to make the crossing between tides. Leave the boat beached with a long line or carry it above high tide mark, close to the Forest Service marker described above, and walk about 50–60 feet from the beach to an old, overgrown road. Turn right (north) along the road where a footpath is brushed out for a little over 200 yards. Watch carefully for a muddy path on the left, crossing the old road ditch. Colored ribbon may mark the trail beginning.

Once found, the path is fairly easily followed upward through the trees (general direction northwest) to the summit ridge. From here the trail peters out, but the route up the ridge is obvious. Before continuing, however, make a mental note where the trail emerges onto the ridge; it is

Bonaparte's gulls in flight (R. T. Wallen)

Grouse or ptarmigan

not so easily found in the opposite direction. Go southwest up the ridge; it rises in steep steps, and travelers are advised to keep to the small trees on the left. Close to the summit, the route becomes a scramble of approximately 20 feet over rock and through some brush.

From the summit, on a clear day, one has superb views of the mainland mountains with their attendant glaciers and icecaps. Spread at one's feet are the town of Petersburg and the greater part of the Wrangell Narrows running south. At certain times of year icebergs drift north in Frederick Sound, toward the northern end of the Narrows. Some become beached under Horn Cliffs to the east-southeast. Their source, Le Conte Glacier, spawns icebergs in a sheer-sided tidal fjord south of Petersburg. On rare occasions the icebergs land in downtown Petersburg!

The boat trip is almost a mile, the trail 2.5 miles. However, this should be considered an all-day hike, and a day pack should be taken.

Grade alpine
Distance 2.5 miles one way
Time 3 hours up, 2 hours down, but allow a full day
Elevation gain 2750 feet ±
Trail condition poor, not readily found
Trail characteristics mountain, forest
Limitations access and time dependent on tides; U.S. Coast Guard-approved lighting for boat if crossing is made after dark
Access by small boat, 1 mile from Petersburg small-boat harbor
Administrative agency: within U.S. Forest Service jurisdiction; trail tagged by local citizens

Si1	**Mount Verstovia (alpine)**	Si4	**Indian River (forest)**
Si2	**Gavan Hill (alpine)**	Si5	**Beaver Lake (sightseeing)**
Si3	**Governor's Walk (sightseeing)**		

Trail. What lovely connotations the word has. It suggests peace, quiet, soft footfalls on forest floor, on grassland, muskeg, and rocky slopes. It whispers of silent creatures slipping away unseen and brings remembrance of others that are not silent — a scolding squirrel, a fawn trilling for its mother, birds saying "I am here!" As distinct from a footpath through a park, pleasant as that may be, "trail" implies wildness. As trail hikers know, there are intangible but priceless things and thoughts to be savored along the way — the odors brought out by the sunshine and by rain; surcease from the tensions and pressures of civilization; a readjustment of one's priorities; a renewed sense of personal identification with nature, which is to say, with wildness, and with wilderness, which is the mother of wildness.

Many thoughtful people, before and after Thoreau, have tried to tell us that the existence of wildness is as important to human survival as the presence of the air we breathe. So in the interest of the preservation of people on the Earth let us be aware as we walk our trails that they are in imminent danger of being destroyed, not by a malignant race of trail-destroyers but by ordinary people who, in the pursuit of other objectives, chisel away inexorably at the wildness that is the essence of trails. They widen the trails to accommodate that peace-shattering contrivance, the gasoline-powered vehicle; they obliterate trails in order to "harvest" the timber; they bury them under airfields and housing developments; they flood them with dams; and all of these things, and more, they claim are benefits to people.

There is no way to save the environment in which trails exist except to draw hard borders around it marked "You may enter and enjoy this land as people, but as engineers, loggers, road builders, or developers you may not enter."

The tool for saving such areas already exists in the Wilderness Act of 1964. Until now the use of the Act has been characterized by foot-dragging on the part of the federal agencies involved, and by energetic and sometimes hysterical opposition on the part of industry. But the power to save is there if you, my fellow trail users, will demand and continue to demand that it be used. It must be used if wilderness trails are to survive outside of museum exhibits. There is no other way.

Jack Calvin
Sitka

SITKA

Sitka, the old Russian capital of Alaska, is situated on the west coast of Baranof Island. Today it retains some of its charm as a historic city despite the changes wrought by modern urban development and the pulp industry. A wooden Russian Orthodox church of classic beauty and Eastern flavor stood in the center of town before it burned to the ground

Sitka harbor

in 1966, but it is being restored by public donations.

Sitka's setting is one of outstanding beauty. Its frontage is on the Pacific Ocean, whose swells are broken on a chain of forested islands guarding the entrance to Sitka Harbor. Shapely spires rise 3000–4000 feet high almost immediately from the outskirts of town and continue round the bay in a glorious sweep of alpine peaks.

Access is by jet airplane or ferry; tour ships visit during the summer. The ferry threads its way through a web of sea passages and narrows to gain sheltered access into Sitka. The great volcanic cone of Mount Edgecumbe stands guard to seaward. Unhappily, this wild, scenic approach has been partially spoiled by clear-cut logging along the ferry lanes and in the bays and inlets.

Sitka's trails range from a stroll along the beach, requiring no special equipment (except perhaps a camera or sketch pad), to alpine hikes with panoramic views of town and open Pacific. All trails are reached from the road system, and most are within walking distance of town. The road system is not too extensive, running from the ferry and Starrigavan Creek Campgrounds 7 miles north of town to just beyond the pulp mill 7 miles south of town. The tour ships either anchor off shore in Crescent Bay or tie up downtown. The ferry arrives 7 miles north of town.

Maps are not required for the Governor's Walk. Sitka quadrangles A-4 and A-5 should give adequate coverage for the other trails.

Si1 MOUNT VERSTOVIA

Mount Verstovia, a shapely, pointed peak, dominates Sitka to the east. Its commanding position over the city gives an ambitious hiker superb, uninterrupted views of Sitka, the coastline with its many surf-washed islands, and the open Pacific. A rough trail gives access to the ridge above tree line, where views start to open up. The trail needs a good dose of maintenance and should be relocated away from a slide area; unfortunately, ownership is currently in a state of limbo while agencies negotiate land selections (a fate suffered by many Panhandle trails sited close to towns). In late summer, after snow has melted, the trail is rela-

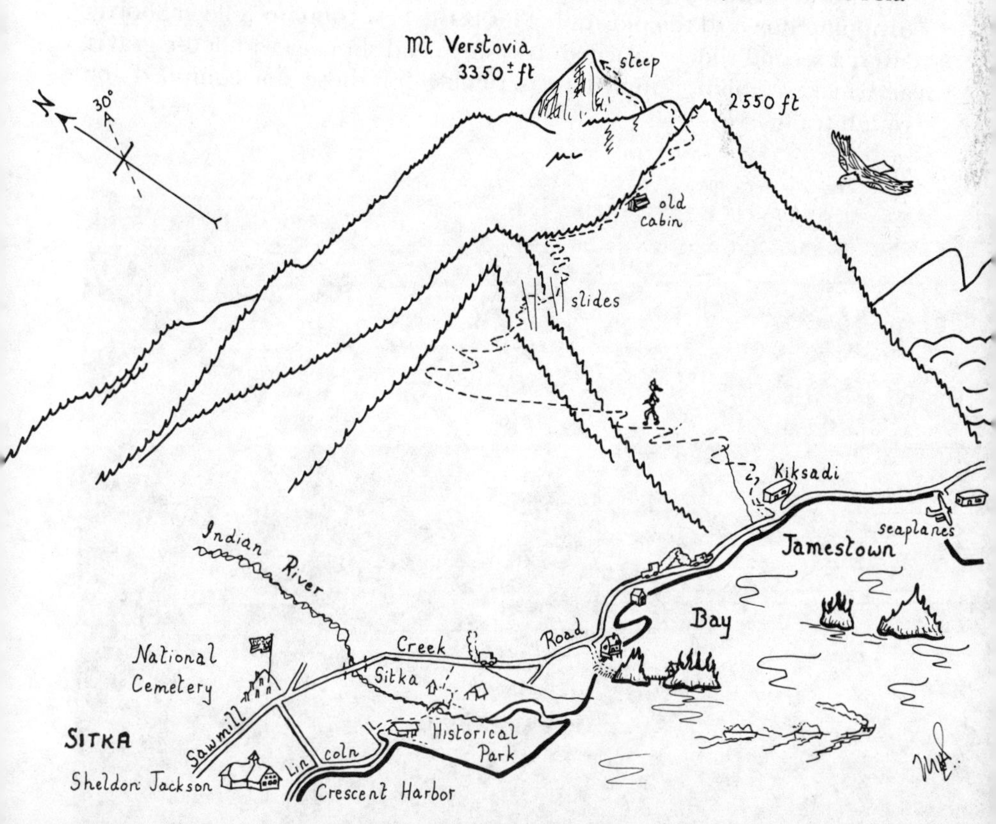

tively dry with only two small streams close to the beginning and some doubtful-looking ponds on a ridge below the final summit of Mount Verstovia. The lower slopes of the mountain were logged by Russians more than a century ago, and signs of their activity may still be seen.

From the center of town, drive 2 miles east along Sawmill Creek Road (beginning two blocks north of the Centennial Building and library) to the Kiksadi Restaurant. Those walking the full distance from town may find it pleasanter to walk around Crescent Harbor on Lincoln Street and through the Sitka National Historical Park to Sawmill Creek Road (see Governor's Walk, Si3).

The Forest Service no longer maintains the trail and their sign has been removed; bulldozers have obliterated the first few yards and the beginning is not immediately apparent. Go to the left (west side) of the Kiksadi Restaurant and scramble up some conspicuous bare rocks. On the far side a path leads away from the road through a stretch of brush. It is not difficult to follow as it climbs uphill in a long series of zigzags. Be careful of "ghost" trails at the apex of many turns — they lead nowhere, most disappearing within a few yards of the main trail. About 1.5 miles from the road, elevation 1200 feet, a slide area is reached. Heavy wear shows a new route climbing up for a few feet, traversing the slide, then dropping down to the old trail. This is the best route to follow. Shortly after, a second slide is reached. It is steep and slippery with loose gravel and makes a short, unpleasant scramble for those not equipped for rough trails.

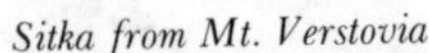

Sitka from Mt. Verstovia

The pathway climbs steeply for another 500 feet to the ridge, running back and forth in tighter turns than before. Once the ridge is reached, the climb is less steep. About 10 minutes farther up, an old cabin in poor condition still stands, partially concealed from the trail on the south side of the ridge. It may be used as a rude shelter, although old fires and garbage litter the earth floor. The trail finally emerges from the trees, and most people stop on the lower peak of Mount Verstovia (marked 2550 on the map). Dwarf mountain hemlock make a fitting foreground to the sweeping views of the Pacific. The city of Sitka lies in miniature at the base of the peak, and on the western horizon the great volcanic cone of Mount Edgecumbe rises from the sea.

A narrower footpath descends from here 300 feet to a saddle between the first peak and the final summit, which towers as a sheer-sided triangular cone nearly 1000 feet over the lesser peak. Experienced hikers may assault the final summit by climbing the ridge above the saddle, then traversing to steep grass slopes on the right of the final rock scarp. Do not attempt the final ascent if winter snows linger on the upper slopes. A slip could land one at the front door of the pulp mill 3000 feet below!

From here, views are even more lofty over sea- and landscape. A wicked-looking, shattered ridge points a tenuous finger inland toward Arrowhead Peak. Behind this rise the shapely Sisters and a tumbled mass of mountains and ice fields forming the backbone of Baranof Island. Below are the somber depths of Silver Bay and the broken coastline of Sitka Sound.

If camping overnight on the ridge or lower peak, please take down all garbage.

Grade alpine
Distance 3 miles one way
Time to first peak 2.5 hours up, 1.5 hours down; to second peak, 3.5–4 hours up, 2.5 hours down
Elevation gain first peak 2550 feet; second peak 3350 feet±
Trail condition fair
Trail characteristic alpine
Access by foot, car, or bicycle, 2 miles from Sitka
Administrative agency formerly U.S. Forest Service; presently in limbo because of State Selection

Si2 GAVAN HILL

Gavan is a little-known old trail that no agency seems willing to claim but is currently maintained by the Forest Service. It starts from the north edge of town and climbs the ridge, a dominant feature on the northern skyline. The way leads upward on a well-defined trail to the summit of the ridge, a little more than 2000 feet above sea level. There is an unexpected glimpse of Sitka through a gap in the trees halfway up, and extensive views of Sitka Sound from the top.

The trail beginning is found by walking up Baranof Street toward the city Pioneer Cemetery. From the center of town walk east toward the Centennial Building and the small-boat harbor at Crescent Bay. Continue along Lincoln Street by the boat harbor; Baranof is the second street going off to the left. It passes a grade school and crosses Sawmill Creek Road and finally Merrill Road. Beyond the last house, shortly before the cemetery is reached, the trail takes off to the right. It is fairly obvious, although not presently signposted.

The trail starts out wet and ambles across muskeg in a northerly direction. It starts to climb seriously when the ridge is reached. The climb is steady as it runs upward and enters groves of huge Sitka spruce and hemlock. It crosses a gully with a stream, then zigzags up the hillside until, after about 1.5 hours of walking, the viewpoint of town is reached. Water may be found close by from small streams; in late summer this is the last chance to collect drinking water. The viewpoint gives intimate views of the city, its barrier of islands, and the Pacific Ocean beyond.

The trail climbs less steeply from here, then becomes less well-defined during another steep section before reaching the summit of the ridge. Careful note should be made of the trail for the return. Continue along

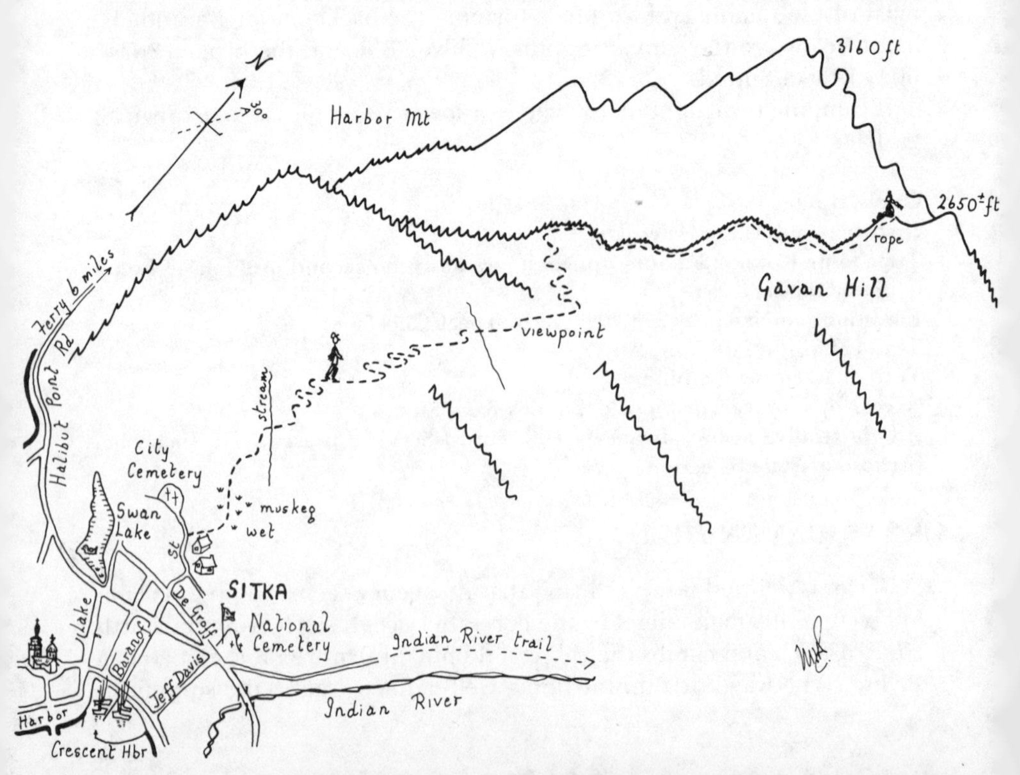

Sitka Sound from Gavan Hill

the ridge in a northeasterly direction. The trees diminish in size as the trail gains altitude. About a quarter of a mile farther along the ridge the shapely, pointed Sisters suddenly come into view between the trees. Small brown peat pools of doubtful drinking quality may be found at this point on the ridge.

A short, steep climb of approximately 200 feet gives access to the first peak. Be sure to stay on the ridge to avoid steep rocks on the left (west side), and do not trust the rope placed as a handrail on the steepest section of the climb, however strong it may seem. Rope left out in all kinds of weather can sometimes be broken with a flip of the fingers! The first peak has the best views.

Another peak 100 feet higher stands about a quarter of a mile behind the first summit. Opportunities for alpine camping are found almost anywhere on the ridge and between the two peaks. A small backpacker's stove is necessary for cooking. If winter snows have melted, water may have to be carried up from the first viewpoint below the ridge.

Grade alpine
Distance 3 miles
Time 3 hours up, 1.5 hours down
Elevation gain 2650 feet
Trail condition fairly good
Trail characteristics wooded hillside, alpine
Access by foot from town
Administrative agency: within State Selection, but presently being maintained by the U.S. Forest Service

Totems on Governor's Walk

Si3 GOVERNOR'S WALK

The tiny Sitka National Historical Park on the eastern extremity of Crescent Bay takes up the half mile of beach to Indian River. Tlingit Indians built a fort close to the river in 1802, but soon after they were defeated in a battle against Russians, led by Alexander Baranof, who were ruthlessly extending their lucrative fur trade down the coast. The site of the fort and its environs are now parkland, containing second-growth trees. The National Historical Park Headquarters are located at the entrance to the Park. From there a short, pleasant, broad trail takes off alongside the beach, in the trees.

The Governor's Walk (colloquially known as Lover's Lane) is liberally sprinkled with totem poles. Visitors with sketch pads and cameras will find a wealth of material in the woods and on the beach; the sweep of the mountains encircles the bay on three sides, with the restless Pacific between.

If walking from town, follow Lincoln Street from the Centennial Building, past Crescent small-boat harbor and Sheldon Jackson College, to the end of the road (1 mile). The National Historical Park headquarters, which also house an Indian workshop and museum, are adjacent to the beach. Walk on the beach side of the building, or through it to the doors on the beach side and at the exit turn left. A broad pathway lined with totem poles enters the trees and follows the beach. Within 15–20 minutes the Tlingit fort site is reached, where the path narrows. From the fort site it is possible to return along Indian River through the woods on the narrower footpath (see map). A fork from this path crosses Indian River by a footbridge to a picnic area on the far side. A short path from here connects with Sawmill Creek Road (Sitka Highway) approximately 1 mile east of Sitka. Another path from the picnic site runs east to a Russian Memorial dating back to the battle of 1804.

Grade sightseeing
Distance 1 mile
Time 40 minutes to 1 hour
Elevation gain none
Trail condition excellent
Trail characteristics historical, shoreline
Access by foot or car from Sitka (1 mile)
Administrative agency National Park Service

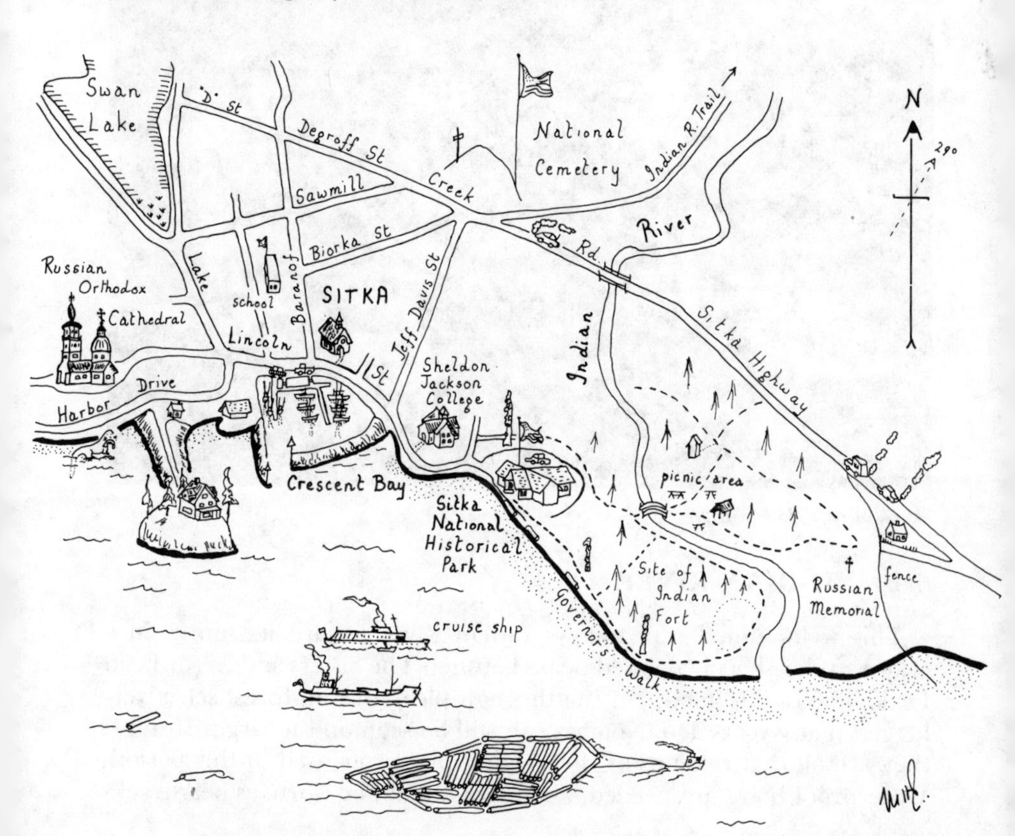

Skunk cabbage, Indian River

Si4 INDIAN RIVER

This well-defined trail follows Indian River toward its source in a cirque under sharply pointed peaks between The Sisters and Arrowhead Peak. The trail is good, passing through pleasant rain forest selectively logged many years ago. Notches can still be seen on the larger stumps; they are all that remains of the logging platforms used in this period. Waterproof boots are needed, and a bell should be worn, as bear tracks are frequently seen. Good fresh water is plentiful for the thirsty. The first mile of trail was damaged by trail bikes that created deep bog holes; these holes discouraged further bike activity beyond that point for a while, until the section was repaired with planking. The trail deteriorates after about 3.5 miles and finally ends at a series of waterfalls.

Find the Centennial Building and Crescent Harbor on the east side of Sitka. Walk around the harbor along Lincoln Street to Jeff Davis Street (immediately before Sheldon Jackson College). Turn left up Jeff Davis Street to the National Cemetery. Then turn right along Sawmill Creek Road, the main road running south out of town. Within a few yards turn left onto a dirt road and walk to its end (0.7 miles from the cemetery and 2.5 miles from town).

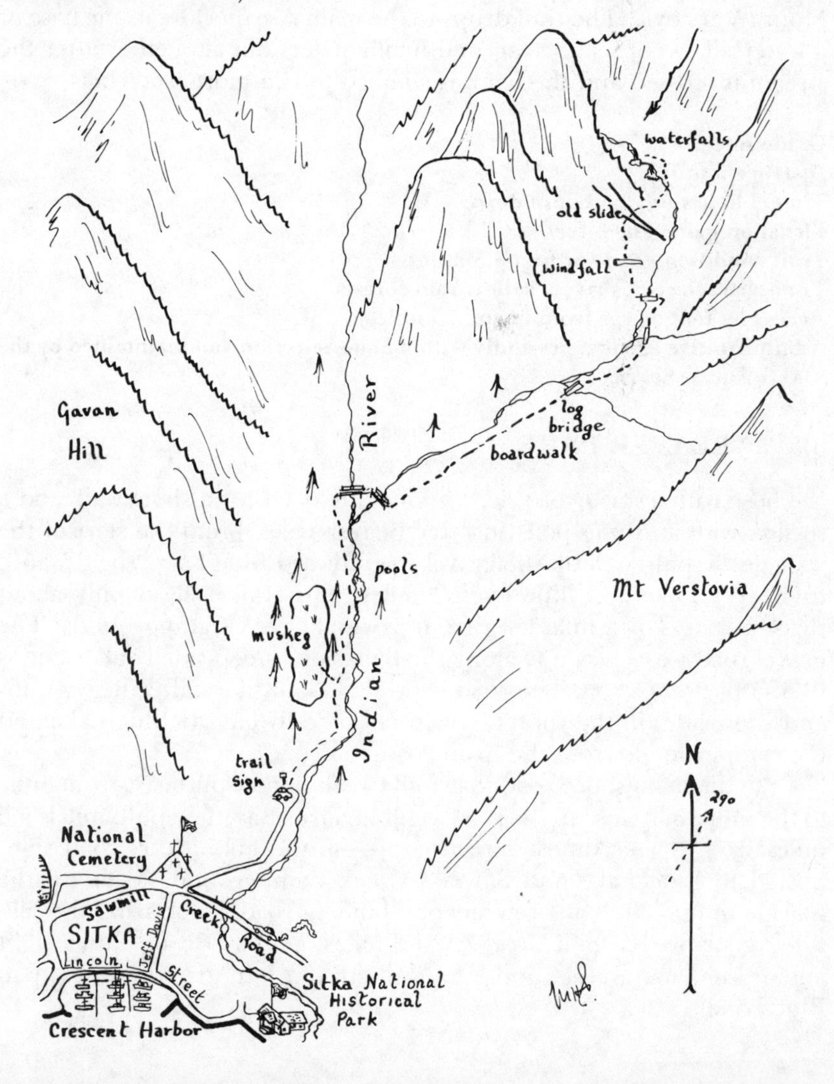

A Forest Service sign marks the beginning of the trail. Follow the pathway along the river by a series of pools and rapids. After about three-quarters of a mile the trees may be abandoned briefly for large open muskeg above and to the left of the trail. From here are views of Gavan Hill and the sharp peaks of The Sisters. After 2 miles the trail crosses Indian River, then its northeast tributary, by new bridges. Then the trail follows the east bank of the tributary and for a short distance becomes boardwalk. The gradually ascending path crosses two smaller streams on log bridges.

The tributary is recrossed to its west bank by a log bridge without a handrail. From this point the route deteriorates considerably. It becomes a steep climb to an open slide with views of Arrowhead Peak and Mount Verstovia. The trail drops to the main stream close to the base of a waterfall, becomes unclear, and finally peters out altogether after the stream is crossed and the bank is climbed to two more waterfalls.

Grade forest
Distance 5 miles
Time 3 hours up, 2.5 hours down
Elevation gain 1300+ feet
Trail condition good for first 3.5 miles
Trail characteristics river, valley, rain forests
Access by foot or car from town (2.5 miles)
Administrative agency: presently within State Selection, but maintained by the U.S. Forest Service

Si5 **BEAVER LAKE**

Those with a car or bicycle, who feel the need for a short walk and a session with a fishing pole, may try Beaver Lake. From the start of the walk at the pulp mill up the gravel road toward Blue Lake, the distance to Beaver Lake is a little over 2 miles. The trail itself is only about three-quarters of a mile long from Sawmill Creek Campgrounds. The gravel road weaves its way along the flanks of a steep-sided valley and is itself a pleasant stroll. The road is prone to landslides after heavy rains and snowslides in the winter, which periodically cut off Blue Lake and the campgrounds from the main road.

Take the main shore road (Sawmill Creek Road) southeast from Sitka to the pulp mill, close to the road's end in Silver Bay. The pulp mill is 5.5 miles from town. Almost directly opposite the mill, a dirt road signposted to Blue Lake and Sawmill Creek Campgrounds leads up the hillside to the left. Take this steeply climbing road, contouring the hillside well above Sawmill Creek. At 1.3 miles the road divides; turn right and descend to the creek and campgrounds (the left turn continues up to Blue Lake).

Walk through the campground, cross the bridge over the creek, and look for the trail on the left. It climbs steeply upward within a few yards of the bridge. Follow the trail in a series of switchbacks up the hillside. Some of the sharp turns abut against an old slide. Do not cross the slide; instead, stay on the trail where it continues to climb to the right, or west, side. It finally traverses the top. The steep climb is about 350 feet.

At the top of the hill a good boardwalk negotiates muskeg across flat countryside to the lake. Note the cedar trees flourishing in the area. At the lake, a wooden landing platform and boat are furnished by the Forest Service. After the boat is used, bring it out of the water onto the platform and turn it upside down before leaving the lake. Fishermen intending to use the boat should take extra oars in case those at the lake are missing.

Beaver Lake is dark in color, effectively reflecting the somber mood of the mountains above. It is trapped between the solid mountain walls on the one hand and wooded knolls and muskeg on the other. The outflow into Sawmill Creek provides good fishing.

Beaver Lake

Grade sightseeing (strenuous climb at first)
Distance from pulp mill, 2.3 miles
Time 1.5 hours from pulp mill
Elevation gain 437 feet
Trail condition good (be careful of slides on the road)
Trail characteristics muskeg and lake, fishing
Access by car or bicycle from Sitka (5.5 miles)
Administrative agency U.S. Forest Service

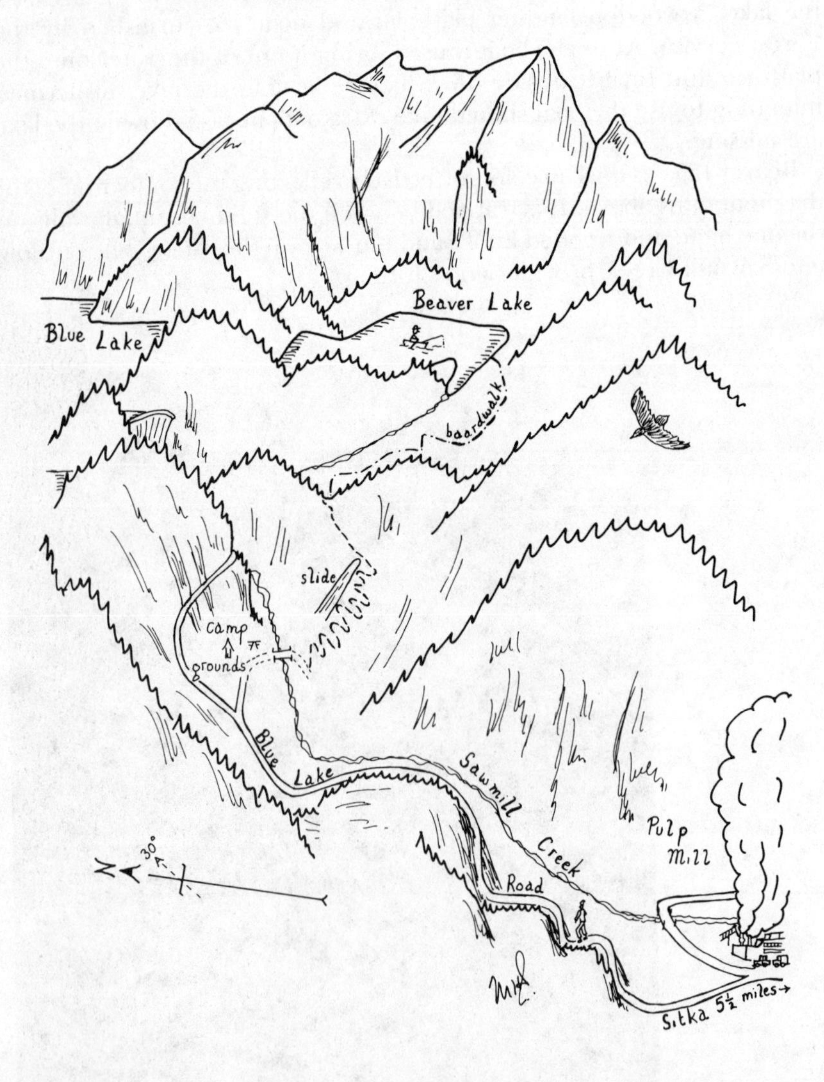

Alaska rainforest

Conservation could be defined as the wise use and rational management of scarce natural resources. Taking the term "use" to include wildlife habitat, aesthetic values, and other values not involving modification of the environment, it is perfectly possible for the existing values of an area to far outweigh any new uses that might be developed. When this is the case, the only wise and rational course is to preserve the existing values. In other words, preservation is an essential component of conservation.

The Tongass National Forest, which covers most of Southeast Alaska, is a case in point. About 30 percent of the Tongass is classified as commercially valuable forest land. This is the old-growth rain forest that lies along Southeast's shoreline and on the lower slopes and valley floors. The remaining 70 percent of the Tongass consists of alpine areas, rock and ice, and scrubby, noncommercial forest. The logging industry, highway builders, and proponents of intensive recreational development all have plans for this area that would destroy the forest. What they overlook is that the forest has enormous value of a different sort in its present, undisturbed state: It is the largest de facto rain forest wilderness in the United States; it provides essential habitat for many species of mammals, birds, and fish (including several species of Pacific salmon that are the basis of Southeast's fishing industry); it offers vast opportunities for dispersed recreation such as hiking, kayaking and canoeing, camping, sport fishing, hunting, nature study, and photography; it is an important scenic resource, especially for tourists traveling by ferry or cruise ship; and finally, it has value for the human spirit by simply being there. Surely the best use for a substantial portion of this forest wilderness would be to leave it as it is — to preserve the wild lands in their present state.

The key question is this: How much wilderness should be preserved and where? Few have seriously advocated that all the forests of Southeast Alaska should be preserved, although this may be more a matter of political realism than personal conviction. (I, for one, feel that enough trees have already been cut.) What conservationists have advocated is that certain high quality areas be preserved, including some areas that contain substantial stands of undisturbed forest that would otherwise be logged (e.g., on Admiralty Island and in the Yakobi-West Chichagof area). If all the preservation proposals suggested by Southeast Alaska conservation organizations were adopted, the total reduction in the volume of timber available for logging would be small compared to the original volume on the Tongass. Surely this is not too great a price to pay to protect key portions of one of the most spectacularly beautiful wild places on Earth.

The unique and irreplaceable resources of the Tongass belong to the American public as a whole and are not the private province of the merchants, industrialists, and politicians of Southeast Alaska. The responsibility falls on all of us to insure that these resources are not sacrificed in the name of "progress" or "development" or "growth," but that they remain as they are in trust for the future. We must see ourselves as stewards whose concern is for the land itself rather than for short-term economic "gains" that can be wrested from the land only at an unacceptable cost.

Joseph W. Greenough
Juneau

JUNEAU

One is struck, when arriving by ferry or tour ship, by Juneau's precarious site on the skirt of sheer mountain slopes. One has the impression that a small shrug from above would send the entire capital city of Alaska into the tidal channel on which it sits, and yet the scene is so unbelievably beautiful it takes the breath away.

Juneau's history and its trails are tied up with gold finds in the 1880s and early 1900s, and many local names reflect the miners' trials, tribulations, and triumphs during that period, for example, Perseverance, Last Chance Basin, Silverbow, Nugget Creek, Bullion Creek, etc. One relic of lasting interest is the Treadwell Ditch traversing the east side of Douglas Island. It carried water from all the major streams to the Treadwell Mine, south of Douglas.

Because of Juneau's close proximity to the mountains and their deep, indented valleys, some of the best trails begin from the downtown area within walking distance of the ferry and tour ships. A year-round bus service goes to Douglas; buses also serve the Mendenhall Valley and Auke Bay and help visitors without their own transportation to gain access to out-of-town trails. The bus starts from the ferry terminal downtown, and stops on street corners almost anywhere en route when flagged.

Juneau's link with the outside world is through the jet airport, 9 miles north of town, and the ferry service. The ferry either docks downtown or uses the Auke Bay ferry terminal 14 miles north of town. Cruise ships tie up in town.

Warning: "Glory holes" (deep, open mine pits) and possibly vertical shafts are present in the Mount Juneau, Mount Roberts, and Dupont areas, plus Douglas Island. Tread with care if you wander off the trail.

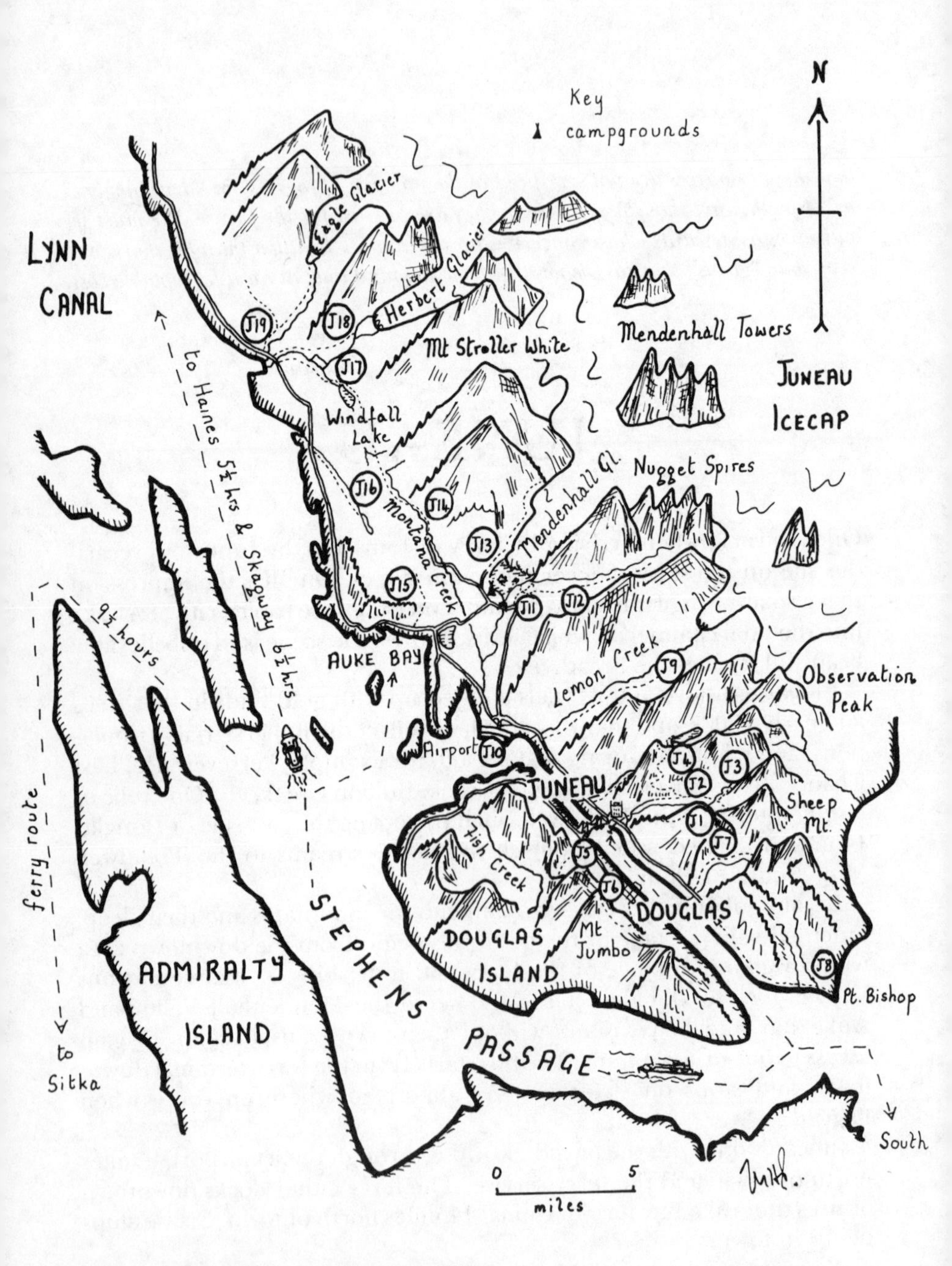

Trails within walking distance of town:

J1 **Mount Roberts (alpine)**
J2 **Perseverance (sightseeing)**

J3 **Granite Basin (forest)**
J4 **Mount Juneau (alpine)**
J5 **Kowee Ski Bowl (forest)**

Maps required: Juneau 1:63,360 series B-1 and B-2 quadrangles; or Juneau and vicinity topographic map, 1:24,000 series.

Douglas (3 miles from Juneau):
J6 **Mount Jumbo (Bradley) (alpine)**

Maps required: Juneau B-2 and A-2; or Juneau and vicinity, 1:24,000 series.

Thane Road (4–6 miles south of Juneau):
J7 **Sheep Creek (forest)**
J8 **Bishop Point (forest)**

Maps required: Juneau B-1 and A-1. Sheep Creek only: Juneau and vicinity, 1:24,000 series.

Glacier Highway (5 miles north of Juneau):
J9 **Lemon Creek (forest)**

Map required: Juneau B-2.

Proximity of airport and Mendenhall Glacier (9–13 miles north of Juneau):
J10 **Wetlands (sightseeing)**
J11 **East Glacier (sightseeing)**
J12 **Nugget Creek (forest)**
J13 **West Glacier (forest)**
J14 **Montana Creek (forest)**

Maps required: Juneau B-2. Additional for Montana Creek: Juneau B-3 and C-3.

Auke Bay and points north (12–28 miles north of Juneau):
J15 **Spaulding (forest)**
J16 **Peterson (forest)**
J17 **Windfall Lake (forest)**
J18 **Herbert Glacier (forest)**
J19 **Amalga-Eagle Glacier (forest)**

Maps required: Juneau B-2, B-3, and C-3.

Maps can be obtained locally, in person, in the Federal Building on 9th and Glacier Avenue.

J1 MOUNT ROBERTS

The hulk of Mount Roberts sits over Juneau like a crouching bear. A trail climbs onto its spine but stops short, by 1 mile, of the summit of Mount Roberts. It ends instead on the summit of Gastineau Peak (3666 feet), a subsidiary peak. From here, commanding views are obtained of Juneau and Douglas, the entire length of Gastineau Channel running into Stephens Passage, and Admiralty Island in the far distance. Silverbow Basin forms a deep valley on the northern side.

This popular mountain has two distinct advantages. The trail is easily reached from the downtown district of Juneau, and the upper slopes are relatively safe during late spring and early summer snows. Care must be taken on the final ridge, however, A hike to the first open views in alpine country, about 200 feet above tree line (1800 feet above the channel), makes a pleasant outing for families. The route boasts an intimate view of the city from above, 15–20 minutes from the start; the trail, though well maintained, is wet and muddy in patches.

From the ferry terminal, turn left up Franklin Street, the main street into town. Stay on Franklin and go straight up a hill past the Baranof Hotel to 6th Street. The last block is steep. Turn right on 6th Street and climb another steep hill to its end against a wooded hillside. A sign to Mount Roberts is directly ahead, on the hillside at the end of the road.

At first the trail climbs steeply in a series of switchbacks, leading onto the wooded ridge. About 200 feet above the sign, the path pauses by a

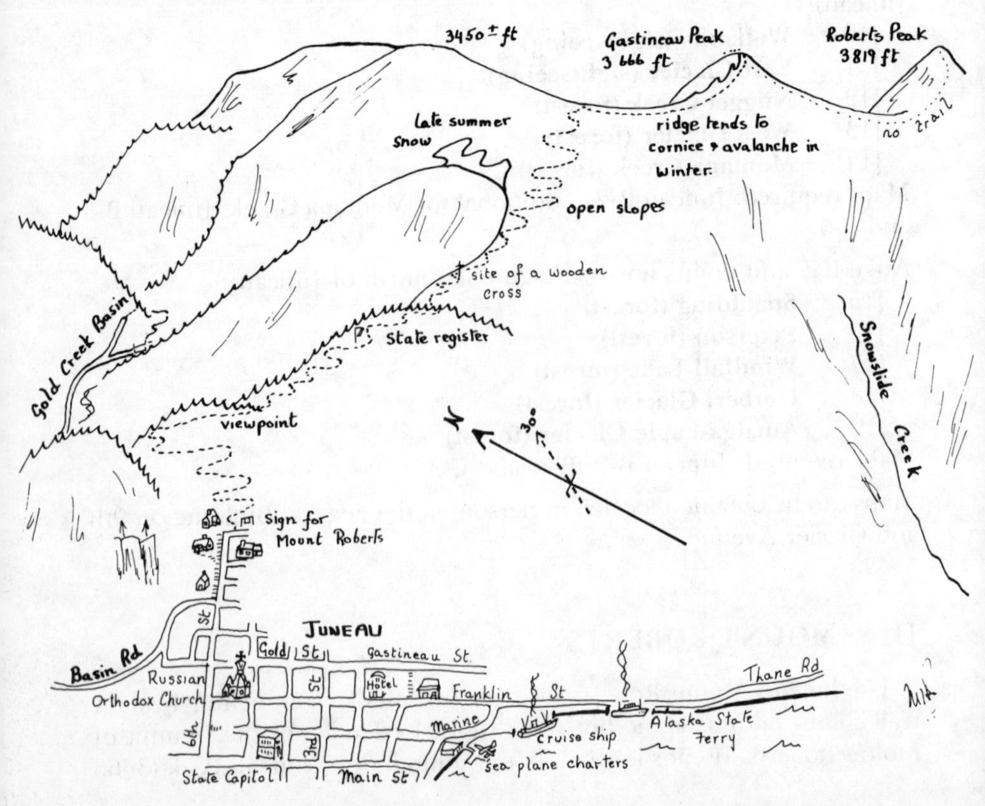

viewpoint of the city. It then climbs through trees in large zigzags, crossing at least three streams en route. In late August and September these may be the sole supply of water, because of the virtual disappearance of snowbanks above. A State register has been placed about three-quarters of the way to the tree line.

Allow about 2 hours to reach open alpine slopes above the trees. A wooden cross once stood here, on a natural platform. The views are superb. The entire Gastineau Channel is spread out below, its surface grooved and ridged by intricate wake patterns in constant motion. Fishing boats, pleasure craft, ferries, tour ships (just disappearing over the horizon with a puff of smoke!), and more fishing boats ply back and forth. Watch for merlins (pigeon hawks) passing through during the late summer.

The footpath continues to climb steeply until the summit ridge is reached at 3000 feet. This runs southeast directly over Gastineau Channel on one side and Silverbow Basin on the other. The ridge to Gastineau Peak is pleasant but airy, and the views are even more expansive from the summit. Early and late in the year a cold wind often whips off the icecap — not very far away — and chills one to the bone. Take warm clothing and extra food.

First viewpoint, Mount Roberts Trail

An extra hour is needed to reach Mount Roberts, 150 feet higher than Gastineau Peak and a mile farther on. Only experienced mountaineers should attempt the final ridge in deep snow, since it tends to develop a cornice and avalanche.

Grade alpine
Distance 0.8 mile from ferry terminal to trail; 2.7 miles trail to Gastineau Peak
Time 3 hours up, 2 hours down (first viewpoint 30–40 minutes from ferry terminal)
Elevation gain 3666 feet
Trail condition good
Trail characteristic mountain
Access by foot from town
Administrative agency State of Alaska

J2 PERSEVERANCE

The approach along Basin Road to Perseverance is a walk unto itself. The road overhangs Gold Creek on wooden trestles and plunges through a cleft overshadowed by Mount Juneau on the one hand and Mount Roberts on the other. Sometimes bears graze in open patches of brush on the opposite mountainside. In spring, the distinctive aroma of cottonwoods coming into leaf pervades the atmosphere, and single whistled notes of varied thrushes flood the valley with sound. Hermit and

Silverbow Basin

Swainson's thrushes perform soprano solos with oft-repeated phrases. Any time of year the valley is overwhelming to visitors from Outside not used to the suddenness of Alaska's vertical scenery. Two waterfalls are displayed along its length, not counting the aqueous display down the sheer flanks of Mount Juneau.

In winter, travel is not recommended along Perseverance trail and associated trails (Mount Juneau and Granite Basin) because they are subject to avalanche activity.

From the ferry terminal take the same route up Franklin Street to 6th Street as for the Mount Roberts trail. On 6th Street turn right, then left up Gold Street (the next turning). This climbs steeply to 8th Street. Turn right, then immediately left onto Basin Road; this rounds a corner on trestles following Gold Creek, until within half a mile it crosses the creek and shortly after divides. Keep left up the hill. In half a mile the road ends at a stile and signpost — the beginning of Perseverance trail. The trail continues to climb and soon comes to a viewpoint of Snowslide Gulch across a deep canyon.

The waterfall seen round the next corner is Ebner Falls, and within a quarter of a mile of this point a short footpath goes to the top of the falls. Almost opposite the trail junction are the start of the path up Mount Juneau, and a State register. Perseverance trail proceeds up the valley, and after crossing Granite Creek it once again divides. The well-defined path to the left up a steep hill leads to Granite Basin (described in J3). Go straight on and within half a mile a spur trail on the right leads to the Glory Hole.

The main trail ends 0.3 mile farther on in Silverbow Basin. A waterfall seems to remain permanently suspended in space, like a long white tassel, from a ridge above. Derelict mine buildings and other remains of the gold mining era are scattered around. Allow 3.5 hours from town to reach the end of the trail and see the points of interest (not including Mount Juneau and Granite Basin).

Glory Hole

The spur is probably no longer than 400 yards and at first drops steeply downhill. It follows a stream for a few yards, causing some wet moments for those not practiced at boulder-hopping. The path climbs steeply and ends abruptly on an edge close to some ruined mining buildings. Parents are urgently advised to hold children by the hand before approaching the edge. The man-made pit is at least 300 feet deep and 200 yards across.

Grade sightseeing
Distance 2 miles, ferry terminal to trail
Trail to Silverbow Basin 2.7 miles

Trail to Ebner Falls 0.6 mile
Trail to Glory Hole 2.4 miles
Time 2.5 hours to Silverbow Basin and Perseverance Mine from town; 3.5 hours with diversion
Elevation gain 1100 feet
Trail condition excellent
Trail characteristics historical, scenic valley
Limitation avalanche danger in winter
Access by foot or car from town
Administrative agency State of Alaska

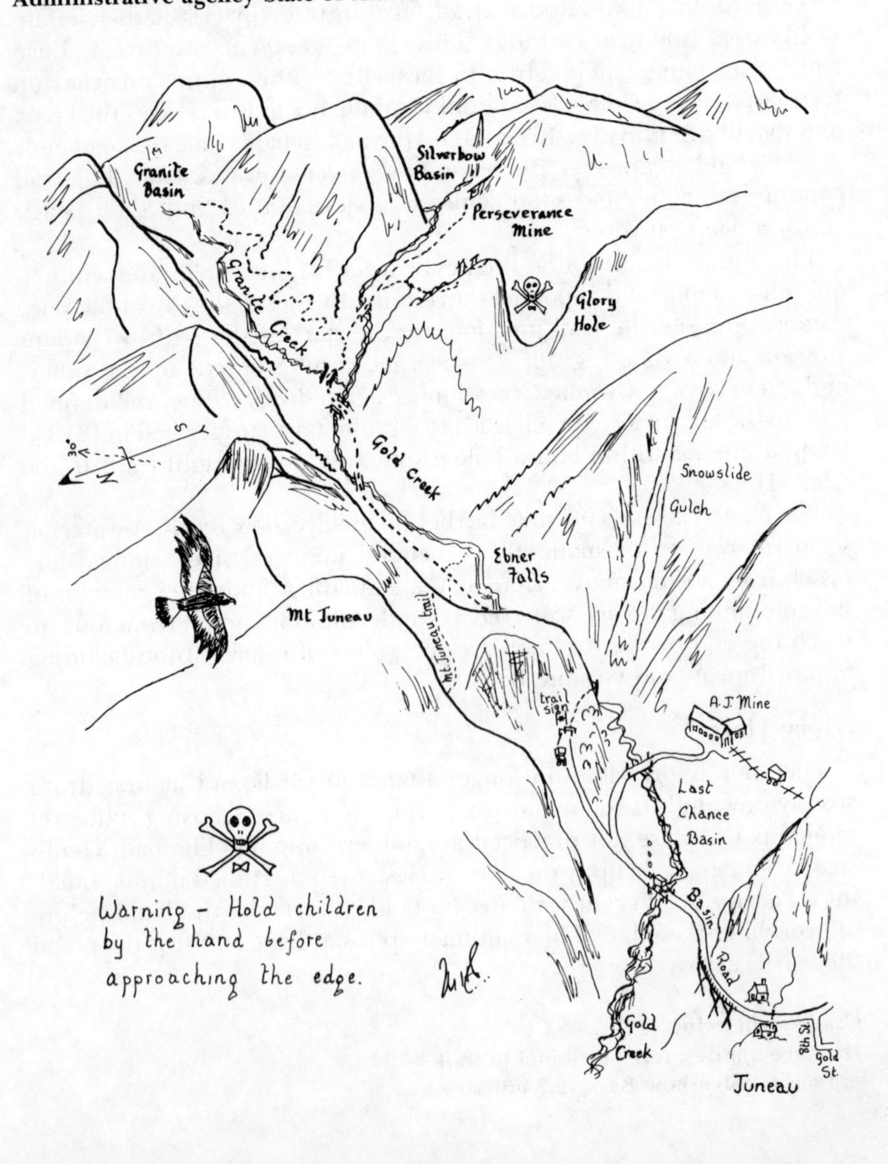

J3 GRANITE BASIN

Granite Basin is a mountain bowl accessible via a spur trail from Perseverance trail. The basin is 1.5 miles and 700 feet above Silverbow Basin, which may account for its solitude, even though Perseverance is well traveled. The beauty of the upper basin, and the variety of wildflowers in early August, are impressive. Some of the flowers are blue cranesbill (wild geranium), forget-me-not (Alaska's State flower), delicate clusters of western columbine peeping out from moss-covered rocks, and white Grass of Parnassus. Growing in profusion (on both Perseverance and Granite Basin trails) are monkshood and blue and yellow daisies. Give yourself an entire day to get up there and back into town. It would be a pity to hurry things.

Refer to the Perseverance trail for the Granite trail takeoff point. The trail junction is approximately 2 miles from the roadhead, shortly after crossing Granite Creek. Almost immediately the trail climbs steeply in a series of switchbacks and passes through a copse of trees. Otherwise it stays in tall brush until the basin is reached. The trail stays above Granite Creek, a cataract spilling through a narrow cleft in the mountains. Even in August snow lingers in the basin, sometimes in photogenic bridges over the stream. The path runs east, then veers northeast as it approaches the lip of the basin.

A short, sharp climb brings one over the lip, where the stream tumbles out of a pool. From this point the entire basin is visible although the trail soon peters out. The bowl is an alpine cirque, and access to the Mount Juneau ridge is possible. Mount Olds, also accessible from the basin, dominates the skyline to the north-northeast.

Watch for golden eagles. In the land of bald eagles, golden eagles are scarce, but a pair is known to be nesting above Gold Creek. Water pipits, savannah sparrows, golden-crowned sparrows (whose spring song intones "oh, dear me" in lucid tones), rosy finches, and rock ptarmigans may also frequent the slopes above and below the basin.

Grade forest
Distance 3.5 miles from road end to basin
Time 3 hours from town
Elevation gain 1750 feet
Trail condition good
Trail characteristics valley, alpine bowl
Limitation avalanche danger in winter
Access by car or foot to end of road, 2 miles from ferry terminal
Administrative agency State of Alaska

J4 MOUNT JUNEAU

Mount Juneau dominates the city of Juneau, leaning over the shoulder of the city, its constant guardian. Every year the mountain shows its awesome power: in April and May the mantle of snow slides off its flanks and tumbles down its gullies with a roar that can be heard for miles. Anyone seeing this will be warned of the danger of setting foot on Mount Juneau while snow lingers. It has already claimed many lives.

A steep trail leads off Perseverance trail and goes to the summit of Mount Juneau. It is subject to avalanches in early spring as well as winter, and the danger persists over gullies and final steep slopes until May and June. In late summer, however, it is within the capabilities of anyone strong enough and sound in wind, but it is a full day's climb.

Hikers with ambition and skill in hiking over mountain terrain can traverse the ridge from the summit of Mount Juneau to Granite Basin or Salmon Creek reservoir. In early summer an ice ax — and ability to use it properly — are needed for long glissades into one cirque or the other; care should be taken on choice of route into either basin because of bluffs and small glaciers. The complete round trip requires at least 10 hours, so be prepared for a long day.

Refer to the Perseverance trail (J2) for directions to the beginning of the Mount Juneau trail. A State register is located at the junction of the two trails. The way up Mount Juneau climbs immediately in a series of switchbacks to the summit of a spur, called the Horn, where it runs inside the edge of a grove of tall hemlock and spruce. A footpath (not readily seen) to the left leads to a viewpoint of Juneau within a frame of trees. A short way farther up, at about 1200 feet, the climb temporarily eases and the trail traverses Mount Juneau for about a mile, running west.

There are splendid views both up and down: an interesting oblique view of the city, the A. J. Mine directly below, and the steep section of trail above. The trail traverse passes a flooded horizontal mine shaft. Mountain streams cascade across the trail and tumble over the cliff edge below. Great care must be taken across the stream gullies when they are covered with snow. If gully crossings cannot be safely protected with ice ax and/or rope, they should not be attempted.

The trail climbs once more through a copse of trees, then runs through brush and onto steep slopes by a small stream trickle. The elevation is about 1800 feet. The stream is the last water, unless there is snow above. The route from here on is steep to within 500 feet of the summit. Avoid snow unless equipped with an ice ax. Views are

Granite Basin

panoramic all the way, and from the top on a clear day the Fairweather Range rises west of Glacier Bay about 150 miles away.

Grade alpine
Distance 2.5 miles from ferry terminal to trail beginning; 2 miles, trail to summit
Time 4 hours from town, 2 hours down (allow a full day)
Elevation gain 3576 feet
Trail condition good
Trail characteristics mountain-alpine
Limitations: in winter and spring, avalanche hazard and steep snow slopes on upper third of trail. Ice ax and ability to use it essential. Best time: late July to first snows in September
Access by car or foot from town, then via Perseverance trail
Administrative agency State of Alaska

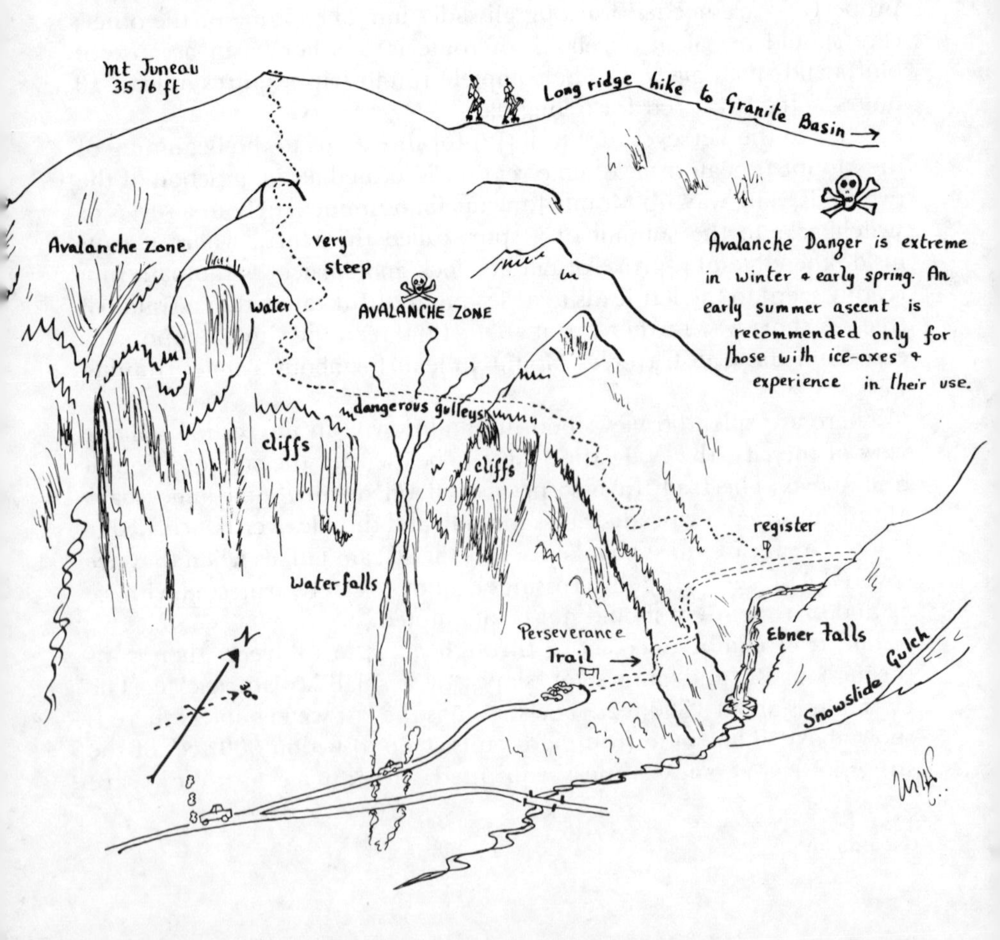

J5 KOWEE SKI BOWL

Otherwise known as the Dan Moller Ski Trail, this is a pleasant walk on Douglas Island, used extensively by skiers in winter. The route gradually ascends to the head of a valley into an alpine basin. It runs alternately through trees and open, muskeg meadows where, in autumn, the Alaska bog cotton grows in profusion and turns the muskeg white. The trail is boardwalk over much of the muskeg stretches but is wet in places. From the end of the trail, access is possible onto a ridge, the backbone of Douglas Island, and to Mount Troy, 3005 feet above sea level.

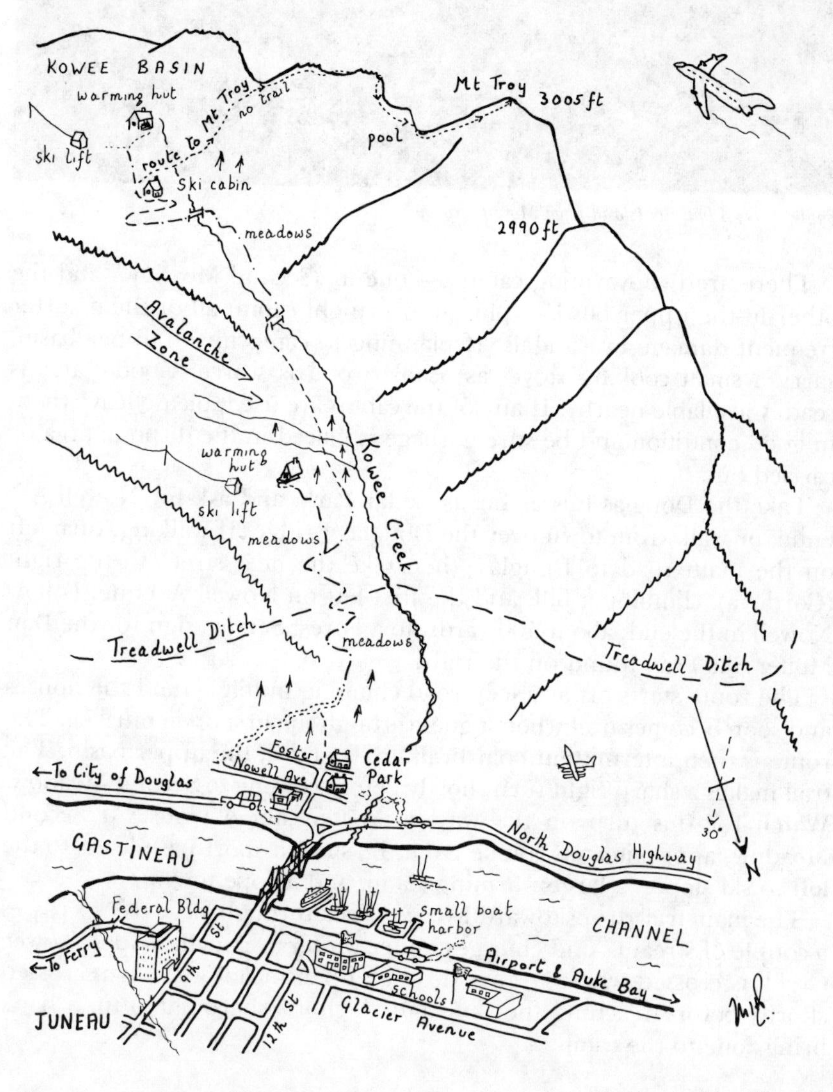

Eagle Peak, Admiralty Island from Mount Troy

There are two warming cabins — one in "Second Meadow" and the other in the upper bowl — plus an overnight cabin; all of them suffer frequent damage by vandals. If planning to camp in the upper basin, carry a small cooking stove, as usable wood is scarce. Good water is readily available nearby. If any of the cabins are used, please leave them in good condition and be sure garbage is placed in the disposal area or carried out.

Take the Douglas bus as far as Cedar Park, and ask for Nowell Avenue; or walk from town over the Douglas Bridge. If walking, turn left on the main road to Douglas, then take the next street to the right (Cordova), climbing a hill, and the first left on Nowell Avenue. Follow Nowell to the end, about 500 yards, to a Forest Service sign for the Dan Moller Ski Trail found on the right.

The route starts off as a jeep road climbing uphill behind the houses and soon becomes trail when it goes through the first open muskeg. The route is then intermittent boardwalk to its end in the upper basin. The trail makes a sharp right turn shortly before coming to Second Meadow. Watch for this turn on the way back; it is not obvious. At Second Meadow, approximately a mile from the start, a short path leads to the left to ski slopes, a large warming cabin, and a rope tow.

The main trail drops toward Kowee Creek through large trees, crosses a couple of streams, and emerges under winter avalanche slopes. Kowee Creek is crossed where it goes through open meadows; it is recrossed shortly before reaching the ski cabin. A short, sharp climb up a bank brings one to the cabin.

The trail continues a short distance beyond here, but fades away in the upper basin after about 200 yards. A large warming hut, unfortunately the worse for wear, is to the right and a ski tow to the left. A low ridge, at the head of the basin, only 600 feet higher, can be climbed up moderately steep slopes. By using game trails, one can travel northwest on the ridge onto Mount Troy. Probably these trails were made by black bears, since brown bears are not normally found on Douglas Island. From the large notch in the ridge, the site of a small pool, ascend diagonally to the right, first through brush, then trees, and follow the ridge by easy scrambling once out in the open.

In spring, steep snow slopes should be treated with respect, and in late summer beware of deer cabbage covering the slopes; it is beautiful with autumn colors, but slippery underfoot. From the top of Mount Troy there are extensive views of Admiralty Island and the interior of Douglas Island.

Grade to basin forest; Mount Troy alpine
Distance 1.6 miles from ferry terminal to Nowell Avenue; 3.3 miles from Cedar Park bus stop to Kowee Basin
Time 2 hours from Cedar Park to Kowee Basin, 1.5 hours return; 4 hours from Cedar Park to summit of Mount Troy, 3 hours down (or overnight)
Elevation gain 1800 feet; Mount Troy 3005 feet
Trail condition to basin excellent; from Basin to Mount Troy no trail
Trail characteristics valley, muskeg meadows; Mount Troy alpine
Access by bus or foot from town
Administrative agency U.S. Forest Service

J6 MOUNT JUMBO

Mount Bradley is the name given on the map, but the mountain is known colloquially as Mount Jumbo, named after one of the mines in Douglas. It is the highest peak on Douglas Island, with a commanding position over Douglas, Juneau, and Gastineau Channel, and sweeping views west to Admiralty Island and northwest to the Chilkat Range.

Unfortunately the trail is in poor shape, and it would be nice to see it adopted by the State or borough when either has final jurisdiction over the land. Currently it is kept open by local residents, but it is miserably wet, with deep bog holes and windfalls bad enough on the steep sections to make a saint curse! It crosses the Treadwell Ditch at a point where the ditch can be recognized as man-made, and crosses wide open muskeg before climbing the ridge. A. J. Industries owns a portion of the right-of-way, but they allow public access through their land.

Ride the bus to Douglas, but do not get off until it has run through town to the far end and started on the return to Juneau along 5th Street. Then, hopefully, ask to be put off by the Mount Jumbo trail; it is unmarked in the 300 block and begins in an empty lot about 50 feet wide between two houses. The empty lot is designated to become "Anderson Street" at some future date; presently it has a staggered crossing with a dirt road extending to 3rd Street.

Do not walk on private property when you start (the trail begins by a private home). Almost immediately, the trail enters brush and becomes boggy. Before long some steep wooden steps in ruinous condition are reached. At this point a slightly better alternative can be taken to the right. The trail traverses the hillside in a southeasterly direction, crosses a small stream, then goes through a clear-cut logged prior to 1905 for the Douglas (Jumbo) Mine.

The trail then crosses Paris Creek and, shortly afterward, at the top of a steep climb, crosses the Treadwell Ditch. Another boggy section must be waded before the trail crosses a stream and runs up a slatted log on a

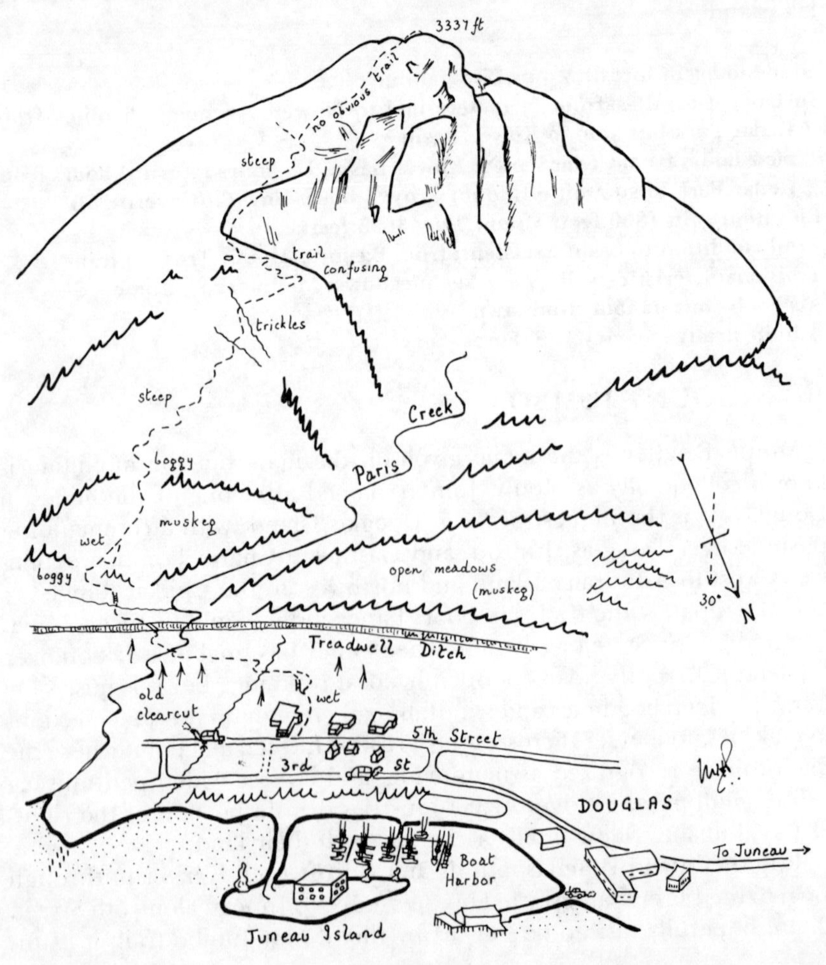

Gastineau Channel from Mount Jumbo

steep incline. (Be careful, wet wood is slippery.) Once more bog, before the trail emerges into open muskeg about 550 feet above sea level and a mile from the beginning of the trail. Go southwest through the muskeg toward the ridge of Mount Jumbo looming above. Note where you exit from the trees for the return, because the tendency is to go a few yards too far to the left. The last of the really mean bog holes is on the far side of the muskeg; then the pathway begins to climb in earnest. It goes almost straight up the ridge and is blocked in places by some particularly difficult windfalls. Just before the path emerges from the trees two small streams may be encountered, depending on the dryness or wetness of the summer. This is the last water before the summit after snow melt, except for a small peat pool on the upper ridge.

The trail comes out onto the ridge and is easy to follow upward, but not down. Note which way it goes, so that the directions can be reversed on the return. (During the descent first go north, then northeast to pick up the trail.) The final summit towers above the ridge at this point. The path follows the edge of the Paris Creek basin, then climbs steeply. If snow lingers an ice ax is needed, since the slope is highly exposed.

An obvious trail traverses to the left, but this may be ignored and a direct approach made to the summit. Almost any route can be picked from this point. The summit, sprinkled with alpine tarns, many still half-covered with snow even in August, makes a good fair weather campsite. Less exposed camping is found on the ridge below at the base of the final summit, by the brackish pool mentioned earlier (water should be boiled before drinking).

Grade alpine
Distance 2.6 miles
Time 3.5 hours up, 2.5 hours down (it takes longer than you think!)
Elevation gain 3337 feet
Trail condition poor
Trail characteristics forest, muskeg, alpine
Access by bus or car from Juneau (3.5 miles)
Administrative agency: none at present; within State Selection. Kept open by local citizens. Part of the lower section owned by A. J. Industries; public access allowed

J7 SHEEP CREEK

Sheep Creek is in a steep-sided, flat-bottomed valley that bustled with mining activity at the turn of the century. Derelict cabins still stand as gaunt reminders of the past. Sheep Creek was named when the first miners mistook the mountain goats they saw on the crags for sheep.

The trail runs through pleasant groves of evergreens at first, then breaks into the open in the valley itself. This trail is not recommended for winter travel because of avalanche activity in the general area. Bear sign is plentiful, but I have never encountered a bear while wearing a bell. In the past the trail could be followed over a 3400-foot summit, alongside some powerlines, to Carlson Creek and Annex Creek in Taku Inlet, at least a two-day journey. But the trail is not maintained beyond the first watershed and is barely passable now.

Drive south out of Juneau along the shore road, called Thane Road, to 4.1 miles (3.5 miles from the ferry terminal). Turn left onto a wide dirt

Sheep Creek

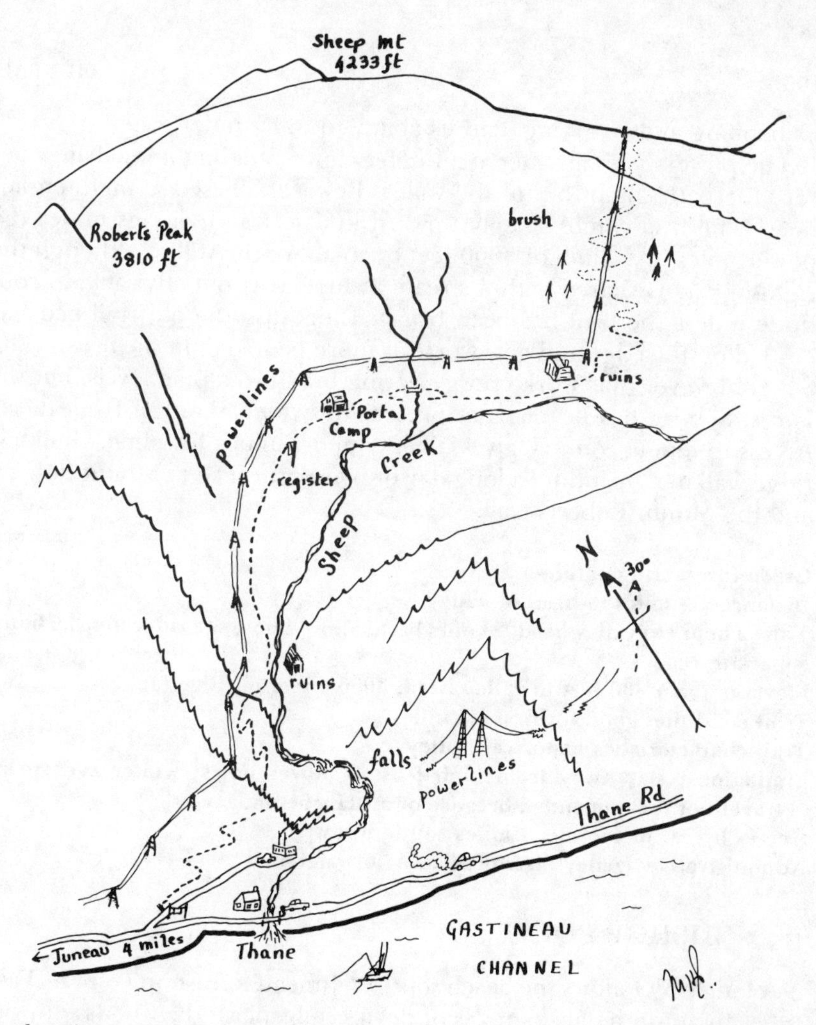

road going up a hill. The trail, starting on steps, will be found immediately on the left. The State trail sign stands between the two roads. Limited parking may be available on the upper road, and at a short distance along Thane Road, at Sheep Creek, there is ample parking.

The trail climbs in tall trees with stretches of corduroy footing (logwalk). A viewpoint of Sheep Creek tumbling over the rim of the valley is passed; immediately beyond this the trail climbs steeply. The steep climb is short and the top is reached half a mile from the road, 1000 feet above sea level. The trail next drops into Sheep Creek Valley, meeting the creek at the first set of derelict buildings (seen on the far bank).

A little over a mile up the valley more buildings in a dangerous state of decay are found at Portal Camp. The trail narrows from here; watch for a short diversion to the left over a log bridge at a stream crossing. A resident dipper, or water ouzel (a small, brown bird), frequents the river's edge at the far end of the valley. It is recognized by a clear song, its bobbing and curtsying, and its ability to walk under water.

The power poles are met at a tumble-down building immediately before the path climbs out of the valley. Beware! These are high tension lines! The trail climbs steeply upward in a series of zigzags under the power poles in a climb of 3000 feet or so above the valley, although the right-of-way is shared with a stream at first. It is not advisable to continue unless the trail has been brushed, because the old trail bed has eroded on the edge and gets worse as more people fight the brush. The State, however, has work crews clearing brush to alpine levels, but the Forest Service has no plans at present to extend the trail from there. Access to alpine country gives hikers opportunities for almost limitless ridge walking, including a long day or overnight hike to Mount Roberts and the Mount Roberts trail.

Grade forest (ridge alpine)
Distance 2.5 miles to head of valley
Time 2 hours to valley head, 2 hours back; allow 4 hours to ridge top, 3.5 hours back to road
Elevation gain 800 feet to valley head; 3000+ feet to ridge top
Trail condition good for first 1.5 miles
Trail characteristics historical, valley
Limitations: stay away from high tension power poles; winter and spring travel not recommended because of avalanche danger
Access by car or bicycle, 4 miles south of town
Administrative agency State of Alaska, to watershed

J8 BISHOP POINT

A long trail follows the beach south of Juneau to Bishop Point in Taku Inlet. In autumn, large groves of devil's club splash the woods with rich yellows and orange, and beyond Dupont deer cabbage covers the ground with lush yellow leaves. The overall effect of somber browns, deep greens, and bright yellows is hard to describe. It is as if nature had donned her best party dress before retiring for the winter.

For the first 1.5 miles the trail is muddy and requires good waterproof boots. Unfortunately, the cabin at Bishop Point is subject to vandalism, possibly because it is easily available to powerboats. It is currently no better than a shelter.

If starting from the ferry terminal, turn right and follow the shoreline road (Thane Road) southeast to its end, 6 miles from town. Park at the road end; a trail sign marks the beginning of the trail above the shoreline. In a few yards it crosses Sheep Creek and then points a long muddy finger at Dupont, an old powder storage dock 1.6 miles away.

After about a mile the path to Bishop Point leads to the left; but if you are a fisherman, stick with the mud for a while. Dupont is a fine fishing

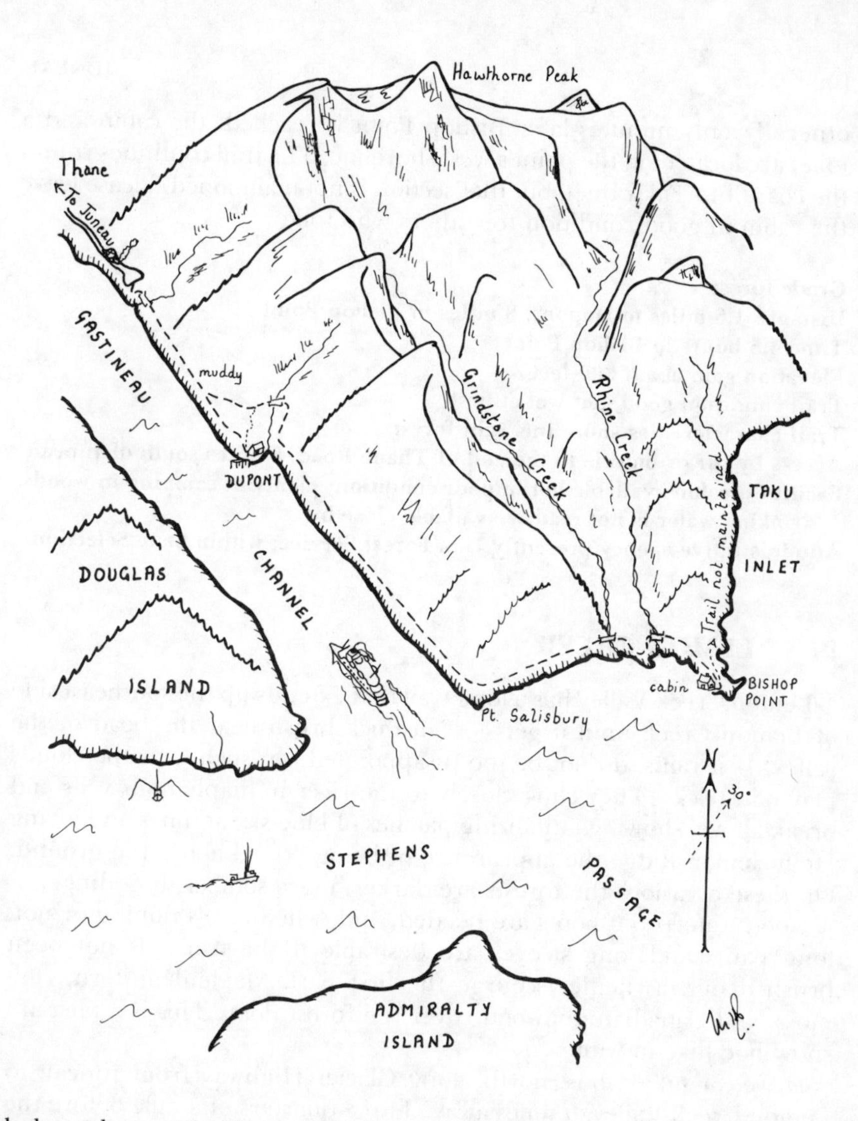

hole and many local people fish off the rocks for halibut and salmon. Stay off the old dock; it suffers from old age, and its rotten planks are liable to give way any day.

The Bishop Point trail is regained by climbing the hill on the north side of Dupont Creek, but stay away from the creek bed — it becomes a steep-sided gully higher up. The trail, less threadbare from fewer feet, is about 200 feet above the Dupont powder house ruins and crosses the creek at this level. It then drops toward the shoreline but stays above it, crossing many streams for most of its course.

Evidence of past selective logging is visible close to Point Salisbury. Six and a half to 7 miles from the road two rushing mountain torrents, Grindstone Creek and Rhine Creek, are crossed within 0.65 mile of each other. Twenty minutes later Bishop Point is reached; the cabin and a toilet are located on the point's west shoreline. The trail continues round the coast into Taku Inlet, but that section is not maintained. Please leave the cabin in good condition for others who follow.

Grade forest
Distance 1.6 miles to Dupont; 8 miles to Bishop Point
Time 4.5 hours to Bishop Point
Elevation gain about 200 feet
Trail condition good, but wet at first
Trail characteristics shoreline, rain forest
Access by car or bicycle to the end of Thane Road, 6 miles south of Juneau
Facilities: cabin available but in poor condition; plenty of camping in woods; drinking water is not readily available close by
Administrative agency presently U.S. Forest Service; within State Selection

J9 LEMON CREEK

Lemon Creek Valley has a long trail that extends up the southeast side of Lemon Creek until it gets lost in thick brush near the head of the valley. If it rains, do not be too disappointed; on such days the clouds play odd tricks. They cling closely to the river in diaphanous veils and break above, showing tantalizing patches of blue sky at times and giving Heintzleman Ridge the appearance of being poised above the ground. On these occasions the forests are darker, more somber, brooding.

Good waterproof boots are needed, and, whether it's raining or not, long pants and long sleeves are desirable if the trail has not been brushed out, as nettles scourge the first part. Maidenhair fern, club moss, and Canadian dogwood cover the forest floor. This is a pleasant snowshoe hike in winter.

Drive, or take a bus, north along Glacier Highway from Juneau to Lemon Creek Valley, 5 miles away. Three-quarters of a mile before the highway crosses Lemon Creek, a trail sign stands on the right side of the road, immediately beyond a modern church.

The trail starts as a jeep road running northeast, and within three-fifths of a mile it plunges through nettle-choked brush (unless recently cut back by trail crews). Luckily this section is short, and the pathway settles down to an amble through hemlock forests with less brush. A log bridge crosses Sawmill Creek. Soon the trail threads through a fascinating miniature forest of skunk cabbage in the center of a wet stretch. There are few more surprises as the path wends its way up the valley, closely following the fast glacial stream of Lemon Creek. Another rapid, unnamed creek is crossed before reaching a campsite in the trees 5 miles from the road.

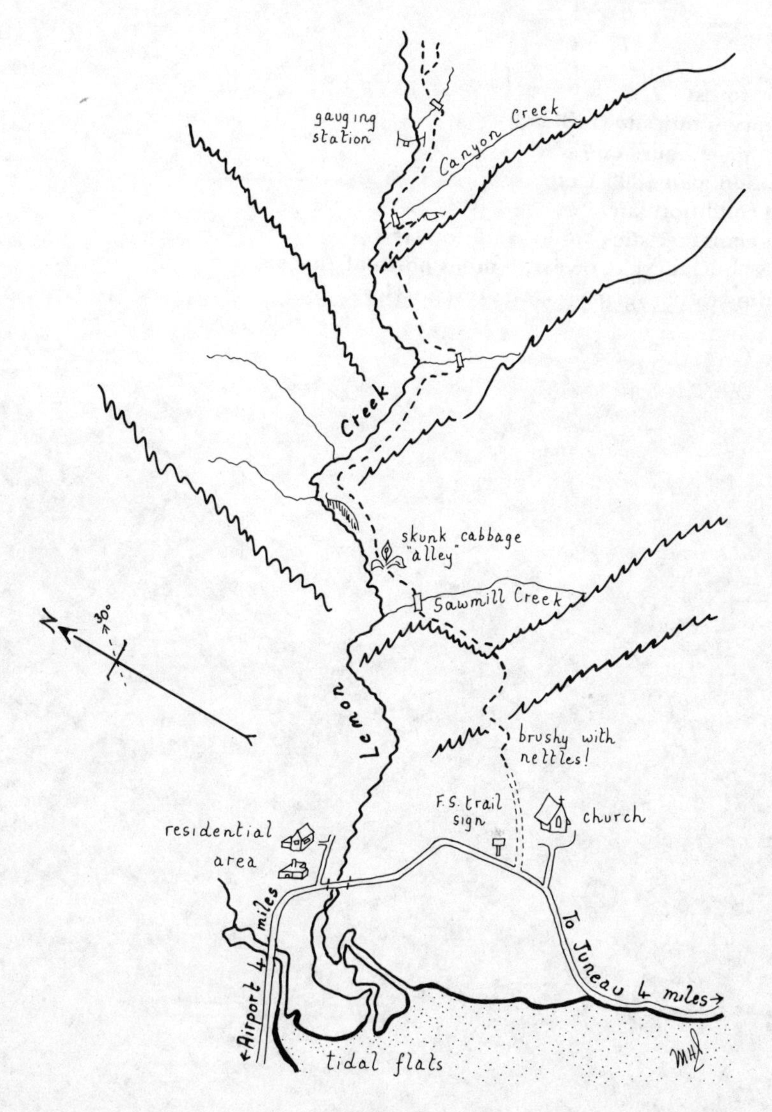

The trail turns back on itself for a few yards to cross Canyon Creek, then climbs a bank on the far side before it enters a short stretch of muskeg. Back in the trees, within half a mile, a tagged trail leads to the right up a steep hill. This is a poorly marked, hard-to-follow trail (definitely not for the non-mountaineer) to Camp 17 on the icecap.

A short way beyond is a gauging station, where the trail opens into long, grassy meadows. In late July and early August a natural garden exhibits a riot of color on the far side of a stream. Monkshood, fireweed, yellow composite, blue geranium, or cranesbill, and other flowers stand unblinking in the sun or rain; it is the last surprise of the walk before it ends shortly thereafter in a small ravine and a welter of brush.

Grade forest
Distance 6 miles to trail end
Time 3.5–4 hours one way
Elevation gain 1000 feet
Trail condition fair
Trail characteristics valley, rain forests
Access bus, bicycle, or car, 5 miles north of Juneau
Administrative agency U.S. Forest Service

Lemon Creek

J10 WETLANDS

The Wetlands beckon to visitors obliged to wait between flights at the airport. They are also for those who have a pair of binoculars and more than a passing interest in birds. The Wetlands — Juneau's tidal marshes — are rich in warblers, waders, bay and pond ducks, swans, hawks, and bald eagles. In spring, aggressive courtship displays are seen and territorial rights are asserted in a riot of song. By late summer, things have settled down a bit, and the birds are not as easily identified.

The airport runway has raised dirt roads around its west end to the south side. One may stay up here and stay dry, or — armed with good boots and tidetables — descend into the marshes to see the shore birds more closely. The walk can be as short or as long as one cares to make it, but allow an hour to walk from the terminal to the end of the runway (three-quarters of a mile) and back.

Leave the terminal building, turn left, then left again up the next obvious street (do not wander onto the airport apron), then left once more toward the runway past private planes and hangers. Turn right on a dirt road which parallels the main runway to the west end.

Motorists driving from Juneau follow the airport signs, but instead of turning left to the passenger and terminal building, continue west a short block, then turn left down a dirt road which leads past the private plane sector. Turn right by the main runway and drive to the runway end, where there is limited parking. A raised dirt road goes to the left (south) across the end of the runway. If permission has been granted, take this road, but *first be sure no plane is landing or taking off*. Shortly after crossing the runway, the road passes tidal ponds on the left, where sometimes trumpeter swans, groups of whistling swans, white-fronted geese, Canada geese, and various types of ducks are visible. On the right are tidal flats and the Mendenhall River. Within 200 yards the road turns left and parallels the runway for half a mile. Another 300 yards from the turn, go left down a short spur road to the tidal pools, or straight on to the end of the dike.

The following check list of birds noted to this time is provided by Rich Gordon of Juneau:

Spring: Migratory whistling swans in groups, migratory trumpeters in pairs, white-fronted geese, Canada geese, bay ducks (e.g., scaup, buffleheads, goldeneyes, etc.), marsh hawks, short-eared owls (now rare, as they are shot at), sharp-tailed sandpipers (rare), pipits, Lapland longspurs, and glaucous-winged gulls (the most common of the gulls), may all be seen.

The visitor cannot count on seeing shorebirds, as they are not consistently present.

Trumpeter swan, Wetlands (R. T. Wallen)

Summer: Herons (rare, like the owls and for the same reason), red-throated loons (nesting), mallards, greenwing teals, shovelers, baldpates, hooded mergansers, killdeers, semipalmated plovers, snipe, least and spotted sandpipers, and possibly pintails are present. Bonaparte's gulls and mew gulls are often seen, but they do not nest on the Wetlands. Lesser yellowlegs and short-bill dowitchers are thought to be nesting. Glaucous-winged gulls and Arctic terns are nesting; the latter not in colonies. Also seen are Traill's flycatchers, tree, bank and barn swallows, northwest crows and ravens, bald eagles, ruby-crowned kinglets, robins, myrtle warblers, red-winged blackbirds, Savannah sparrows and Lincoln's sparrows, plus a pair of nesting song sparrows.
Fall: The area is best avoided because of the duck-hunting season. Bird movements are unknown at this time.
Winter: No birds will be seen if the area is frozen. Otherwise there will be bay ducks seeking shelter, and Canada geese.

More birds may be seen on the tidal flats, but waders would be needed. Consult a tidetable. *Do not get cut off by the incoming tide.*

Grade sightseeing
Distance 2.5 miles from terminal to end of dike
Time 1.5 hours minimum round trip to first ponds
Elevation gain none
Pathway condition excellent

Characteristics wetlands, marshes
Best time May–June
Limitation: Do not cross when aircraft are landing or taking off.
Access by foot from airport, 0.7 mile (by bus, bicycle, or car from town to airport, 9 miles

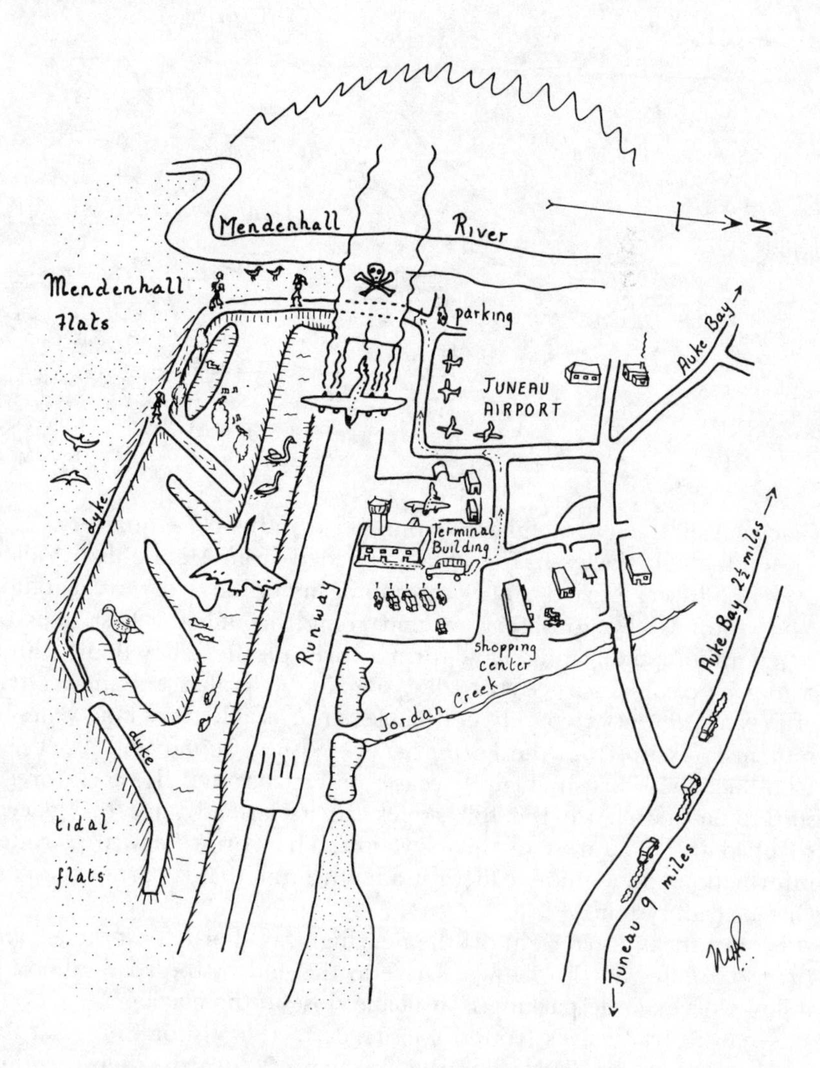

J11 EAST GLACIER

Do not be put off by rain or low cloud when planning to see Mendenhall Glacier; the blues in the ice are intensified and make better photographic material. Allow yourself additional time to walk the East

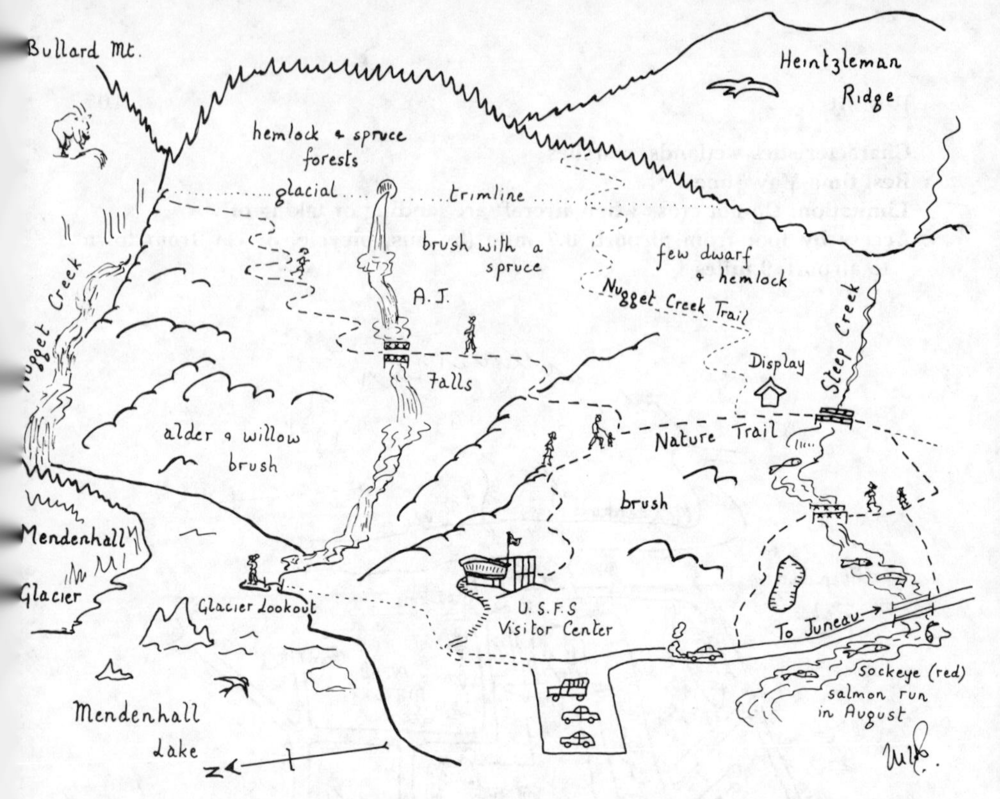

Glacier trail, to view the glacier from above and at close quarters.

Mendenhall Glacier has gradually receded from Mendenhall Valley over a 200-year period and is continuing its unhurried retreat today. The visitor is able to observe a land going through the first steps of regeneration; alder and willow form a cover on the valley floor, with a scattering of Sitka spruce struggling to gain the final ascendancy. Their efforts at present are barely noticeable, since sizable trees take years to return. Look up from the Forest Service Visitor Center and observe a trim line where brush abruptly ceases and spruce and hemlock forests start their march up the hill slopes. In its last advance the glacier stripped the old forest to this elevation. The Forest Service provides information and a guide leaflet for a nature trail that is part of the East Glacier trail system.

From Juneau, turn right off the new highway shortly past the airport turn, 9.3 miles north of town. Drive to the end of the road, almost 4 miles, where ample parking is available close to the glacier.

A nature trail leaves from the east side of the Visitor Center at the head of the stairs. Walk along this for about 200 yards, then turn left onto the East Glacier trail. This angles up a hillside and traverses under the A. J. Waterfall (water diverted by miners through a conduit). The trail then climbs more steeply in a series of sharp-angled turns until views are gained of the abrupt ice walls where the glacier terminates in Mendenhall Lake. On the right, Nugget Creek tumbles into the lake in a torrent of water, carving tunnels or arches in the ice. This vantage also gives extensive views of Mendenhall Valley and reaches of fresh and tidal water glinting in the distance. The trail continues past a short protective cable fence and winds upward to join the Nugget Creek trail.

On the return, an alternative is to turn left at the nature trail, bypassing the Visitor Center. The path traverses the hillside for about a quarter of a mile, passing Nugget Creek trail on the left. It crosses a stream and descends toward the road. When recrossing the stream below, watch for spawning sockeye (red) salmon from mid-July to mid-August, or coho (silver) salmon from mid-September to November. Males are recognized by a large, fierce beak and aggressive behavior. Fishing is not allowed nor is it advisable, since the salmon are in the first stages of decomposition before death overtakes them. The pathway ends on the road a few yards behind the parking area.

Grade sightseeing
Distance 1.5 miles one way
Time 2 hours round trip
Elevation gain 600 feet
Trail condition excellent
Trail characteristics open valley, glacier views
Access by tour bus, car, or bicycle, 13.5 miles north of Juneau, 4.5 miles from airport, 4 miles from Mendenhall Lake campgrounds
Administrative agency U.S. Forest Service

Mendenhall Glacier and Nugget Creek

Derelict bridge, Nugget Creek

J12 NUGGET CREEK

Nugget Creek discharges a torrent of water through a gorge into the east side of Mendenhall Glacier. A path threads through the valley in hemlock and spruce rain forests to a three-sided shelter at Vista Creek. It is possible to penetrate a mile farther up the valley, to Goat Creek and a view of Nugget Spires, but this section of trail has reverted to forest and brush, is difficult to find, and requires an extra hour each way.

Start from either end of the Mendenhall Glacier nature trail (see East Glacier trail and map, J11, for details). The Nugget Creek trail branches off the nature trail at a covered display about a quarter of a mile from the Visitor Center. The trail ascends through heavy brush, with occasional views of the glacier and Mendenhall Valley. Watch for toads contemplating in the middle of the pathway during August and September. Also notice how, within the trim line, spruce and hemlock are beginning to get a toehold among the alder. Saplings may occasionally be seen struggling for position and light.

The path climbs into forest, and before long the skeleton of an old flume is passed. Within a mile a trail junction is reached. If the left trail is taken it will lead to an observation point of the glacier and valley. A right turn can be made off this spur, and by going straight over and down, a spillway and now-defunct suspension bridge across Nugget Creek may be found. The upper part of this path connects with the East Glacier trail.

Nugget Creek trail leads off to the right at the junction, running east up the valley through rain forest. At one point it divides, with two trails running parallel for a way, then reuniting. About half a mile before reaching the Vista Creek shelter, shortly after crossing Falls Creek, a ridge rises steeply to the right or south. This may be used for access into Heintzleman Ridge, although no route is marked and it is recommended for experienced hikers only.

The path, which deteriorates rapidly past the shelter and is hard to follow, climbs the lip of a deep, beautiful gorge. Devil's club and nettles must be waded through and windfalls climbed, but, once the top is reached, views of Nugget Spires are striking. The nebulous path vanishes altogether in thick brush beyond Goat Creek, a short way beyond the viewpoint. However, within half a mile of here, open, easy hiking country is attained. The Forest Service plans to brush the last 1.5 miles of trail in the near future.

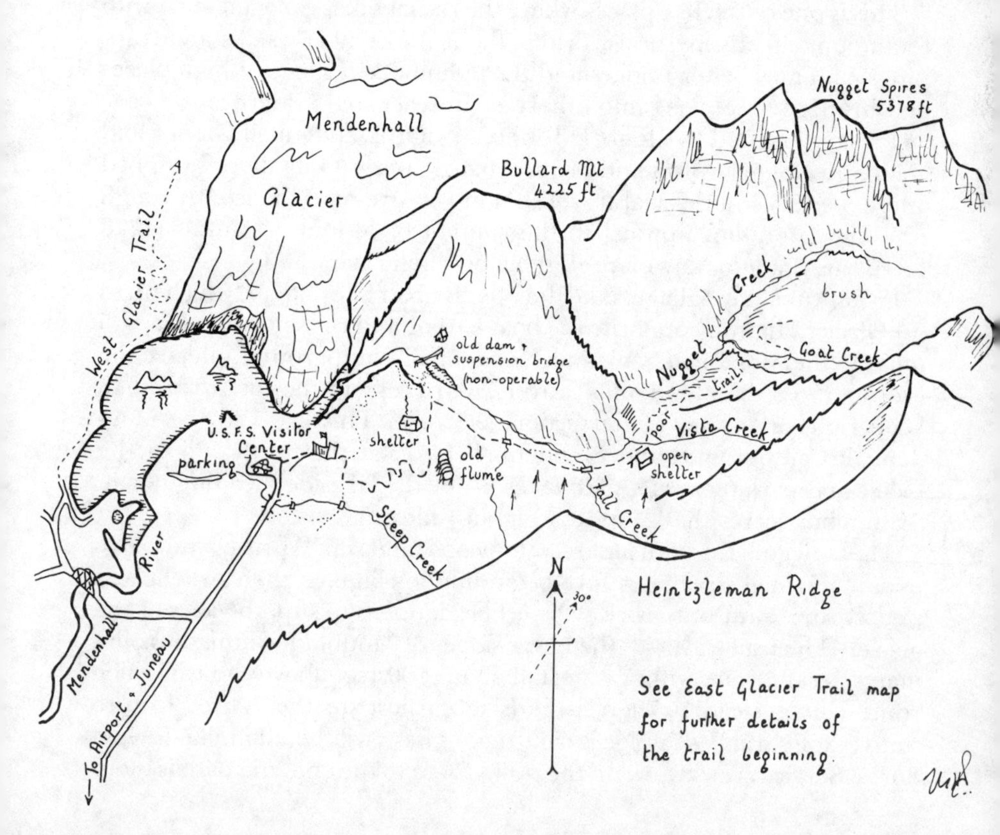

Grade forest
Distance 3 miles to Vista Creek
Time with side trip to the spillway, 2.5 hours one way
Elevation gain 1200 feet to Vista Creek
Trail condition good
Trail characteristics valley, rain forests
Access see J11
Administrative agency U.S. Forest Service

J13 WEST GLACIER

The trail running on the west side of the Mendenhall Glacier is a revelation to those who have never had the opportunity to see a glacier at firsthand. It offers intimate views of the slowly flowing river of ice, to a point above the icefall where the trail ends in a gigantic cirque. Great spires and black towers encircle the large, broken mass of blue ice, and hanging glaciers spill down from upper cwms. The glacier ends 1200 feet below, in a fan-shaped, smooth sheet of ice above Mendenhall Lake, into which the ice occasionally calves.

This is one of the few places where the casual hiker can gain entry into the mountaineer's mystical world without the climber's skills and trappings, and may better understand the mountaineer's love of high places and his urge to journey into otherwise unreachable wilderness.

This trail is used by climbers for access onto Mendenhall Glacier and climbs on Nugget Spires and Mendenhall Towers. (Only those equipped and experienced in glacial travel should venture onto the ice.) A rough trail also continues upward to the summit of Mount McGinnis (4228 feet); this is a long day or preferably overnight trip.

From Auke Bay Village, take the Mendenhall Loop Road, which turns off Glacier Highway opposite the boat harbor and runs northeast for 2.5 miles to the Montana Creek and Mendenhall Campground intersection (do not cross the Mendenhall River). Turn left up the dirt road, then keep right at the next intersection, 0.3 mile. This leads to the Mendenhall Campground and Mendenhall Lake; at the north end of the picnic and parking area a path takes off by the lakeside, heading north. (A minibus serves the Loop Road from Juneau.)

The trail goes through alder, cottonwood, and small spruce, and crosses several small streams before beginning to climb. It then switchbacks steeply up a bluff onto rock slabs, where it opens to superb views of the glacier. The trail traverses the lower slopes of Mount McGinnis, crossing many streams, one with a waterfall about 100 feet above the trail. The route climbs steadily, then ascends in earnest up the "Aztec torture steps," aptly dubbed by local children. (These will be eliminated when Forest Service crews work on the trail.) Close to the end, the path is more difficult to follow (keep left and upward when in doubt). If the route is not immediately apparent, retrace your steps to the last known section of trail and try again. It should not be lost for more than a few yards at a time.

A large rock platform above the first icefall (an abrupt drop in levels characterized by a jumbled mass of broken ice) is finally gained. The glacier widens above, forming a "bay" under the lower, more abrupt, slopes of Mount Stroller White, surrounding the rock promontory on three sides. Mountains rise almost sheer from the ice on all sides.

From this point a flagged route runs up the ridge of Mount McGinnis. It goes first through trees, then shortly runs out onto brush and alpine slopes, From here it is a long climb to the summit and overnight gear is recommended.

Grade forest; Mount McGinnis alpine
Distance 3 miles one way
Time 3 hours up, 1.5 down; Mount McGinnis add 4.5 hours up, 2.5 hours down (this is best as an overnight trip)
Elevation gain 1300 feet; Mount McGinnis 4228 feet
Trail condition good except for last half mile which is confusing; Mount McGinnis no trail
Trail characteristic glacial overlook; sunglasses advised because of glacial glare
Access by foot from Mendenhall Campground; by car or bicycle from Auke Bay (3.5 miles) and Juneau (13 miles)
Administrative agency U.S. Forest Service

Mendenhall Glacier

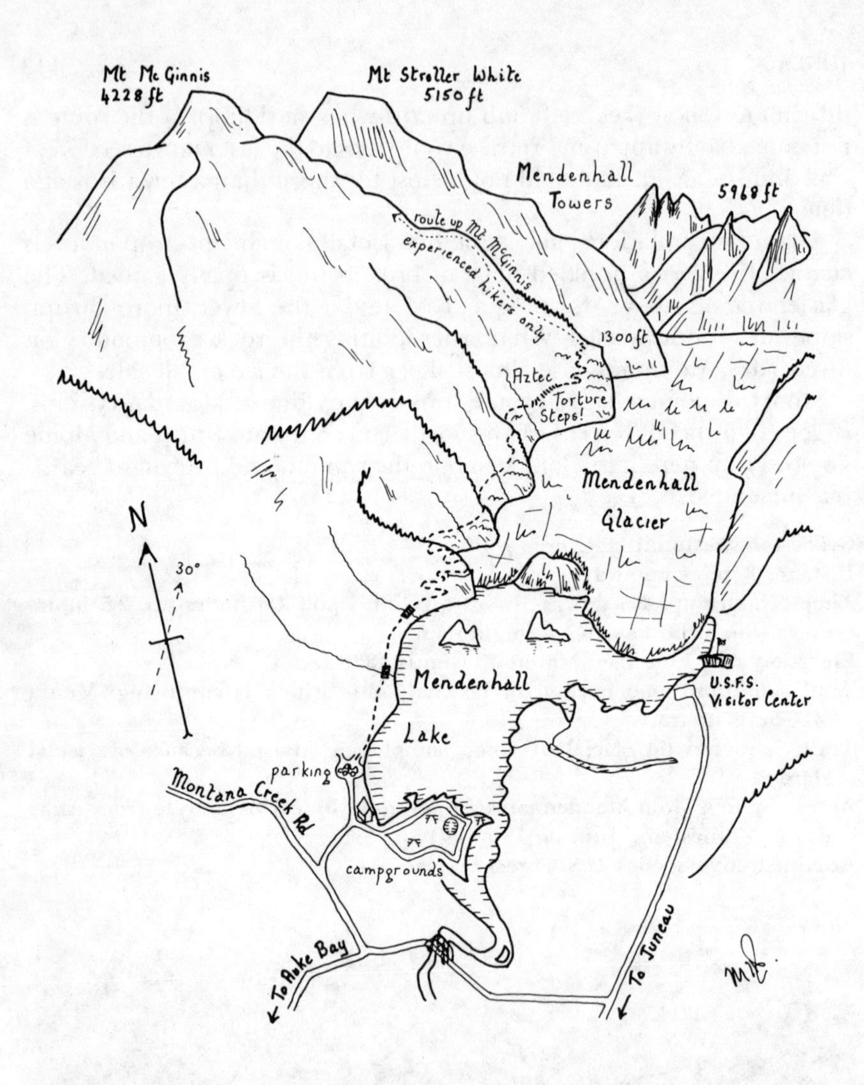

J14 MONTANA CREEK

A trail connects Windfall Lake with Montana Creek Valley. It is about 7 miles long (10 miles from the Herbert River roadhead) and makes either a good summer hike through forests, open meadows, and over a watershed to the Montana Creek river system or a winter snowshoe or cross-country ski run. Many people fear bears along this route and carry a gun. However two of us with warning bells on boots and pack had no encounter with bears. The going is rough through deep, boggy patches, and waterproof boots to mid-calf are necessary to stay dry. In summer waterproof trousers are useful after recent rain to protect the legs from wet brush. The trail can be walked either way: from Windfall Lake trail, which starts 27 miles north of Juneau, or from the end of Montana Creek Road.

If walking from Montana Creek, take the Mendenhall Loop Road from Auke Bay (see West Glacier trail, J13), and after about 2.5 miles turn left up a gravel road (shortly before the main road crosses the Mendenhall River) to a fork which is reached within 0.3 mile. Take the left turn and drive to the end, about 3 miles, where ample parking will be found by Montana Creek. A few yards from the end of the road, look for a trail on the left which follows the creek bank upstream.

Parties doing the trail one way may have access problems, unless

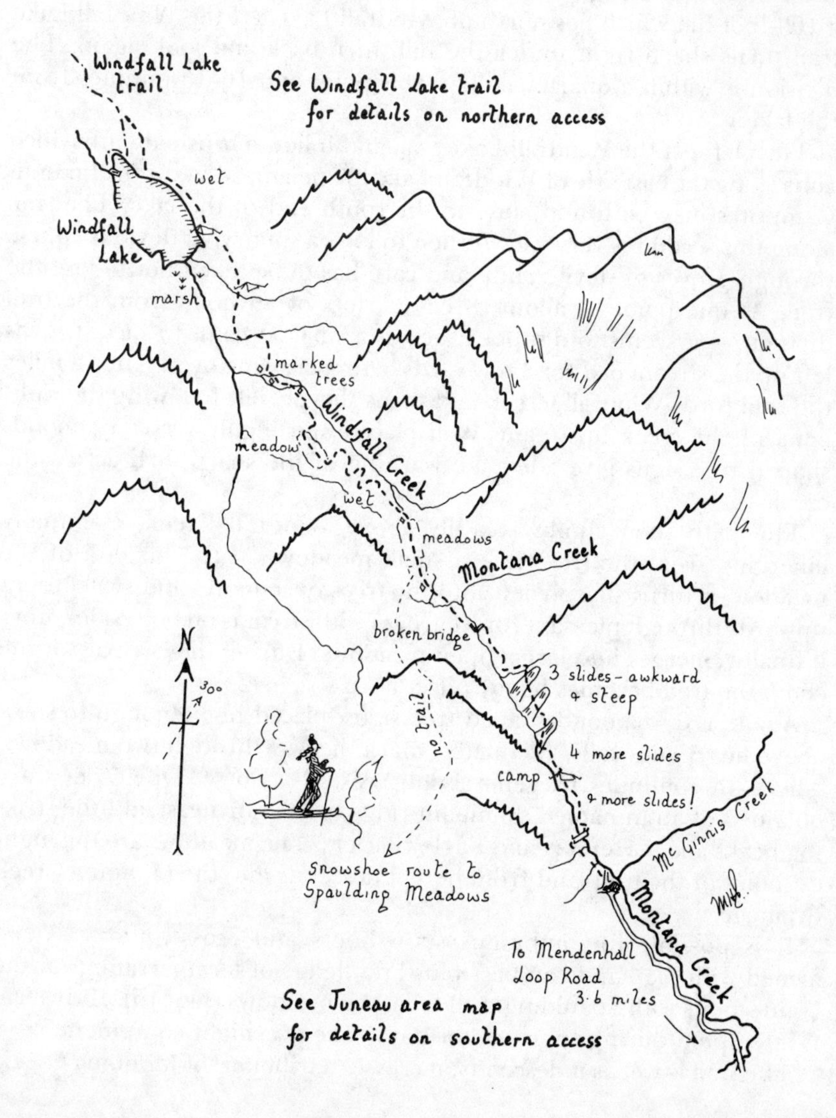

someone is available to drop them off at one end and pick them up at the other. Another solution is to have two parties going in opposite directions; car keys can then be exchanged somewhere along the trail. Those traveling south who care to walk the extra 3 miles to Mendenhall Loop Road — making the hike 13 miles in all — can return to town by bus. Bus schedules should be checked first, however.

Those starting from the north end should refer to the Windfall Lake trail description (J17) for the beginning of that trail. After about an hour of walking (2.8 miles) look for a trail leading off to the left. It will be seen at the end of planking, shortly before reaching the last beaver ponds and a 100-foot hill which lies north of Windfall Lake. (If the Windfall Lake trail turns sharp right under the hill, turn back and look again. The division is within a quarter mile of this point and 10–15 minutes from the lake.)

Turn left off the Windfall Lake trail and follow a brushed path which runs along the east side of Windfall Lake to open meadows at the far end. Campsites may be found close to the south end of the lake. The trail along this section is very wet. It then follows a somewhat devious course through groves of devil's club, and care has to be taken not to lose the trail. At one point — about three-quarters of an hour from the trail division — it seems to disappear across a small stream. In fact, it turns left up the stream bed for a few yards before crossing over. After 2 miles the trail fords Windfall Creek and turns sharply left following the right bank of the creek upstream. Well placed and highly visible diamond-shaped tree signs give adequate warning of the sharp turn across the creek.

The path then climbs steadily above Windfall Creek, eventually emerging from the trees into a small meadow. At the far end of the meadow, it turns sharply left into the trees once more, and switchbacks upwards through pleasant forest groves with streams on both sides, until it finally emerges into large, open meadows. During the last part of the climb the trail becomes boggy once more.

Again, red, diamond-shaped tree signs, placed high enough to show above heavy snowfalls, adequately mark the way through two meadows. The path continues its general southeasterly course. Open views are obtained of an unnamed dominant ridge to the northeast and the striking peaks above Herbert and Eagle Glaciers. The meadows are the highest point of the trail, and from here it descends into the Montana Creek drainage.

It is possible for ambitious snowshoers and cross-country skiers, armed with map and compass plus knowledge of local terrain, to make connections with Spaulding trail from the meadows (see J15). If this trip is attempted during short winter days, take overnight equipment.

The trail is wet as it descends; it crosses a tributary of Montana Creek, and, shortly afterward, the main stream by a broken bridge. Take care on the bridge; it is slippery. The trail then follows the east side of Montana Creek and goes across a series of slides. The first is awkward, as a climb is necessary over an old, broken plank bridge across a steep gully, and the first slide is crossed on a faded trail. The second slide is steep and exposed with poor trail, and care is needed in crossing. (Winter travel, in this section, is best along the frozen riverbed.) On the third slide the path drops to river level, then climbs once more and crosses about four more slides to a campsite by the river.

From here the trail is much improved. It is trampled by many feet and the slides it crosses are less awkward. The trail finally crosses a good footbridge to the west bank of Montana Creek and coasts about a quarter mile across some tributary streams to the road.

Grade forest
Distance 9.5 miles from beginning of Windfall Lake trail to Montana Creek Road
Time 6 hours
Elevation gain 850 feet ±
Trail condition poor
Trail characteristics forest, meadows
Access by car, 27 miles north of Juneau or 15 miles north of Juneau
Administrative agency U.S. Forest Service

J15 SPAULDING

This is a wet trail which needs maintenance, but it is so beautiful it should not be passed by. Good waterproof boots are needed, and a map, a compass, and sharp eyes, as the trail can be missed on the return from the last muskeg meadows.

The views over Auke Bay are wide open, and in August the meadows are white with Alaska bog cotton. Earlier, they are covered with white orchis, and if one kneels, the minuscule world of insectivorous plants — sundew and butterwort — will come into focus. One can wander for miles over the last meadow, which forms a gently shelving platform 1500 to 1700 feet above sea level. Spaulding was also a mining trail at one time, and some workings may be found if one looks hard enough for them, close to a derelict cabin which the trail passes just before it fades out in the meadow.

Bears have been seen on the meadows, so attach a bell to your boot or carry a can full of pebbles as a noisemaker. Spaulding meadows are highly recommended for cross-country skiers and snowshoers. Also, connections can be made with Montana Creek trail by cross-country experts, summer and winter (see J14).

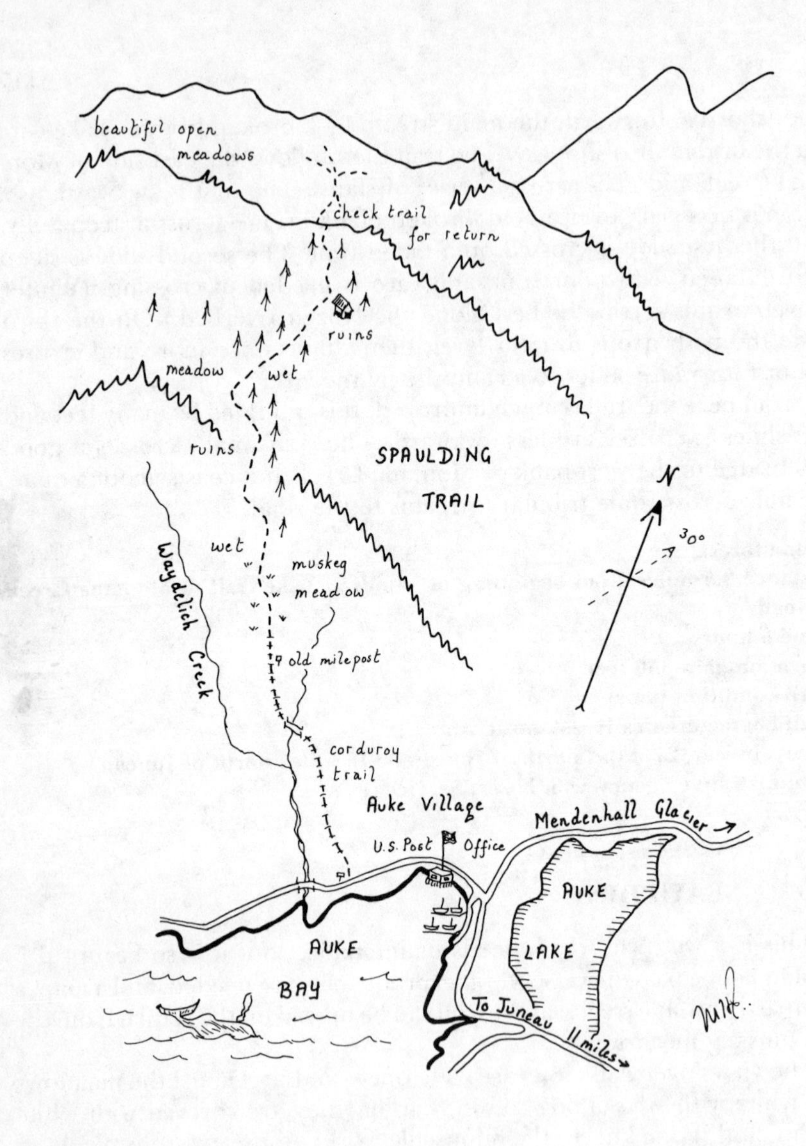

Take the only road out to Auke Bay Village, 12 miles north of Juneau and 3 miles from the airport; about 200 yards beyond the Auke Bay Post office, a trail sign is visible on the right of the road. (Do not cross Waydelich Creek.) Parking can be found in the village.

The trail starts climbing almost immediately on an old corduroy road. It then turns sharply to cross a stream ditch, and just before emerging onto the first muskeg meadow, passes an old milepost. The trail is well trampled through the muskeg and horribly wet. Look back, as views of Auke Bay have already opened up. The path then goes back into trees and traverses a hillside, climbing gently, and reaches a second meadow within another mile. Stay with the edge of the trees on the right, and the path will be picked up once more without difficulty. It then goes back into trees through deep bog holes and emerges eventually in a smaller meadow containing an old cabin which has seen better days.

A further short section through trees, and the trail finally emerges and disappears into the final meadows. Surprisingly, drinking water is scarce on the trail as no major streams are crossed, but small pools may be found in the meadows with runoff; camping is otherwise good.

For the present, until this trail is worked on by the Forest Service, watch very carefully where it emerges into the meadows and make a mental note of what part of the hillside you are on. If you do get lost on the way back, don't worry — you are in good company; many others have. But do not go crashing through the trees. You are probably too low: return to the meadows and walk up the edge of timberline until you find the trail.

Grade forest
Distance 3 miles
Time 2.5 hours up, 1.5 down
Elevation gain 1500 feet ±
Trail condition poor, wet
Trail characteristic mountain meadows
Access by foot from Auke Bay Village, or bus from Juneau (12 miles)
Administrative agency U.S. Forest Service

Spaulding Meadows

J16 PETERSON

Peterson is another legacy from Juneau's past, and in fact, remains of an old tramway serve as a trail base for the first mile or so. The route passes a waterfall — a good fishing place on a short side trip. The trail climbs gradually to Peterson Lake; almost the entire walk is in forests. Good waterproof boots are needed, as the trail has been sadly neglected over the years. There are many deep bog holes and the corduroy roadbed is slippery. The route is not difficult to find, however, and the fishing under the waterfall and in the lake is fun.

Drive north from Juneau, past Auke Bay, to the 24-mile post almost a mile beyond the Shrine of Saint Therese. A Forest Service Sign indicates the beginning of the trail. The path climbs a bank through some brush, then enters the forest. Within 15 minutes an indistinct spur trail forks to the left. This goes to some falls; be sure to take the right fork at the junction a few yards from the main trail (the left branch was swept off a cliff and is now impassable). The right fork branches left after another few yards, then drops down a steep bank to the bottom of the waterfall. A rope serves as a handline to a pool at the base of the falls.

The main trail emerges into muskeg on rotten boards which have to be circumnavigated in places. It then divides at a signpost, the path to the left being a very old trail which virtually disappears on the other side of Peterson Creek. Take the right fork, which leads into trees and follows Peterson Creek upstream, through uncountable bog holes, until the lake is reached roughly 2 miles from the sign.

Grade forest
Distance 4 miles one way
Time 2 hours one way
Elevation gain 750 feet
Trail characteristics forest
Trail condition poor, very wet
Access by car, 24 miles north of Juneau
Administrative agency U.S. Forest Service

Canadian dogwood

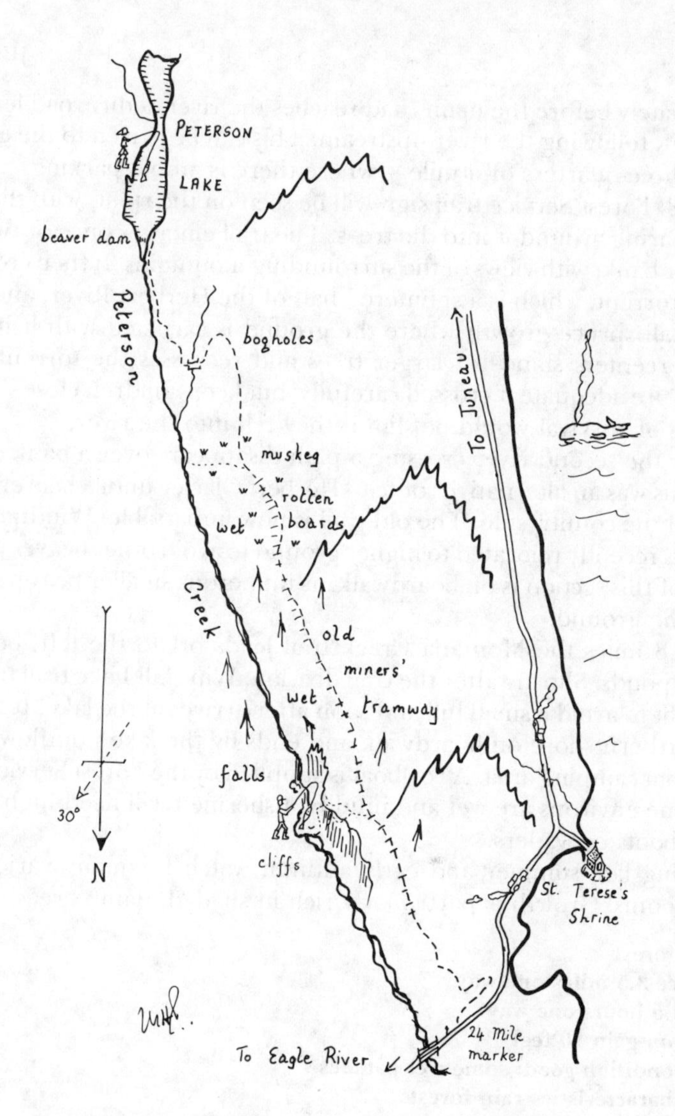

J17 WINDFALL LAKE

Windfall is one of three trails found almost 28 miles north of Juneau. It is partially boardwalk and easily followed, but wet in places. Take your fishing pole, as the lake is stocked with Dolly Varden and cutthroat trout. Many people snowshoe the trail in winter and fish through the ice. The route to Windfall Lake wanders by Herbert River for a distance, with open views up the river to the ragged, striking peaks above Herbert Glacier, then penetrates deep forest of old moss-covered trees and mature devil's club.

Drive north out of Juneau past the airport and Auke Bay to Herbert River, which is crossed by the road between the 27- and 28-mile posts.

Immediately before the main road reaches the river, a dirt road leads to the right, following the river upstream. This can be driven to the end — about three-quarters of a mile— where there is ample parking.

A U.S. Forest Service trail sign will be seen on the right, with the trail disappearing around it into the trees. The trail emerges once or twice at the river bank, with views of the surrounding mountains. It then crosses a raging torrent, which is a splintered half of the Herbert River, and goes into small spruce growth where the ground is carpeted with lichen. It shortly reenters stands of larger trees and recrosses the torrent. The bridges are adequate if crossed carefully, but keep children close — their chances of survival would be slim if they fell into the river.

After the second river crossing a path disappears over a bank on the left. This was an alternative route to Herbert Glacier until a beaver chose to flood the countryside. The old trail is now impassable. Windfall Lake trail was recently relocated to higher ground to avoid other beaver ponds. Much of this section is on boardwalk, as numerous smaller beaver ponds flood the ground.

At 2.8 miles the Montana Creek trail leads off to the left, between beaver ponds. Shortly after the trail division, Windfall Lake trail turns to the right to avoid a small hill and soon after arrives at the lake. It follows the northern shore on boardwalk and ends by the lake's outflow and a small, flat camping area. A rowboat is supplied by the Forest Service. The shoreline environs are wet and muddy; fishermen will need high waterproof boots or waders.

During late summer and early autumn watch for many varieties of mushrooms. Growth is particularly rich in shaded, damp areas.

Grade forest
Distance 3.5 miles one way
Time 1.5 hours one way
Elevation gain 80 feet
Trail condition good; some wet patches
Trail characteristics rain forests
Access by car, 28 miles north of Juneau
Administrative agency U.S. Forest Service

J18 HERBERT GLACIER

Until recently, the route to Herbert Glacier was called the Goat Mountain trail because a poorly marked spur is used for access onto Goat Mountain, a prominent landmark over the valley. Another trail, in need of restoration, leads from Windfall Lake trail along the south bank of the Herbert River to Herbert Glacier, but this trail is now impassable.

Once out of an initial long stretch of forest, the Herbert Glacier trail is fascinating. It meanders through groves of small spruce, the ground

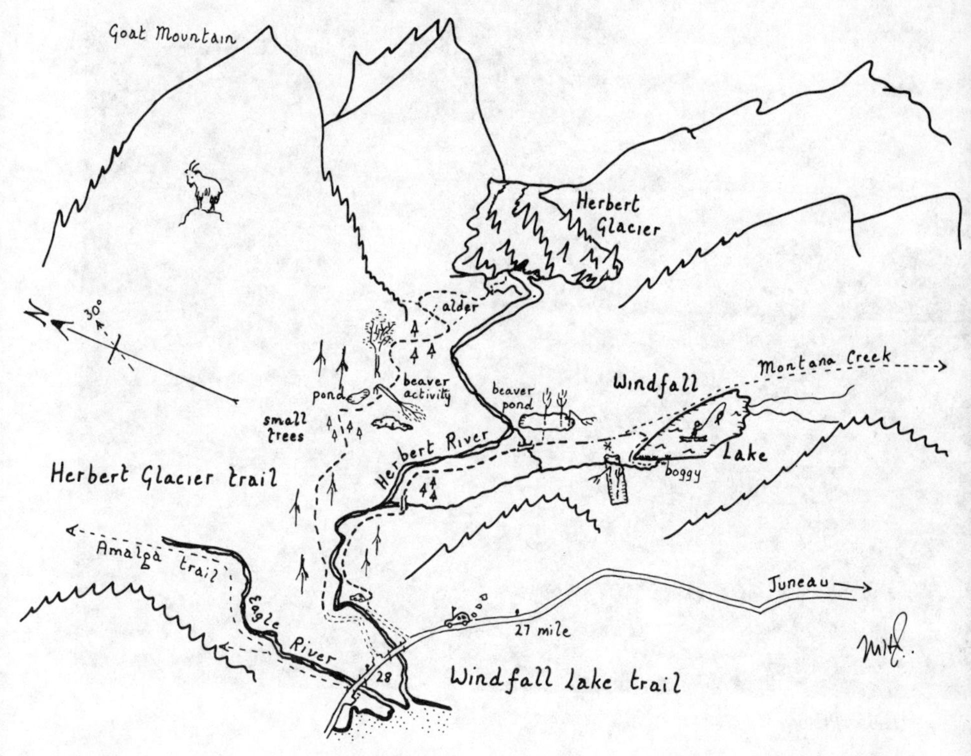

carpeted with mosses and lichens and the skyline dominated by the bulk of Goat Mountain. The trail then wanders through a delightful beaver totemland by a small lake. Look for trees, still standing, scored with tooth marks and with trunks half chewed away. It is a wonder they remain upright. Sometimes the travels of a tree felled by beavers are written in the mud of the trail or pool bank. The walk ends at the glacier terminus; access is possible onto the terminal moraine, though the last half mile through alder is confusing.

This route makes a pleasant snowshoe outing in winter, but old tree blazes have to be carefully followed to avoid losing the way during the second mile. Take map and compass. Do not wander onto the glacier itself unless roped and knowledgeable in glacier travel and rescue techniques.

Drive to Herbert River, 28 miles north of Juneau. Cross the river and within a few yards turn right into a gravel parking lot. The trail starts from the parking area along a narrow dirt road, formerly an old tramway route. The road ends about a mile from the highway. The trail continues into the trees closely following the Herbert River at first. It then enters a young uniform hemlock forest carpeted with moss. The plank boardwalks are currently too narrow for comfort; judging by wear, many hikers take to the bog on one side.

Within a mile the trail emerges from the tall, thin hemlock stand into small spruce and partially open country. Enchanting woods with a velvet

Herbert Glacier

mossy floor are reentered; here is the small lake with obvious beaver activity along its shore. Once more out of the trees, the glacier is visible in the distance, and again the ground is richly carpeted with lichens and moss.

The path then enters alder and its route becomes somewhat tortuous. It turns sharply left, then goes across a trail crossroads heading toward Goat Mountain, now almost directly above. At the next junction the trail turns sharply right. It traverses the lower slopes of Goat Mountain and comes out onto a moss-covered moraine close to the river. (Note where the trail emerges for the return.) It is then easy to follow across a couple of pleasant small streams before finally arriving in open moraine country. The glacier is at least half a mile away but is easily approached along the river bank, then over terminal moraine. Do not walk onto the glacier itself, unless familiar with and equipped for glacier travel.

Grade forest
Distance 4.5 miles one way
Time 2.5 hours one way
Elevation gain 300 feet
Trail condition good at first, confusing toward the end
Trail characteristics young forests, beaver activity, glacier
Access by car, 28 miles north of Juneau
Administrative agency U.S. Forest Service

J19 AMALGA-EAGLE GLACIER

Amalga is an old mining trail along Eagle River to Eagle Glacier. The mine workings are on a hillside about a mile west of the glacier, but they are hard to find. The trail was recently rehabilitated by the Forest Service personnel, who brushed, cleared, and put in boardwalk part way. The route wanders through spruce and hemlock rain forests, past beaver ponds and muskeg pools sometimes alive with wildfowl. Some areas are wet, so good boots are advisable. A couple of camping spots are available, one about a mile from the glacier with good water close by.

Drive north out of Juneau just past the 28-mile post. Cross Eagle River,

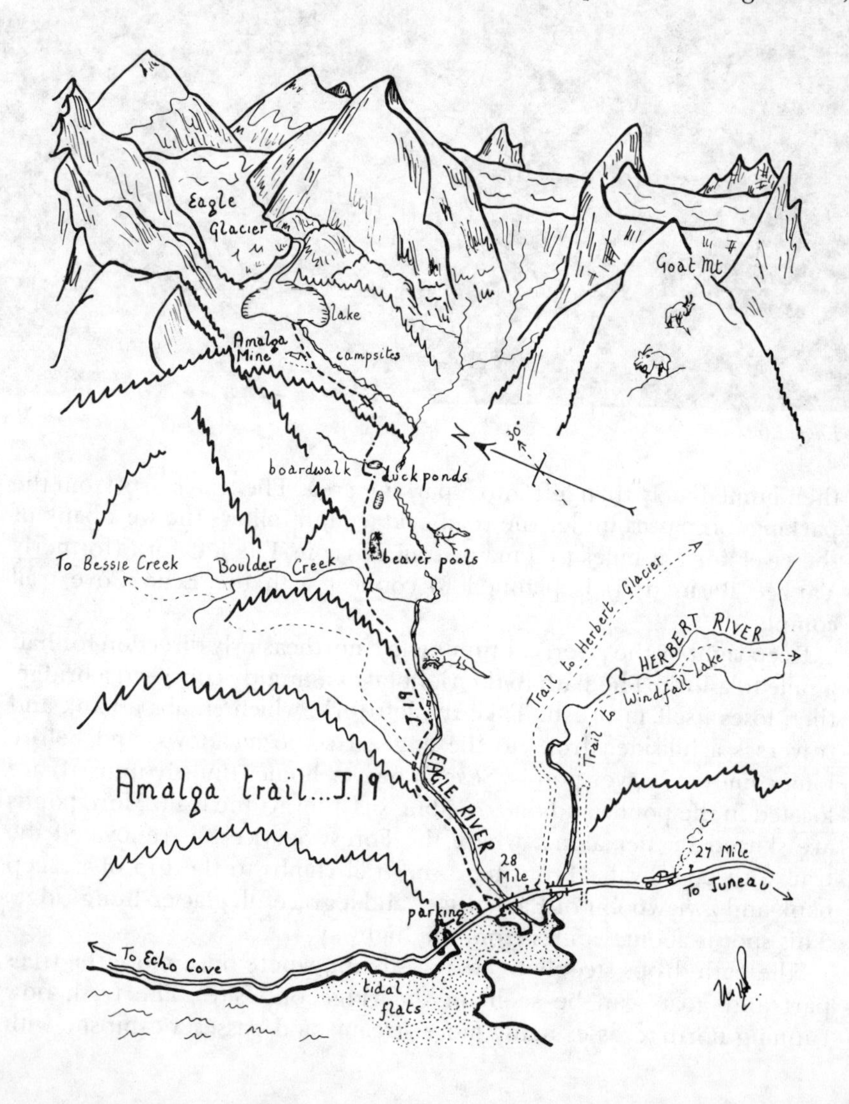

Eagle River

then immediately turn left into a parking area. The trail starts from the parking lot, passes under the road bridge, and follows the west bank of the river for 1.3 miles to a major trail division. The left fork (formerly Yankee Basin trail) is planned to connect with the Echo Cove trail complex.

Keep right by the river, continuing in a northeasterly direction for half a mile to a fork. The path to the right takes a muddy course to a bridge, then loses itself in brush. Take the left fork, which climbs a bank and traverses a hillside, drops to the edge of some meadows, and before long comes to beaver ponds. Several beaver homes (mostly unused) are located in the ponds and one dwelling sits athwart the trail. More ponds are skirted farther along, where the Forest Service has renovated the trail with boardwalk. From here the trail climbs to the top of a steep bank and a viewpoint of Eagle River and a graceful, glacier-hung ridge. This spot is about 4 miles from the highway.

The path drops steeply to cross a stream, where once more the trees part and goats can be seen on the ridge opposite. The trail, now running north, crosses many more streams and passes a campsite with running water. Within a mile the glacier is reached, but separated from the trail end by a glacier-fed lake. The Forest Service plans to extend the trail to a better viewpoint. Even so, this view is unforgettable, and the shoreline makes a good picnic site. According to sign discovered, otters occasionally cross the beach. Bear sign is distinct along the route, so a bell, whistle, or can of pebbles should be taken.

Grade forest
Distance 5.5 miles to Eagle Glacier
Time 3 hours in
Elevation gain 300 feet
Trail condition good
Trail characteristics rain forests, beaver activity, glacier
Access by car, 28 miles north of Juneau
Administrative agency U.S. Forest Service

Devil's club and rainforest moss

H1	Mount Ripinski (alpine)
S 1	Chilkoot (Dyea) (alpine)
S 2	Lower Dewey Lake Complex (sightseeing)
S 3	Upper Dewey Lake (forest-strenuous)
S 4	Devil's Punchbowl (alpine)

What is it that makes one's feelings change toward the land, one who has fought his way through devil's club, brush, and heavy timber for years, regarding them as obstacles to progress, to be overcome and eliminated? For some the change never comes, but for others the years mellow the view that the value of life forms is determined only by their usefulness to man.

We walk through the forests now with a more balanced view. We cry out against the abuses that man has inflicted. For us the question is, how can we teach our children to respect life before it is too late, to walk through the forests with awe rather than with impatience?

Richard C. Folta
Haines

HAINES

As one cruises north from Juneau the scene changes dramatically. The pattern of islands has dissolved into the mists below the horizon, and glacier-hung mountains with crenelated ridges embroidered against the sky, beautiful in their majesty and isolation, have stepped forward to contain a sheer-walled fjord, Lynn Canal. The single-minded rain forests of Sitka spruce, western hemlock, and cedar have also disappeared, and here the autumn gold of birch and the light green of deciduous trees, showing through the evergreens, make a palpable difference in the scene.

The tidal finger of Lynn Canal was first recognized as the logical access to the Yukon in the 1890s when thousands of desperate souls suffering from gold fever funnelled through the Chilkoot Pass. Haines-Port Chilkoot lies on a northwest finger of Lynn Canal, on an isthmus above the Chilkat flats and close to the beginnings of another historic but less well-known trail into the Interior. This is the Dalton Trail, now a tenuous thread through the wilderness rapidly becoming lost to willow and cottonwood encroachment; it may soon be just a memory unless rescued by a sympathetic agency.

S 5 **The Magic Forest (Sturgill's Landing) (forest)**
S 6 **Lower Reid Falls (sightseeing)**
S 7 **Skyline Trail and A.B. Mountain (alpine)**
S 8 **Denver Glacier (forest)**
S 9 **Laughton Glacier (sightseeing)**
S10 **Lost Lake (forest)**

The Chilkat Valley is unique because of a resident and transient bald eagle population equal to the total bald eagle population of the contiguous United States. As many as 3000 concentrate on an unfrozen stretch of river close to Klukwan, 24 miles northwest of Haines. During November, eagles can be counted in their hundreds, in one glance from the highway. They are dependent on a late run of spawning salmon which take advantage of the unfrozen river. This phenomenon is caused by upwelling of relatively warm ground waters through the alluvial gravel beds and is crucial to the survival of the salmon and hence the bald eagles.

Nature shows the delicacy of her inner mechanism with this combination of factors, each one dependent upon the other for survival, and like any delicate machinery, it can be irrevocably damaged by man's heavy-fisted methods of utilizing the environment. This may shortly be the case if a proposed strip mining operation of the alluvial flats for low grade iron ore is permitted. The Chilkat Valley is faced with a choice between retaining its dazzling beauty and its bald eagle population, or having the strip mining operation. Involved is a Japanese firm which would also like to mine the 4000-foot mountain behind the river flats.

Haines is the Southeast Alaska terminus of the Alaska Highway, and is regularly visited by the ferry service, which docks 7 miles north of town. Its only trail is up Mount Ripinski; others are planned south of town.

Maps required are Skagway A-2 and B-2.

Lynn Canal and Kakuhan Range from Mount Ripinski

H1 MOUNT RIPINSKI

Haines and the Chilkat Valley are so well endowed with glacial-hung peaks it seems almost surprising that Mount Ripinski, dominating the city from the north, can be climbed easily up the back side without the equipment and skills of technical mountaineering. From the summit can be seen a staggering array of ice and snow peaks marching down the upper Lynn Canal like sentries on guard duty, and more peaks — stark and glistening, black and white — on the south side of the Chilkat Valley. These form a wall between the valley and tidal inlets of Glacier Bay. At Mount Ripinski's feet lie the twin cities of Haines and Port Chilkoot. In 1971 an old, unused trail to the summit was resurrected by Haines citizens, who continue to assume responsibility for its maintenance.

A long day is needed for the climb, or overnight camping is possible high up for those who prefer. In early summer an ice ax would be helpful for the snow-covered upper slopes.

Find Main Street, the broadest boulevard running through the heart of Haines. Walk east (toward the harbor) one block from Haines Public School, or half a block from the ferry information office, to Lutak Road, the main road to the ferry terminal. Turn left (north) on Lutak Road past the fire station and Legion Hall on the right, toward Mount Ripinski. Leave the main road when it turns right to Lutak Inlet; go straight on, up a hill along Young Street. This leads to the now unused oil pipeline to Fairbanks, situated directly under the steep scarp of the lower ridge. The pipeline is similar to a jeep road; the pipe itself is buried. It makes easy walking, although it is muddy in places. Turn right along the pipeline, climbing steadily uphill. The Mount Ripinski trail turns off to the left, at 1 mile, shortly after the pipeline tops a rise and descends to its source — the tank farm — now just visible.

The trail crosses two streams and goes by an old city reservoir. It climbs steadily, through mountain and western hemlock and spruce stands, and passes open muskeg and a small pool at the 1300-foot level, about one-third of the way up the mountain. The path then climbs more steeply, pausing briefly at a viewpoint of Haines, and finally emerges into open alpine meadows at the head of Johnson Creek — a good resting place with drinking water readily available, pleasant heather slopes, and expansive views to the southeast. Allow 3 hours to get to this altitude (about 2000 feet above sea level and almost two-thirds of the way up to the first peak).

The route stays above Johnson Creek and the lovely alpine pool which is its source, and wanders through a thicket of dwarf mountain hemlock before emerging once more onto open slopes. A steep grass gully leads the way to the ridge, which is followed in a northwesterly direction to the first summit. The gully keeps the snow until late summer and provides glissading for the return. The ridge has a sheer southern scarp slope standing directly over the Haines highway, yet its angle relents enough to retain within its folds a small, lonely alpine lake, seen on the left.

The first peak, 3563 feet high, is enough climbing for most people. It has a bench mark and a high wooden surveyor's platform. The second, or far peak, is almost half a mile away and a little less than 100 feet higher. It is advisable to watch for sudden shifts of the weather from this lofty perch; the beginning of the return may be difficult to locate in conditions of poor visibility.

Grade alpine
Distance 5.2 miles to the far summit from the center of Haines
Pipeline 0.9 miles
Trail to first peak 3.2 miles
Time 4–5 hours up, 3 hours down
Elevation gain 3563+ feet
Trail condition good; rehabilitated and maintained by local citizens
Trail characteristics mountain, panoramic views
Access by foot from town

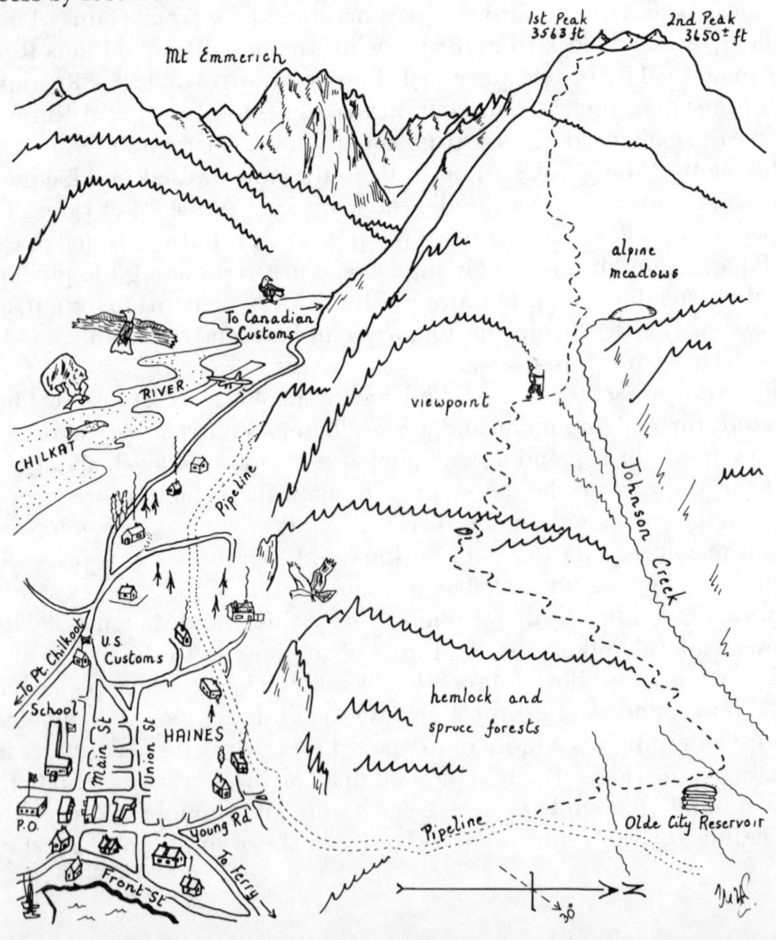

I told my grandchildren that the mossy big woods are a magic forest, and they accepted this description unquestioningly and quickly recognize the magic forests as we pass into them from the old burn areas.

Barbara Kalen
Skagway

SKAGWAY

Skagway is the northern terminus of the ferry service in Southeast Alaska, lying at the head of a long finger of Lynn Canal called Taiya Inlet. It is overshadowed on all sides by mountains rising 4000 to 5000 feet above the narrow valley — a beautiful sight, especially in the autumn when the birches turn a shimmering gold, sharply contrasting with the first snows on the mountain tops.

Skagway has regular ferry service all year, but sometimes in winter it is necessary to abort a docking or cut short the layover time because the terminal is exposed to powerful gusts of wind, common at this time of year. A narrow gauge railway, its history tied in with the gold rush, connects Skagway with Carcross and Whitehorse, Yukon Territory, and parallels the Dyea Valley, separated from Chilkoot Pass by a range of mountains.

The history of the 1897–99 gold rush lies over Skagway and Dyea like a mantle. No sensitive person can walk the dusty main street downtown between the straight-fronted wood-frame buildings, or hear the hollow ring of his footsteps on the old boardwalks, without thinking of the past. The Chilkoot Trail shows evidence of the great human activity and the terrible toll on horses at the turn of the century. Many of the miners made other, less famous trails, leaving a fine system as a legacy.

The Skagway-area trails vary from a 4- to 6-day hike to a 30-minute stroll. The Chilkoot is an international right-of-way that sees more than 2000 hikers a year. Laughton Glacier is reached via the White Pass and Yukon Railroad, and the others, except Lost Lake in the Dyea Valley, are close to Skagway.

Anyone visiting or hiking in the area should do some reading beforehand to acquaint himself with the history and atmosphere of the town and surrounding countryside.

Maps required: Skagway B-1 and C-1 quadrangles. For Chilkoot Pass, apply to the Department of Indian Affairs and Northern Development,

Box 1767, Whitehorse, Yukon Territory, Canada, for the White Pass sheet 1:50,000 104/11 East and the Homan Lake sheet 104M/14 East, in addition to Skagway B-1 and C-1.

S1 CHILKOOT (DYEA)

Introduction

The Chilkoot, or Dyea, Trail is famous for its gold rush origins. It was one of the most successful routes used by the Klondike "stampeders" to penetrate the interior. The trail is still littered with the bones of thousands of horses; their shoes are cast aside in a large heap below Crater Lake. There are sledges and cables and an assortment of rusty pots and pans and other litter (or artifacts, depending on the point of view of the beholder). In 1974 a series of explanatory signs were installed on aluminum posts, each containing a photograph from the 1898 era. The text is given in both English and French on both U.S. and Canadian sides of the border.

As one wanders through the pass, the atmosphere of gold rush fever still hangs in the air. Derelict cable housings stand like gaunt scarecrows on rock outcrops, mute testimony to the past and to the dreams of thousands of men — and for many, their epitaph. Like ghostly fingers from the past, rust-bitten cables point the way to the summit for the increasing tide of modern pilgrims.

Before following in their footsteps, bear in mind this is an international trail. Check with the National Park Visitor Center or Headquarters for the latest information on the trail. It is advisable to find out the times of the trains leaving Bennett for Whitehorse or Skagway before leaving Skagway if the trail is to be hiked from south to north. Tickets from Bennett must be bought in Skagway.

The start of the trail northbound is 8.5 miles from Skagway, and for those who plan to hike to Bennett and catch the train back to Skagway, transportation by taxi to the trailhead would be the best solution. The trail is a 3- to 6-day hike (depending on the party's stamina or interest in gold rush history) and the traveler can return by train to Skagway, unless the decision is to go on to Carcross or Whitehorse. It would therefore be better, if one has a vehicle, to leave it in town. At least a 2-days' supply of extra food should be taken for emergencies, and a cooking stove, weatherproof tent or tarp, and a ticket for the train from Bennett. The hiker should be in good physical condition and should already have struck a lasting partnership between himself and his boots. Maps and compass are necessary, as well as the other Ten Essentials.

For those who decide to drive to the start of the trail, go north on State Street, one block west of the downtown area (see the map for the Skyline trail, S7), until it meets the White Pass and Yukon Railroad marshalling yards, where it veers westward to cross the Skagway River by the only bridge. It then turns north again past a tank farm. Take the first dirt road to the left, beyond the tank farm, signposted to Dyea. This road makes a sweep up the hillside in a southerly direction, then closely follows the coastline in a narrow tortuous, hair-raising fashion to Dyea. It is nonetheless a delightful road, and its beauty and open vistas of water and mountains compare favorably with those of any other road in Alaska. After 8.5 miles the Chilkoot Trail signpost is seen on the right side of the road, shortly before the Taiya River is crossed by a steel bridge.

Chilkoot Trail: Section1

Beginning to Sheep Camp (to Mile 13)

The trail climbs over a hill in the first 0.5 mile, then follows the Taiya River for 2 miles. An old wagon road (also used in the 1950s for logging)

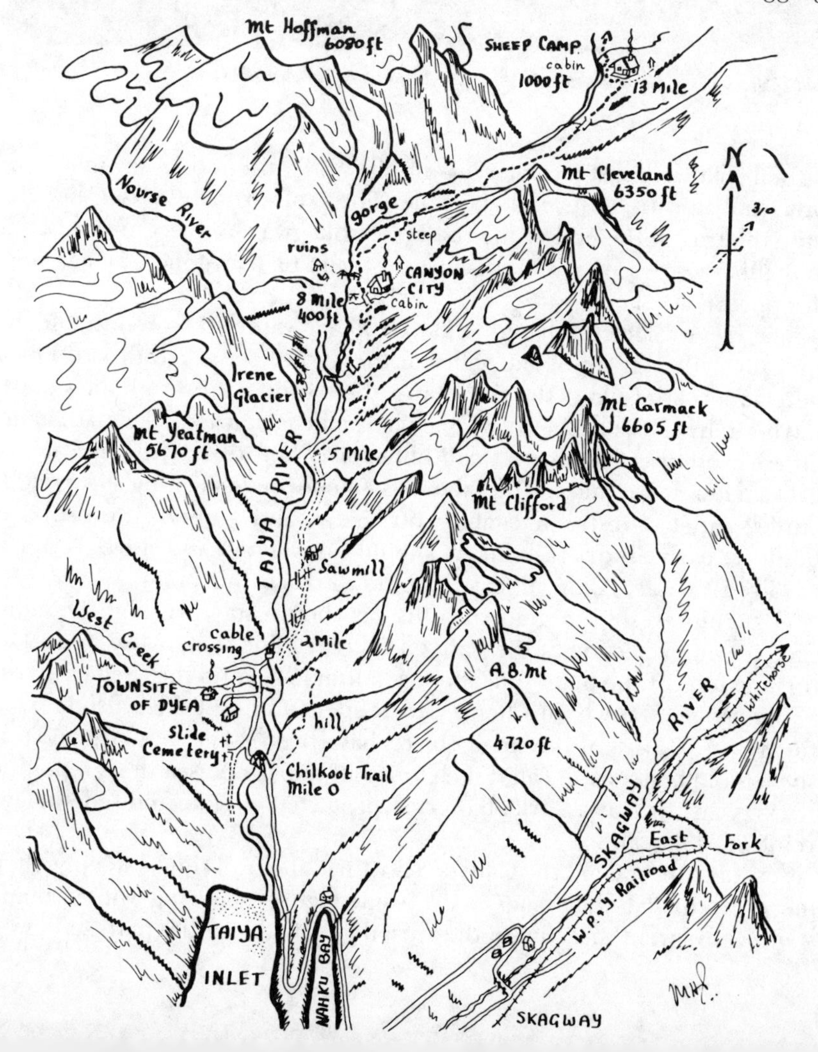

Old cable crossing, Chilkoot, now fallen victim to erosion (Barbara D. Kalen)

is then followed past a cable crossing site and a time-worn sawmill, now practically a ruin, to its end at 5 Mile. The cable crossing was a shortcut onto the trail at the end of the road from Skagway. Subject to vandalism and the vagaries of river erosion, this relic of a bygone era has now disappeared.

The Irene Glacier, a hanging glacier like a waterfall frozen in midair, spills over the far lip of the valley at the end of the wagon road. From here a footpath follows the river bank, then wanders through the woods, staying fairly close to the river. Each half mile is marked. The path gains little elevation except for a small hill shortly before arriving at Canyon City shelter at 7.8 miles. The cabin has an enormous heating stove, eight bunks, rudely constructed table and chairs, and a good wood supply, but it is nearly always full; hikers should carry a tent and stove. Water is readily available. Allow at least 5 hours to reach this point.

Hikers interested in gold rush history should stay overnight to allow time for an inspection of the Canyon City site. The remains are found by turning left off the main trail about a half mile beyond the shelter, across a footbridge. Many happy hours can be spent amongst the brush looking for treasure. Most of the small objects have been taken, but large objects such as old boilers and cabin skeletons still remain. Resist the temptation to carry any find away. All objects are protected by state and federal law; removal is illegal.

A short way beyond the Canyon City turn, the trail climbs steeply, then more gradually, traversing a steep-sided gorge. During winter many stampeders went directly up the frozen riverbed, but the path stays well above the gorge on the east side and occasionally offers views of the river and valley upstream. After about 2.5 miles it drops to Pleasant Camp, a campsite during the gold rush, then gradually rises to Sheep Camp at 13 Mile (elevation 1000 feet). Although the trail crosses many streams, it becomes rather featureless as it winds through the thinning trees, and to the tired hiker it seems endless. About the time the traveler is convinced the cabin was moved up the valley by gremlins, the roof becomes visible through the trees on the left.

Sheep Camp shelter has a good supply of wood, a stream nearby, a register fascinating to read for the mistakes of previous hikers, a good stove which heats the cabin both summer and winter, eight bunks, and an authentic poker table that has survived since the turn of the century. This is another site that is nearly always full, especially during the summer. The trek to Sheep Camp from Canyon City takes 3 to 4 hours.

Chilkoot Trail: Section 2
Sheep Camp to Ptarmigan (Deep) Lake (Miles 13 to 25)

From Sheep Camp the footpath runs northeast and climbs steadily as the valley becomes narrower. Once above the alder and onto rock, the pathway is more difficult to find. Care must be taken, when boulder-hopping, to keep a sharp lookout for cairns and any visible markers, if the intention is to stay on the trail. However there is no real danger of losing the way if the right bank of the stream is followed until a well-marked crossing is reached. From here, large stone cairns can be followed, with the stream now on the right, until the Scales are reached. The Scales are unmistakable: situated almost at the head of the valley close to the 16-mile post, they are identified by mounds of old articles left by the human tide around 1900. From the Scales to the summit, the route is marked in summer with snow markers.

The area should be avoided during spring and after heavy snowfalls in winter, since it is highly susceptible to avalanche. Many gold rush miners were killed in a slide which occurred one April close to this spot. Their graves will be seen in Slide Cemetery, Dyea. Also, in early summer, while last-winter snows still linger on the ground, watch for deep holes and rotten snow bridges across streams.

Almost immediately above the Scales, the head of the valley has two obvious routes over the pass. To the right, or east side of the valley, is the Petterson Trail, formerly used by dog teams and pack horses, which is longer and not a practical route today. To the left, or west, of the Petterson Trail is the more famous steep scree slope, immortalized on film when it became a living staircase of stampeders in the winter of 1897–98.

Cairns erected by the Park Service lead directly onto the steep screes. Even in thick mist, the cairns can still be seen from one to the next, but

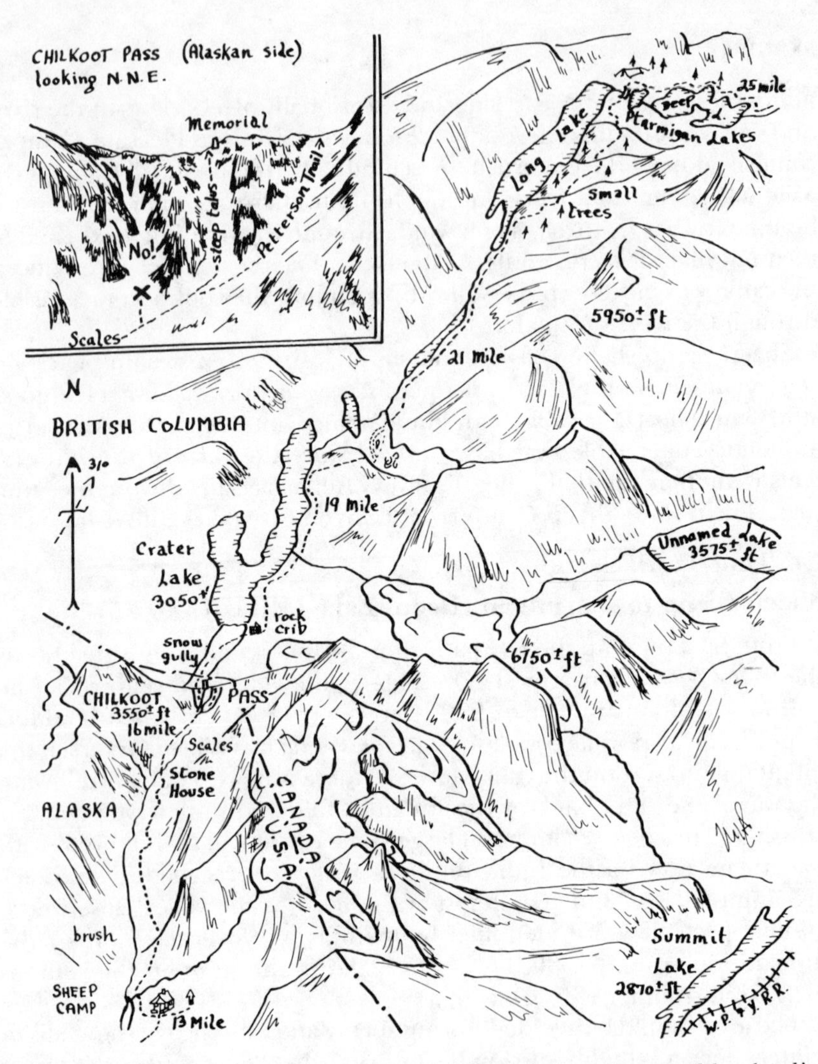

keep alert. Cairns give way to flagging affixed to long cables leading almost to the summit. The scree or talus is loose, so large parties should attempt to stay together to lessen rockfall onto stragglers. These slopes will probably still be covered with snow in late July.

There is an Alaskan Centennial commemorative marker close to the international border between Alaska and British Columbia. From here follow the trail in a narrow declivity to the left of the marker, to the last rise. The compass bearing through the pass should be 23° east of true north (declination to the Canadian map grid is 30.5° east). Those lucky enough to have a clear weather view can look back over the route just taken and see the narrow cleft of the Dyea Valley. The height of the pass is a little over 3500 feet and takes 4 to 10 hours to reach from Sheep Camp. There is no camping between Sheep Camp and the summit.

Storms roar through Chilkoot Pass every week or so, and the summit is exposed to the unmitigated fury of a southeasterly blow. In winter, as much as 3 feet of snow can fall overnight, with temperatures well below zero, and as much as 30 feet can accumulate on the summit during a winter. Anyone caught in a storm is advised to seek shelter directly over the summit, if possible, or by Crater Lake. A tent would be useful and a stove essential for cooking, as firewood is nonexistent and fires are prohibited in Canada. Water is plentiful once over the summit.

If the far side of the summit is in heavy clouds, proceed with care. The snow slope descends directly into Crater Lake with a sudden, sharp drop into deep water. Traverse to the right off the snowfields below the pass and pick up the trail on the southeast side of Crater Lake. An old stone crib is located above Crater Lake at this point, with evidence of a disused wagon road.

The country changes quite dramatically over the pass. Sharp glacier-hung peaks and the dour, narrow-sided valley with its somber, forbidding crags on the Alaskan side give way to wide-open country, liberally sprinkled with lakes and streams, smooth-sloped mountains, and ice fields which spill over the upper slopes to the east.

Mallet-shaped Crater Lake, about 2 miles long, is 500 feet below the summit on the Canadian side. The trail is not well marked for conditions of poor visibility; it follows the east side of the lake, and if the hiker stays low and close to the eastern shore it cannot be lost for long. It becomes very clear about 1.5 miles farther on, toward the lower end of the lake, where it runs by the lakeshore, then turns east, then northeast away from the lake over a small rise or "pass." It is well marked by the Canadian wardens with snow markers and rock cairns as it drops to the river running northeast out of Crater Lake to a couple of small lakes and a heap of artifacts. A wagon road will again be found, and there should be no more trouble following the trail as it descends on the east side of the river to Long Lake, mostly staying close to the river. Southwesterly gales funnel down the valley on storm front days, but a few small, sheltered campsites may be found. There is never any problem finding water.

The trail, which has been brushed and marked by Long Lake, climbs almost 500 feet above the southeast shoreline and runs into sparse, small tree cover once more. But it is a poor campsite as the trees give poor cover in strong blows, and the wind, seemingly with malicious delight, merely flits over the trees and pounces on a tent, temporarily flattening it. Cooking with a small stove under these conditions is virtually impossible.

About 7 miles from the pass the trail drops to a stream connecting Long Lake with Deep Lake — the latter known locally as Ptarmigan Lake. Here it crosses to the north bank by a recently constructed bridge. This is an idyllic spot containing many patches of level ground for camping between the lakes and on the shore of Ptarmigan Lake. There is some shelter from the prevailing winds, and plenty of water. The scenery has softened considerably from the wild, open country of the pass and the somber, black crags of the upper Dyea Valley. There are lovely extensive views down Ptarmigan Lake to distant mountain ranges on the far side of the White Pass and Yukon Railroad.

Chilkoot Trail: Section 3
Ptarmigan Lake to Bennett Station (Miles 24 to 35)

The trail skirts the north shore of Ptarmigan (Deep) Lake, which is about a mile long, then gradually drops 800 feet to Lake Lindeman, following the north edge of a river gorge (Ptarmigan Lake outflow). At

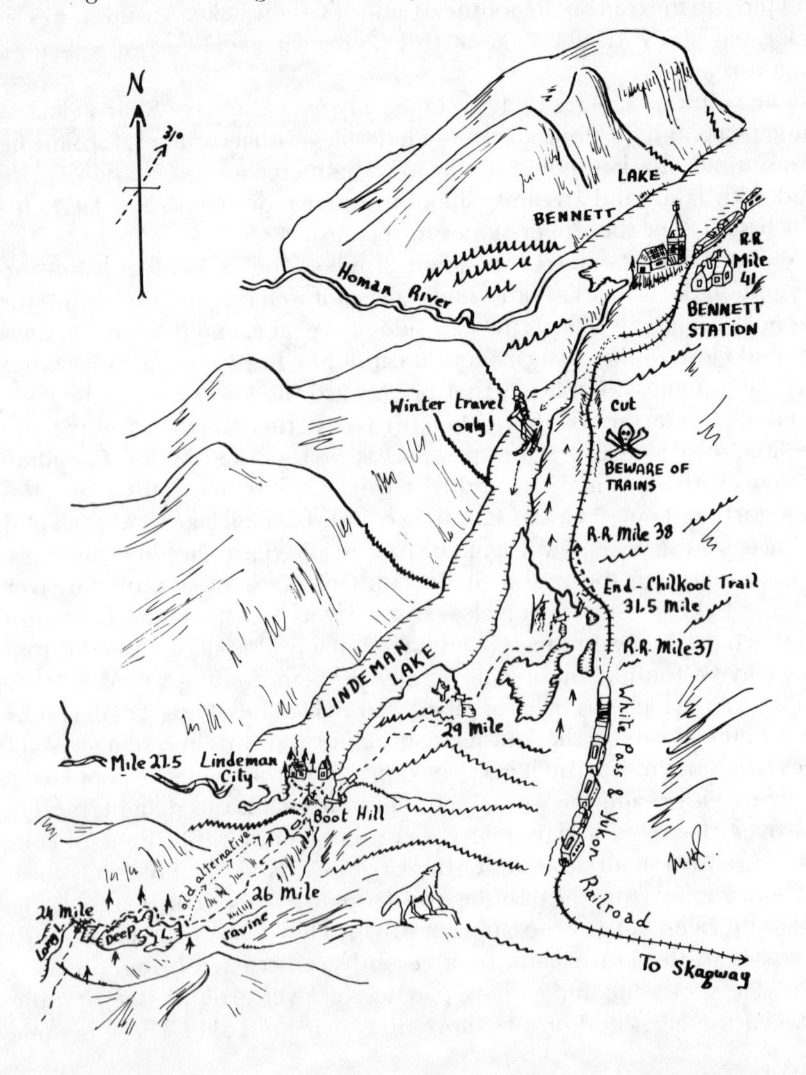

Lindeman City

the east end of Ptarmigan Lake watch for old sledges and runners left behind by stampeders. Distant mountain ranges form a backdrop to the wooded slopes; alpine fir is more prevalent here, with occasonal pines mixed in. A view that should not be missed is that of Lake Lindeman, a little off the trail to the right about halfway down the gorge.

Shortly after passing a pool on the rim of the gorge, the trail turns a corner and the southern end of Lake Lindeman lies at one's feet. As the trail then eases gently down the hillside to the old city of Lindeman, a cabin built in 1968 by the "W.C.I. Engineers" (Whitehorse Correctional Institute) should be visible facing west, close to the shore. A more recent cabin, built in 1971, is about 600 yards east, close to the river mouth, facing northeast up the lake. Both are rudely constructed and exposed to prevailing winds. The stoves are adequate for cooking, but there is no ax and wood is limited, as the indiscriminate cutting of trees is discouraged. They are welcome shelter, nonetheless, and a register has been placed in the west cabin by the Southeast Alaska Mountaineering Association.

Here the trees are gradually coming back after being decimated by stampeders in their near panic to build boats in time for the long trip down the Yukon to Dawson. At this altitude, lodgepole pine has ascendancy over alpine fir.

If one continues east from the first cabin along the main trail toward Bennett, a fork will be encountered about 300 yards away under Boot

Hill, a recently restored graveyard situated on a hill, with views of the lake and surrounding mountains. A tiny pathway to the right goes up the hill, the left fork connects the second cabin with the first, and the right fork curves around the hill, then crosses the river after following it upstream for a short way. This is the trail to Bennett.

Follow the trail around the lower end of the river gorge, across the river, and up a hill — about 200 feet of climbing — where on looking back there is a last view of Boot Hill and the south end of the lake encircled by mountains. About three-quarters of a mile farther on, one has a fleeting glimpse northward down the length of Lake Lindeman to Lake Bennett in the far distance. The trail then crosses Totem Pole Creek No. 9 close to a small lake with a prepared campspot. About a mile farther on it skirts the western edge of a large unnamed lake and crosses the stream by Hangman's Creek. This section has been cleared by the "Engineers" with verve and imagination and a certain whimsical humor. Paint is liberally splashed down the trail and tree blazes are executed with wild abandon.

A mile beyond Hangman's Creek the trail nears the White Pass and Yukon Railroad. This point is a little over 4 miles from Lindeman City

Bennett

and takes 2 to 3 hours to walk. The trail has been rerouted in recent years to avoid walking the railroad tracks for the last few miles to Bennett. It now comes over the hill by the old church above the Bennett Station.

For those going from Bennett to Skagway the trail is easily seen and well signposted where it leaves Bennett up the hill past the old church. For the rest, one will have to reverse these directions. If crossing the pass in poor weather conditions, follow fairly close to the shore of Crater Lake, which runs southwest. At the end of the lake, find the crib and traverse onto the snow to the right. Climb the 500 feet or so to the top by following a compass bearing of 23° west of true south or 203°. (It may be sufficient to follow the south compass needle). If the trail and the Alaska centennial marker are not found immediately below the summit, turn back. The mountains on all sides of the pass are steep and cliff-hung, and it is not worth the risk of straying onto them.

On a clear, crisp winter day, the hike in on skis or snowshoes on the ice of Lake Lindeman is a wonderful experience for the hardy, although temperatures can dip below −50°F in this area. As mentioned earlier, snowfall is sometimes as much as 30 feet on the pass; temperatures in the winter change dramatically from one side of the Coast Range to the other. It is usually much colder on the east side of the Divide, although the winter storms invariably come from the west. A chill factor of a little over 1°F for every mile per hour of wind speed must also be taken into account when attempting the pass. A knowledge of ski mountaineering is helpful, and care must be taken over the avalanche zones in the upper reaches of the Dyea Valley. Survival gear is essential for such an undertaking.

The Chilkoot is a fascinating and beautiful trail for those sound in wind and strong enough to undertake the journey on foot. Attempts have been made to take snowmobiles over the Chilkoot Pass, but this is no place for modern mechanics. The trail should be left solely for those pilgrims who, on foot, follow in the footsteps of the gold rush stampeders. Otherwise the pass is diminished as a challenge.

Grade alpine
Distance 33 miles from Dyea to Bennett
Time 4 days or more
Elevation gain 4700 feet, south to north; 2550 feet, north to south
Trail condition good
Trail characteristic historical, valley and alpine
Limitations: Beware of avalanche hazard in winter and spring, severe weather in winter, and 1000-plus hikers in August. Must buy Bennett-Skagway train ticket before leaving Skagway.
Access by taxi to Dyea (8.5 miles from Skagway) and (return) White Pass and Yukon Railroad, Bennett to Skagway

Facilities: three cabins available to date; always full. Guided tours available in Skagway.
Administrative agencies: in agreement with the Bureau of Land Management, the National Park Service and State of Alaska jointly manage the U.S. portion of the trail at time of writing. The government of the Yukon Territory, in agreement with the government of British Columbia, administers the Canadian portion. Rangers at Sheep Camp; Canadian warden at Lindeman.

S2 LOWER DEWEY LAKE COMPLEX

This is a pleasant short hike for visitors in Skagway for a few hours who wish to see the harbor and town from above and obtain good views across the valley and inlet. In winter, once the bench is reached, the trail complex affords excellent opportunities for snowshoeing. The bench is 500 feet above tidewater and contains a small reservoir and lake stocked with rainbow trout — good skating ponds in the winter. The trail to the bench is steep in places, but the only real difficulty encountered is during March and April, when sheets of ice necessitate the use of creepers or crampons on the lower sections.

Skagway small-boat harbor, Lower Dewey Lake trail

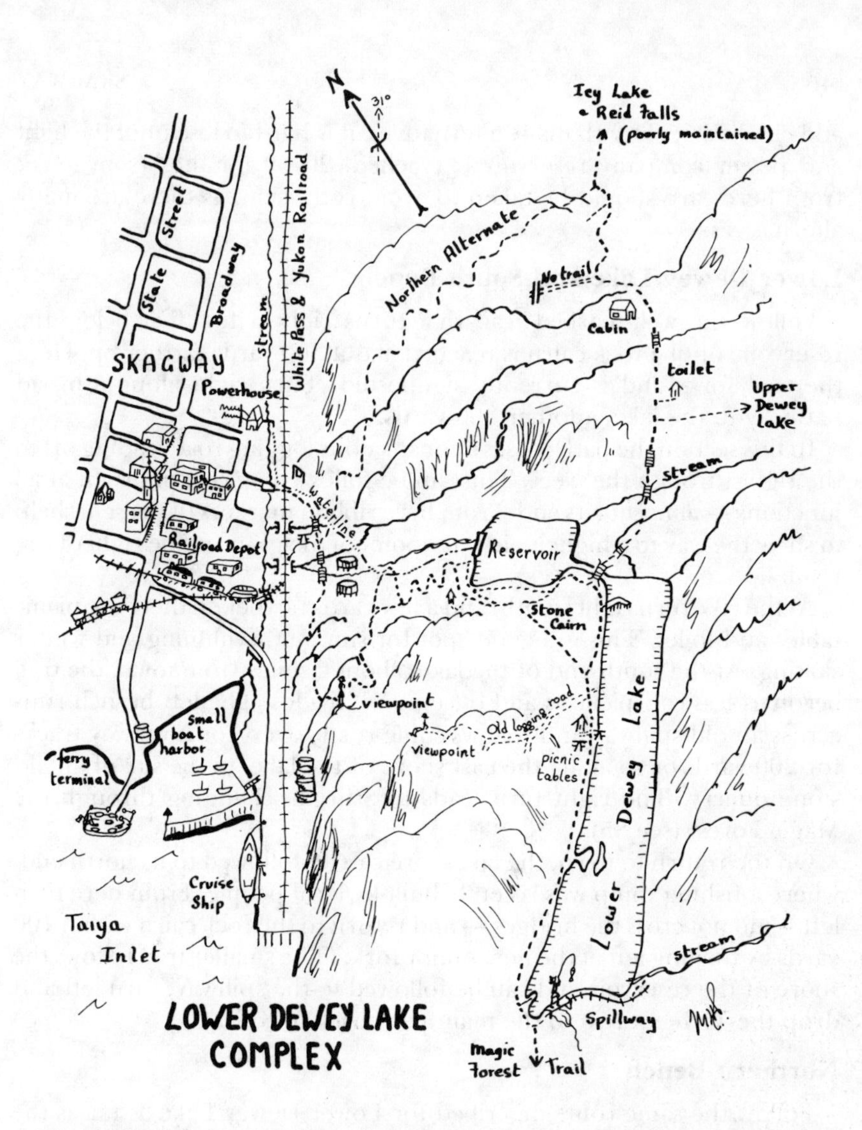

The trail starts across the railroad tracks on the east side of the valley, east of the downtown area. From the ferry terminal, walk into town (the main street is Broadway) across some tracks by the railroad depot, to the Golden North Hotel. Turn right and within the same block turn left by the Klondike Hotel, then immediately right toward the hillside. The Dewey Lake sign will be plainly visible ahead and can be reached by crossing a footbridge over a stream and the railroad tracks. (Cross with care.) The trail will then be seen running up the hillside at an angle. Follow it past a couple of picnic tables on an overlook about 70 yards from the sign and 100 feet above sea level. The trail continues uphill over two wooden bridges past two water towers, and a little over a quarter of a mile from the beginning reaches another viewpoint. Although the trail winds and climbs steeply with many alternatives, it is hard to lose until the light and power company reservoir is reached, 20–30 minutes from town; from here care should be taken to avoid confusion, as there are many alternatives.

Lower Dewey Lake and South Bench

Follow the well-marked trail that turns right a few feet below the reservoir, until a rock cairn is reached about 300 yards farther on. Here the trail forks and is currently signposted. Turn right along a broad pathway to the lake, another 300 yards.

In this section the path passes a conspicuous logging road leading off to the right through the trees. This can be followed — keeping right at all junctions — almost to its end. From here ribbon markers (if present) help to show the way to a higher, airy viewpoint of Skagway on the right of the road.

At the lake turn right (south) and a few yards farther on there are picnic tables and toilet. This is a good spot for summer swimming and winter skating. At the south end of the lake, about 2 miles from town, the trail becomes less conspicuous and once more divides. The left branch runs across an old spillway and follows some rusty, overgrown railway tracks for 200 yards or so along the east shore of the lake, to the site of an old stone quarry. The right turn leads to Sturgill's Landing through the Magic Forest (see S5).

On the return to town, the lakeshore can be followed to its north end, where a fishing ramp was recently built by local people. From here turn left — do not cross the bridges — and return to the rock cairn within 100 yards by turning left at the next minor fork. (The smaller trail follows the shore of the reservoir and can be followed to the spillway; turn left and drop the 15 feet or so to the main path back to town.)

Northern Bench

Follow the same route described for Lower Dewey Lake as far as the rock cairn. Turn left and, after about 100 yards, left again across three bridges. The third bridge crosses the Upper Dewey Lake stream, and shortly beyond on the right is the trail to Upper Lake. Continue north along the bench and within a few yards of the Upper Lake junction there is a toilet in the trees. In another 250 yards, a recently renovated shelter is passed; it is currently in good condition and will hopefully remain so.

Past the shelter, the trail wends its way to the left, then after about 200 yards turns sharply right. A disused logging road, barred by windfalls, goes straight ahead, leading nowhere in particular. Ignore all other small trails off to the left until a major junction is reached half a mile (15–20 minutes walking time) from the cabin. The junction is well marked with arrows and multicolored circles of paint on rocks and trees. The trail

Lower Dewey Lake (Barbara D. Kalen)

climbing the hill straight ahead leads to Icy Lake and Reid Falls but is not well marked or maintained. Turn left and follow the paint marks, first uphill then down a series of switchbacks until the path crosses the waterline. The original trail is reached immediately above the first picnic tables, a few yards above the railroad tracks.

This route can be used as a northern alternative onto the bench and is especially useful when the main trail is icy. The complete circle, walked in the direction described, is marked with painted circles as a guide for the Skagway July 4 marathon run.

The absence of large evergreen trees on both north and south benches is due to a devastating fire in 1912. Mushrooms are plentiful on the bench from late July to September, and edible mushrooms such as *Lactarious deliciosus* (orange delicious), *Russula*, and *Boletus* may be found. Pick at your own risk!

Grade sightseeing
Distance 0.7 mile to Lower Dewey Lake; complete circuit by reservoir and north bench, 2.5 miles
Time 40 minutes to Lower Dewey Lake; circuit 1.5 hours
Elevation gain 600 feet
Trail condition excellent except icy in April
Trail characteristics recent-growth forest, mountain bench
Access by foot from Skagway
Administrative agency State of Alaska

S3 UPPER DEWEY LAKE

To enjoy vistas of upper Taiya Inlet and the surrounding mountains, a hike to Upper Dewey Lake is a must. It can be an all-day or overnight

Mountains above Skagway, Upper Dewey Lake trail (Barbara D. Kalen)

trip, with a good trail all the way. There is a primitive cabin by the lake, 3000 feet above the Skagway valley. Breakfast can be supplemented by eastern brook trout for those who take their fishing poles and licenses. The local people and children use this cabin, and I think it says a great deal for them that vandalism is kept to a minimum. I hope the general public will extend the same courtesy. Those staying overnight should take a cooking stove, as wood is scarce and the cabin stove inadequate.

Upper Dewey Lake trail can be reached by following the trail to the reservoir on the east bench above town (see Lower Dewey Lake, S2). Turn right just below the reservoir, left at the stone cairn, then left again across the bridges. After the third bridge watch for a junction (about 1.3 miles from town). Take the signposted trail to the right, which climbs steeply almost immediately in a series of switchbacks. The climb is long and relentless but is relieved once — about 800 feet above the bench — by a viewpoint of the town and reservoir. The trail is close to the stream from Upper Lake but not yet close enough for hikers to obtain drinking water.

After another 200 feet of climbing the slope eases off, the trail crossing a subsidiary stream by a log.bridge. It then eases upward, with less gradient than before, in a series of pleasant switchbacks through groves of diminishing trees. Another stream is crossed shortly before the trail emerges onto a short stretch of muskeg. Here there are views of the inlet below and Mount Harding. Note the point of reentry for the return, and cross the last open meadow in the same general direction (east), toward a great cirque. The dam at the lake outlet is directly ahead. Turn right along the dam and across a spillway; the cabin is on the right above the stream, protected by a screen of alpine fir.

The lake is a gem captured in a bowl of 5000- to 6000-foot peaks which back onto the Skagway icecap; its overflow spills almost directly into the beautiful fjord below, by a series of cascades. There are many camping spots around the lake, and hiking in the lovely semi-alpine bowl above.

Grade forest (strenuous)
Distance 3.5 miles from town
Time 3 hours up, 2 hours down
Elevation gain 3097 feet
Trail condition good
Trail characteristics mountain
Access by foot from Skagway
Facilities: overnight shelter available; wood is scarce — take a backpacker's stove
Administrative agency State of Alaska

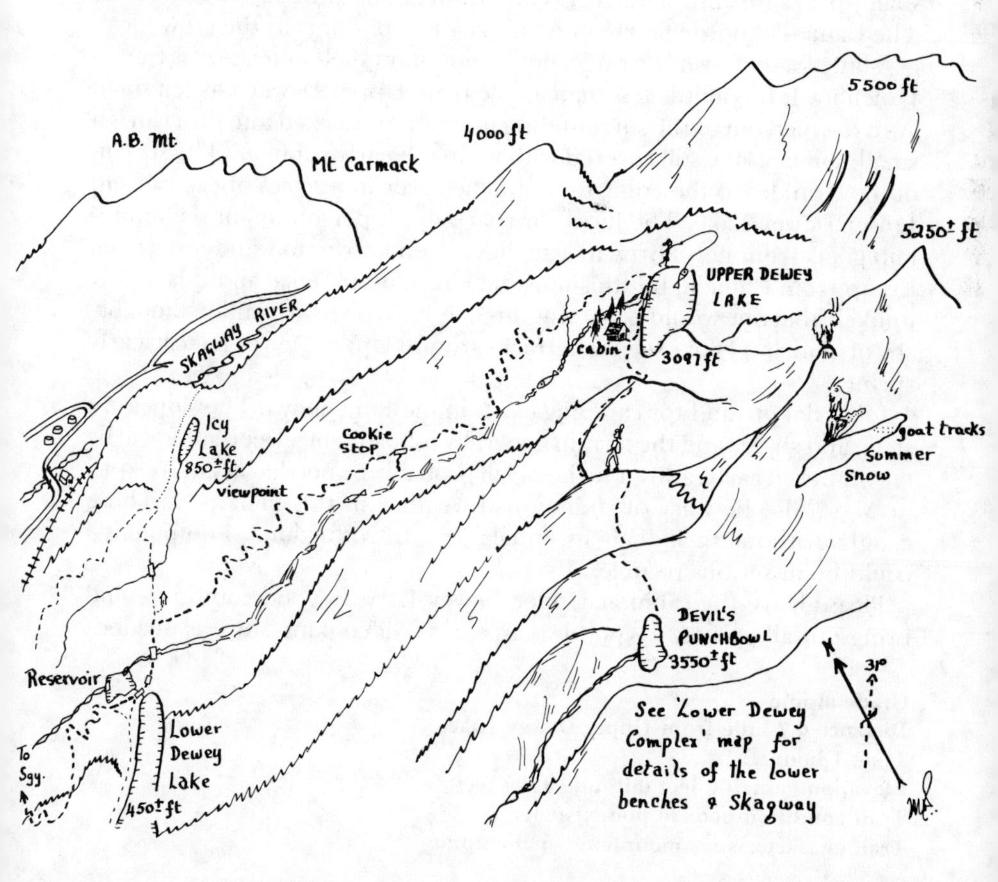

S4 DEVIL'S PUNCHBOWL

The trail starts from the cabin at Upper Dewey Lake or by the lakeside (see S3) and is a delightful evening stroll or afternoon saunter.

From the lake walk south up a ridge which becomes a terrace under the unnamed peak on the southern lip of the Dewey bowl. The trail is indistinct at times, as it runs over boulder jumbles and through dwarf hemlock, but the ridge is obvious and not difficult.

The trail leads above the tree line, and at one point — about 20 or 30 minutes above the cabin — the view is so all-encompassing and magnificent that one has to stop and enjoy it for a while. In the words of a 6-year-old local boy, Skagway is seen as a "toy town" almost 4000 feet below. Toy ships arrive at the dock and toy planes land on the miniature runway far, far below. The entire upper fjord (Taiya Inlet) can be seen surrounded by a complete sweep of mountains, most of them unnamed and unclimbed. For those unused to this country the experience can be overwhelming. Behind the traveler the slopes soar upward to sharp, shaley peaks forming a wall between the hiker and the Skagway ice fields. The Canadian border is about 6 miles east — but only as the crow flies!

A little farther over the ridge, now a mountain shelf or terrace, is Devil's Punchbowl. It is a little less than a mile from Upper Dewey Lake, a small cwm scooped out of the surrounding mountains. Locked into the cwm is a small, somber lake still covered with ice in the early summer. The stream outflow tinkles to the edge, then tumbles over in a series of cataracts to Lower Dewey Lake. The lucky, or sharp-eyed, person might see mountain goats from here. Brown bears have been known to wander over the icecap from Canada, but this must be a rare occurrence and it is highly unlikely that one would be seen at this height. Wolves are understandably shy of man, but I have seen wolf tracks around Upper Dewey Lake in early spring.

Little flat ground for camping exists in the Punchbowl. The slopes are steep and shaley and the terrain generally inhospitable. Deep snow will be encountered early, and snowshoes will probably be needed as late as April or May. Also be wary of sudden bad weather in this high area. Those caught without their Ten Essentials (see Introduction, "Equipment") could be in serious trouble.

Please leave the cabin at Upper Dewey Lake in good condition, and bring out all garbage. Wood is scarce; a small cooking stove is needed.

Grade alpine
Distance 0.7 mile from Upper Dewey Lake
Time 1 hour
Elevation gain 700 feet (altitude 3700 feet)
Trail condition poor to nonexistent
Trail characteristics mountain bench, alpine

Taiya Inlet from the bench above Upper Dewey Lake

Access by foot from Skagway via Upper Dewey Lake trail
Facilities: cabin available at Upper Dewey Lake

S5 THE MAGIC FOREST (Sturgill's Landing)

I had already completed the description of the Lower Dewey Lake Complex and had dismissed the trail leading to Sturgill's Landing as being of no consequence, because no one would ever find it, when Barbara Kalen said I could not leave Skagway until I had seen her Magic Forest; it was somewhere on that trail at the lower edge of the lake. Within a week, three of us were irresistibly drawn into the forests, on a totally separate trail-blazing and cone-collecting expedition, but luckily armed with ribbon, clippers, map, compass, flashlight, and some chocolate. We quite expected to get lost, but never did, and I went convinced I would find just another southeast Alaska rain forest (which are magnificent in their own right). We descended into a grove of pine and hemlock, tall and stately in their search for light, with only a carpet of moss at their feet. The light filtered through in much the way it filters through a stained-glass window in a cathedral. There were two such forests separated by a logged patch, now grown back with small pine, birch,and hemlock, then the trail ended with a long downward swoop above a steep stream gully to the beach. At the bottom was Sturgill's Landing, with picnic tables, a garbage pit, and toilet on the site of the old Sturgill cabin. The trail was so different from any other I had seen in the Panhandle that I realized it had to be included. So Barbara and I went back with our clippers and cleared and marked the trail in earnest, hopefully eliminating the bad spots.

The trail is about 2.5 miles long from the south end of Lower Dewey Lake, or 4.5 miles from Skagway (see S2, Lower Dewey Lake Complex). At the trail division at the lower end of the lake, turn right and after a short way arrive at a ruined cabin. The trail slopes downhill to the site of a second cabin. The trees thus far are a mixture of types and are small, due to the forest fire of 1912. Ignore an unmarked trail leading off to the left. The Magic Forest is entered shortly thereafter, through a thicket of young hemlock which choose to seed directly in the pathway.

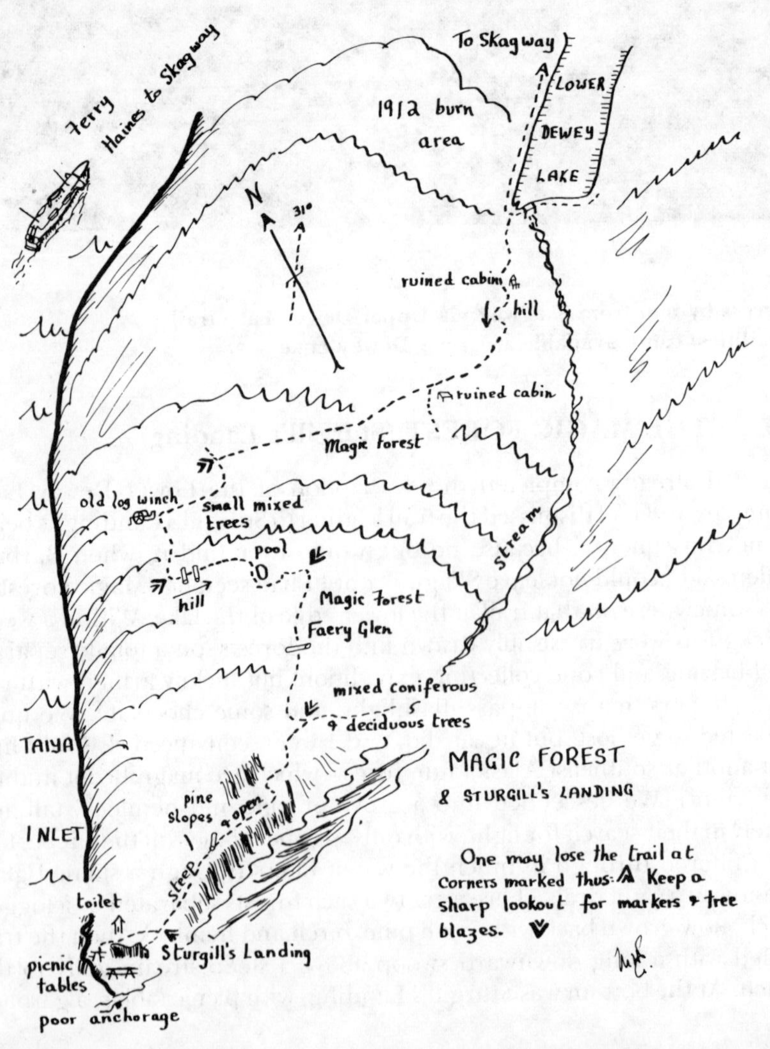

The tendency is to daydream as you wander through the big trees, but do not! Keep a sharp lookout for orange painted blazes as the trail makes some unexpected turns. About 1.5 miles from the lake, one breaks out of the large trees and has a view across Taiya Inlet. Up to 1920 logs were winched and rolled into the sea from here, and some of the old equipment is still lying scattered about.

A short walk farther on will bring one back into the hemlocks and pine once more. Again resist the temptation to daydream — the trees definitely have that effect on one — and follow the orange blazes past open muskeg containing a small pool. The trail skirts the pool, then plunges into the enchanted trees once more. Watch carefully for a sharp right turn shortly after this. The trail then dips into a small mossy gully in which there is a deadfall, and finally runs into small pine, hemlock, spruce and birch forests once more. Shortly before a stream is sighted the trail again makes a sharp right turn. (Its apparent continuation drops to a stream, providing access to drinking water for the thirsty.) The path then traverses and descends the steep side of the stream gully through pine forest. This section of trail is steep and exposed and is not recommended for snowshoe travel. A few feet above the beach the path again turns sharply right for the only feasible route to the picnic spot at the Landing. Anchorage is poor, so the picnic tables are rarely, if ever, used except by hikers who stay with the trail to its end. Visitors wishing to walk the trail one way can be dropped off by small boat at the Landing.

The general direction of the trail from Skagway to the beach is southwest. If you get lost on the way back to town, travel east to the Lower Dewey Lake outflow (the same stream met at the Landing) and follow this upstream to the lake.

Grade forest
Distance 4.5 miles from Skagway to beach
Time 2 hours either direction
Elevation gain 500 feet to lower Dewey Lake, with equal amount lost between lake and beach
Trail condition fair but confusing
Trail characteristics differing forest types, bench, and beach
Access by foot from Skagway to the north end; by small boat to the south end. Anchoring is not recommended, as the beach at Sturgill's Landing is exposed to northerly and southerly blows
Administrative agency: The U.S. Forest Service provided the campground but does not maintain the trail, which needs adoption

S6 LOWER REID FALLS

Almost everyone who comes to Skagway wants to know where its most famous and infamous gold rush characters are buried. "Soapy" Smith, a small-time gambler and crook who once had Skagway by its tail, and Frank Reid, who dispatched Soapy in a gun duel and was himself mortally wounded, are both buried in the Gold Rush Cemetery.

Behind the graveyard a short trail of about 300 yards goes to the base of Reid Falls. The falls are unexpected and attractive, particularly in winter when they become almost totally frozen over. The whole area makes a pleasant afternoon or evening stroll — 1 hour with a car or 2.5 hours on foot from the ferry or cruise ship.

From the ferry terminal walk into town. The continuation of this road, Broadway, passes through the historical center of town. Walk up Broadway as far as you wish, then go left one block to State Street, a wide, black-topped boulevard, and turn right. Watch for the 1-mile post on the right as the railroad marshalling yards are reached. State Street at this point makes a wide sweep to the left and crosses the Skagway River. (See Lower Dewey Lake and Skyline trail maps, S2 and S7.) Keep straight on along a dirt road across the shunting lines and follow the main White Pass and Yukon Railroad line on its west side. After a little over a quarter of a mile the dirt road crosses the railway and ends about 300 yards farther down, with sufficient parking and turning space for those who are driving.

The cemetery is situated directly above the railway tracks, and one can either walk along a broad trail close to the tracks and into the cemetery

Gold Rush cemetery (Barbara D. Kalen)

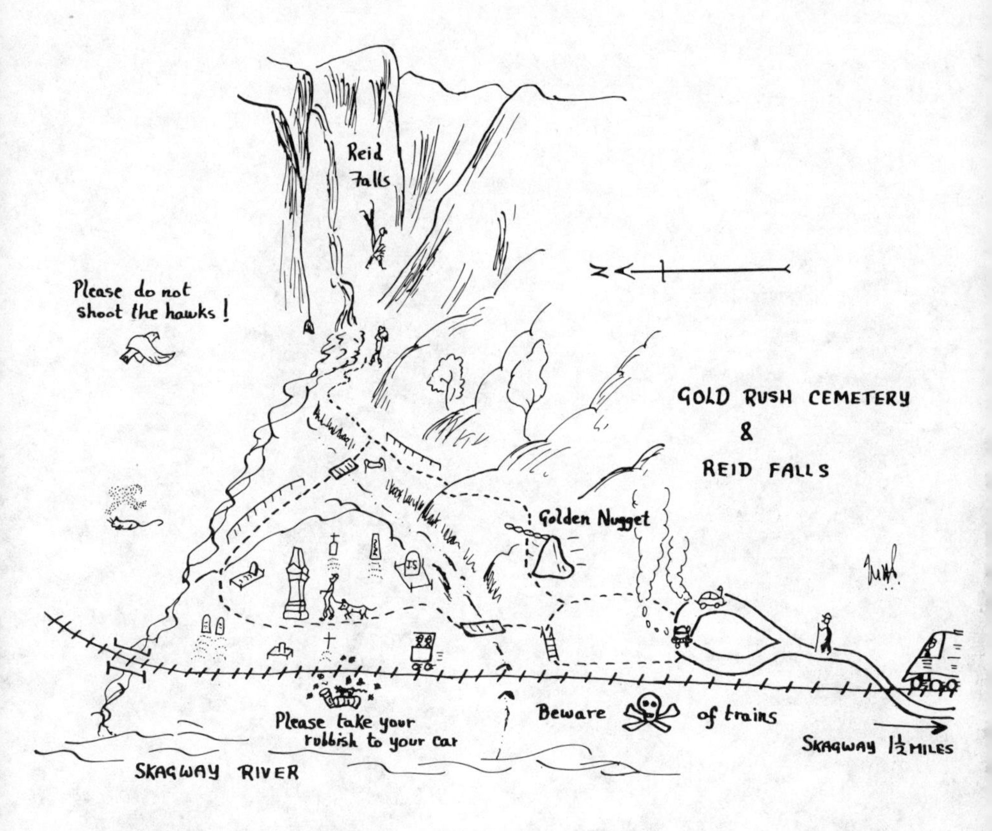

up a ladder, or go directly up a small hill behind the parking area and turn left at the large "gold nugget."

The graveyard is an intriguing place, and most people will find for themselves the things of great interest. Walk past Frank Reid's grave, up a hill and across a bridge, then turn left at the next fork. A few yards farther on the trail ends under Reid Falls. Do not attempt to scramble on the cliffs above for better photographs; the rock is loose and not worth the extra risk. During March and April the trail to the falls may be icy, but the falls will be frozen over and are sometimes highly photogenic.

On the return to the road the left turn can be taken. This leads through the woods to the "gold nugget." From here one can either go down to the railway tracks or turn left down the bank to the parking area.

Grade sightseeing
Distance 2.5 miles from ferry terminal
Time 40 minutes from town
Elevation gain none
Trail condition excellent
Trail characteristics historical, falls
Access by foot or car from town

Skyline trail in winter (Barbara D. Kalen)

S7 SKYLINE AND A. B. MOUNTAIN

It is very hard to have favorites when around Skagway — all the trails are beautiful and seem to have something unique to offer — but I seem to gravitate to the Skyline more than the others. This trail is particularly rich in moss- and lichen-covered rocks, sudden delightful glimpses of tidal waters and the town, and fairly open mixed pine and fir forests. The trail continues up the mountain, where sweeping views of Taiya Inlet, the Tyea Valley, and surrounding sharp, glacier-hung peaks are to be had. A. B. Mountain is the peak on the west side of the Skagway valley and dominates the town from this angle.

One can be satisfied with an hour to the first viewpoint or spend an entire day on the mountain. An especially attractive time is late September or early October when birches, willows, and cottonwoods in the lower woods turn a brilliant gold. On sunny days the woods are radiant, and at these times it seems as if the whole mountain smiles — even when clouds threaten from above.

Drive north out of town across the Skagway River and turn left just beyond a tank farm, up a gravel road signposted to Dyea. (For greater detail see the Chilkoot Trail introduction, page 134.) The road swings south and climbs for 1.5 miles to a "Y" junction. Keep right, and a few yards beyond the "Y," before the road descends, limited parking space is available off the left shoulder. The trail begins from the top of a steep gravel bank directly opposite.

Those without transportation can use a shortcut. Turn left off the road from town onto a bridle path, immediately after crossing the Skagway River. The path climbs a series of sharp turns and intercepts the Dyea road at Mile 3. Turn left and walk up the road past the houses and the "Y" junction to the trail sign on the right.

From the top of the bank the path goes north, by a derelict building and through birch and willow woods. Watch for orange paint and tree blazes. After about 20 or 30 minutes of steady climbing through mixed deciduous and evergreen woods, a viewpoint of Skagway and the inlet is attained. The viewpoint is off the trail, about 20 paces to the right.

The path climbs steadily upward with occasional views back over tidewater and, to the east, to Twin Dewey Peaks dominating the valley. About 2 miles from the road there is a convenient place to stop by a stream for a snack. The path enters mixed hemlock then alpine fir forests, but is not as well traveled. Watch for a sharp left turn (around a windfall) then a right bend as it continues to climb. Later a glimpse of Twin Dewey Peaks, framed by alpine fir, is seen once more from a huge lichen-covered rock platform.

Those going beyond this viewpoint should be prepared for mountain travel (see Introduction). The trail traverses the base of the mountain,

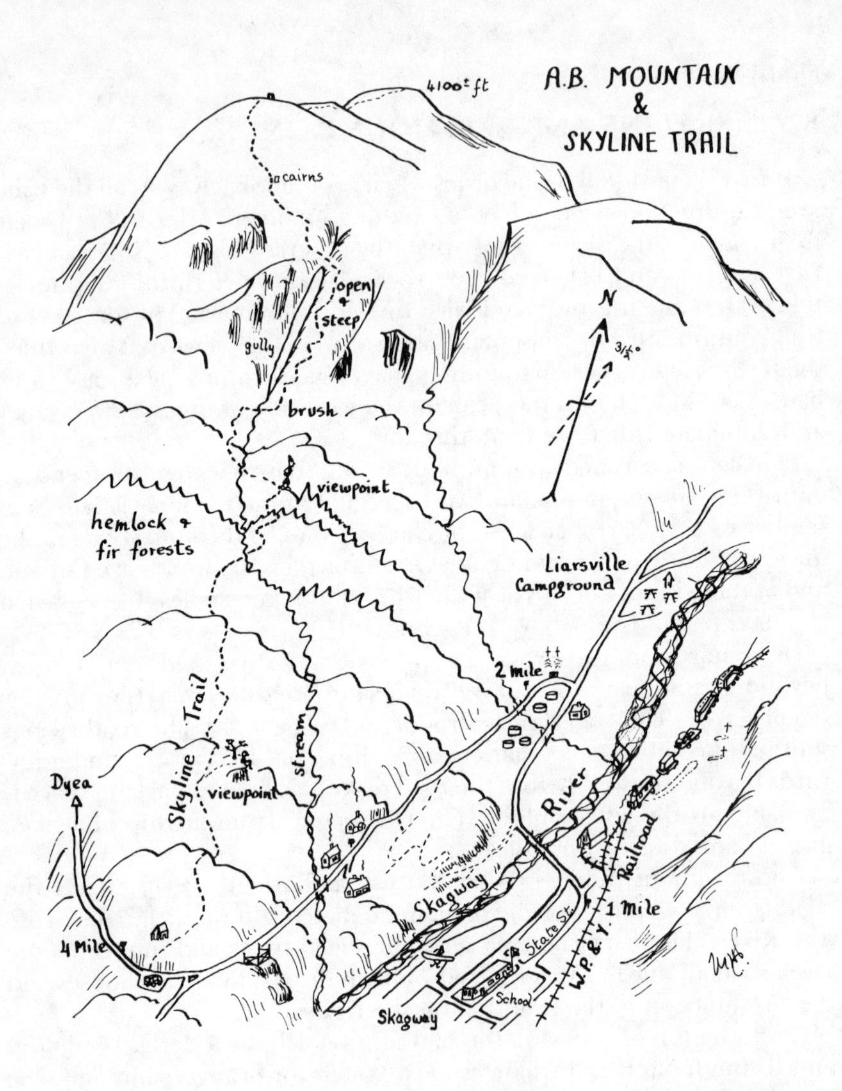

recrosses the stream, then climbs steeply. This part was recently brushed, but it reverts rapidly if left for long. The climb is steep and slippery, and the stream is crossed once more. The route then goes straight up, keeping to the right, or east, of an obvious gully.

Views from here are panoramic. Skagway, the ore-loading facility, and the ferry terminal are laid out like a map, and the graceful, snow-covered peaks around Haines are revealed on a clear day. Close to the top of the gully, cairns lead northwest to the main ridge. It is important when returning to find the correct gully. In bad weather follow the cairns closely. *Do not attempt to come off the mountain any other way.*

The ridge may be climbed as far as is desired, with ever expanding views. The final peak, visible from Skagway, is about 4100 feet high, but A. B. Mountain is approximately 2 miles farther back along the ridge, which runs north then northeast and is over 5000 feet high. Very few stray this far; most are content with the view of Skagway from the first peak.

Grade forest; A. B. Mountain alpine
Distance 2 miles Skyline to second viewpoint
A. B. Mountain 5.5 miles
First peak visible from Skagway 3.5 miles
Time 1.5 hours; A. B. Mountain (first peak) 6 hours
Elevation gain 1800 feet; A. B. Mountain 5000 + feet; first peak 4100 feet
Trail condition good; deteriorates on A. B. Mountain; above 2500 feet tagged route only
Trail characteristics ridge, mountain, alpine
Access by foot (3 miles) or car (4 miles) from Skagway

S8 DENVER GLACIER

The trail starts 3.5 miles from the Gold Rush Cemetery (see Lower Reid Falls, S6); the beginning is reached by walking alongside the railroad tracks. The hike gives an insight into the overwhelming stature of

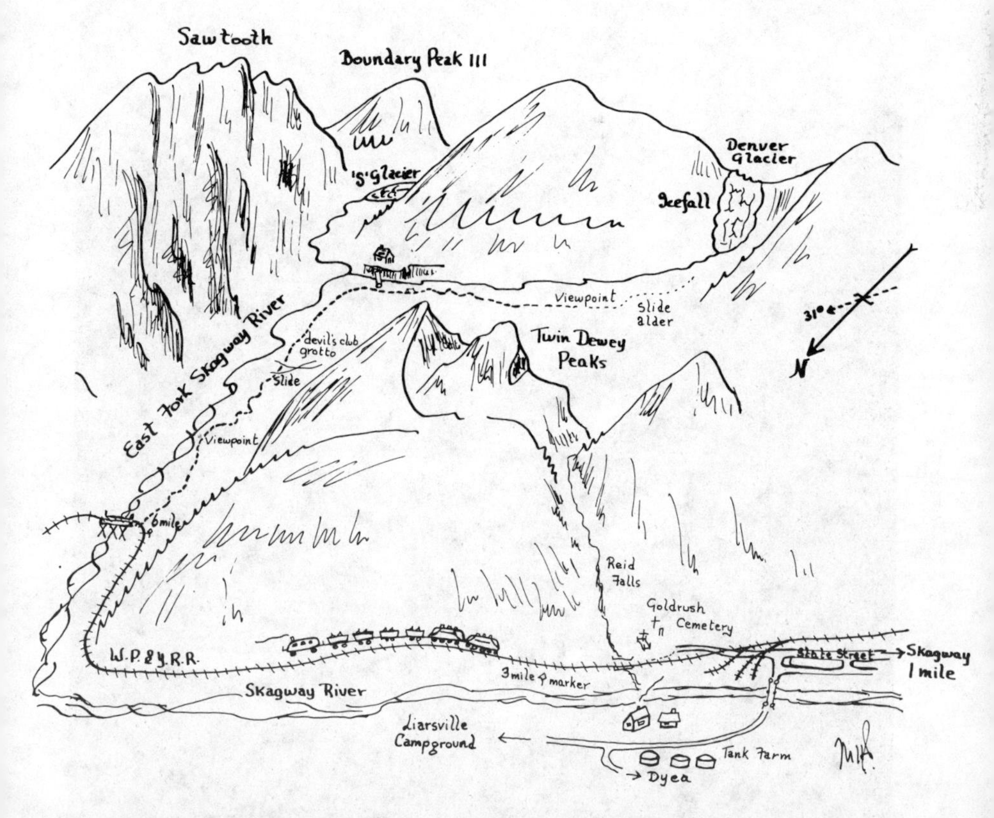

the mountains around Skagway, as the route is locked within the narrow confines of a sheer-walled valley, with the Sawtooth Range (5000 to 7000 feet high) to the north and Twin Dewey Peaks (5645 feet) to the south. The Denver Glacier icefall, the overspill of the Skagway icecap, is receding and hangs frozen in midair, 4000 feet high over the lip of the mountain opposite the trail end. Occasionally huge seracs overbalance and topple forward to disintegrate on the ice below, a potential danger to those who wander too close.

Drive or walk to the Gold Rush Cemetery. Follow the railway tracks — beware of trains — to the 6-mile post where the line crosses the east fork of the Skagway River and runs up the opposite hillside. The Sawtooth Range dominates the skyline to the north with a jagged array of peaks.

The trail begins to the right, immediately before the railroad bridge, and follows the south bank of the river upstream. The route has been kept open by local residents in the past, but the Forest Service has recently brushed the entire trail and will be responsible for its periodic maintenance. For part of its length the trail plunges into spruce and hemlock forests, then emerges on the bank of the swiftly flowing glacial

Denver Glacier, 1971

river. Here is a better opportunity to observe the steep gullies and black spires of the Sawtooth Range directly opposite.

The path climbs a steep hill and traverses a slide area, now covered with alder and devil's club. The latter were left purposely by trail work parties, when the plants were not in the way, since they form an attractive green corridor, 7 to 8 feet tall. The trail leaves the East Fork Skagway River after 3 miles and veers south to enter a side valley — the stream outwash from the Denver Glacier. Two small streams, in devil's club grottos, are crossed; then the path opens onto a rock platform over a miniature gorge, a good snack stop. At one time a bridge straddled the stream from the rock to continue the trail to a partially ruined cabin on the far side. The path also went to the "S" Glacier, another 3 miles, but is now hard to find because of lack of maintenance.

The Denver Glacier trail was recently extended by the Forest Service to the glacier's terminal moraine, another 2 miles. Hikers are warned not to approach the glacier too closely. A snowshoe or ski trip can be made to the glacier, but keep away from steep avalanche slopes toward the end. Also, cross the first slide area with care.

Denver Glacier, about 30 years ago (Barbara D. Kalen)

Grade forest
Distance 8.5 miles from Gold Rush Cemetery
Time 4.5 hours one way
Elevation gain 2000 feet
Trail condition fair
Trail characteristics valley, hanging glacier
Limitations stay well clear of glacier; in winter beware of avalanche slopes at the trail end
Access by car or foot from Skagway to Gold Rush Cemetery (1.5 miles)
Administrative agency U.S. Forest Service

S9 LAUGHTON GLACIER

A short trail north of the Sawtooth Range runs through fir and hemlock woods into a gigantic cirque. Here Laughton Glacier forms the base of a series of cascading glaciers, which start their dizzy descent on the upper reaches of the sheer 3000-foot walls of the Sawtooth Range. The jagged summits atop the walls soar upward to 7000 feet and partially encompass the cirque. It is one of the few spots where the stark splendor

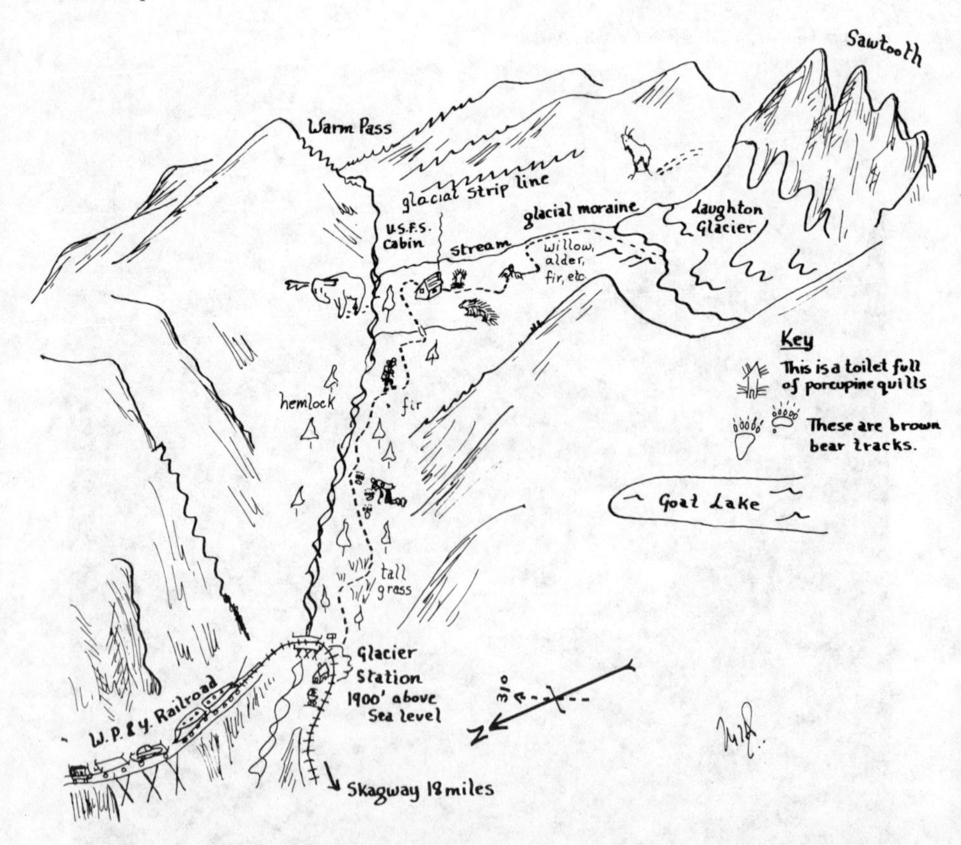

Laughton Glacier (Barbara D. Kalen)

of mountain scenery can be viewed at such close quarters by people not trained and equipped for technical mountaineering. (For another such spot, see West Glacier trail, J13.) A Forest Service cabin sits in a strategic spot, about 1000 feet below and a mile distant from the glacier, at the confluence of two rivers. An overnight stopover may be necessary because of train schedules and is, in any case, highly recommended.

Ride the White Pass and Yukon Railroad to Glacier Station, 18 miles from Skagway, to reach the beginning of the trail. The train will stop on request and can be flagged down for the return, or for an onward journey to Whitehorse, although prior arrangements should be made. One should register with the U.S. Forest Service, Chatham Ranger District, Box 1049, Juneau, Alaska 99801 (see Introduction) for use of the cabin.

The signposted trail takes off by the station, on the east side of the tracks immediately before reaching the railway bridge, and follows the south bank of the river upstream toward Warm Pass to the east. It passes through tall grass meadows shortly after leaving the railway, then enters the forest. River and trail continue in close proximity, the two meeting at a point where the river narrows and runs through a rock cleft. Some of the small streams that are crossed have dangerously slippery logs as bridges; also recent windfalls cause occasional interruptions in what is otherwise smooth traveling.

The cabin, useful as a base for mountaineering parties, is in good condition and has wood and water readily available. It is supplied with an ax and cooking utensils and has enough sleeping space for six people. The stove is adequate for cooking but gives small comfort in winter. Despite repeated attempts to keep the privy in good shape, porcupines insist on chewing through the walls and seat.

A small footpath continues from the cabin to Laughton Glacier, 1000 feet above the cabin and about a mile south. Go past the toilet and walk along the footpath through thinning trees until, within a quarter of a mile, a 1200- to 1500-foot morainal hill is reached. From the top of the hill there is a stunning view of the Sawtooth pinnacles and cascading glaciers, dominating the upper reaches of the valley. The path disappears shortly thereafter, so find the easiest way to the river and follow the stream bed upstream to recent terminal moraine. Do not venture onto the ice unless experienced in glacier travel; glaciers have hidden dangers for the uninitiated.

The trim line, or lower limit of trees, on the ridge opposite clearly demonstrates the height of the glacier before recession. Watch for mountain goats on the surrounding slopes, and do not be surprised if moose knock on the cabin door in the middle of the night. The trail is recommended for both summer and winter travel.

Grade forest
Distance 2 miles to cabin; 3 miles to Laughton Glacier
Time 1 hour to cabin; 2 hours to glacier
Elevation gain 300 feet to cabin; 1300 feet to glacier
Trail condition good
Trail characteristics valley and glacier
Limitations: overnight gear is mandatory because of train schedules. Do not venture onto the glacier
Access by White Pass and Yukon Railroad, 18 miles from Skagway
Facilities: cabin available; beware of porcupine quills in privy seat
Administrative agency U.S. Forest Service

S10 LOST LAKE

A little used and locally maintained trail climbs steeply to a small lake nestled in a fold of a hill above the Taiya (Dyea) Valley. In places the trail is difficult to follow, although it is blazed all the way. It leads to an unexpected viewpoint of upper Taiya Inlet and the Taiya Valley, on a large, steeply angled rock, and through a glorious "garden" of lichen before reaching the lake. Rainbow trout may be caught in the lake and many good campsites found along its shores.

The trail starts on the west side of the Taiya Valley about 10.5 miles northwest of Skagway. Drive north out of Skagway on State Street (one block west of downtown), which makes a sharp left turn by the railroad

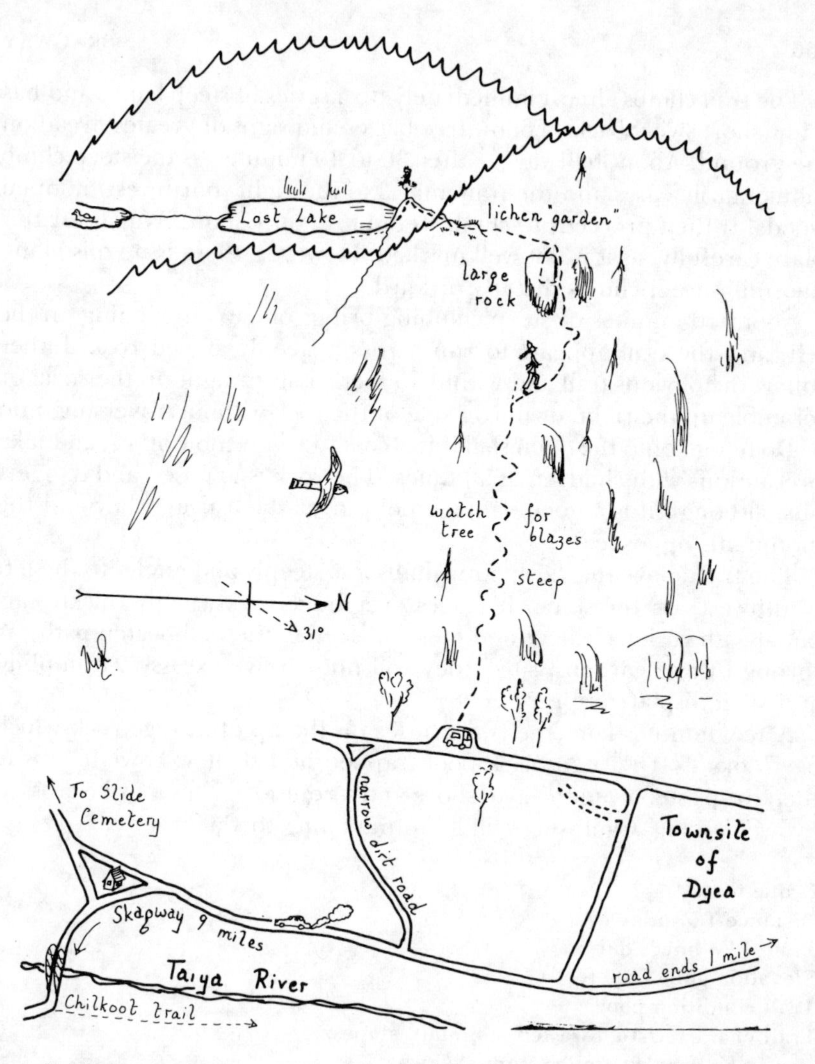

marshalling yards after 1 mile to cross the Skagway River. Turn left just beyond the tank farm up a gravel road which loops back and traverses the hillside southwesterly. It is signposted to Dyea. (See the Skyline trail map, S7, for further details.) Drive with extreme care: the road is narrow and dangerous, although the scenery is superb. Cross the Taiya River (shortly after passing the beginning of the Chilkoot Trail) and turn left at the second obvious turning, about half a mile from the bridge. (A road not evident to most newcomers runs back at an obtuse angle to meet the first turning; see accompanying map). Drive toward the western walls of the valley for about a quarter of a mile, and turn right at the next intersection. Within 75 yards of the turning, a clearing in the trees and a trail leading toward the hill slope are seen on the left. Limited parking may be found off the narrow dirt road.

The trail climbs almost immediately up a series of steep banks and has a few short switchbacks. Follow tree blazes and signs of greatest tread on the ground. About halfway — after 30 to 40 minutes — the steep climb momentarily eases and the trail angles to the right (northwest) in open woods. It then proceeds to climb straight up once more. Watch for this place carefully, as it is not well marked. However, there is no mistaking the trail once it climbs directly upward.

About 10 minutes of steep climbing brings one to an opening on the left, and the trail appears to run across a steeply angled rock. Either follow the obvious trail and within 15 feet climb straight up the rock, or scramble up the right, or north, side of the rock without traversing onto it. Do not go onto the open slab if it is covered with snow or ice, and take precautions with children at all times. The rock is exposed and dangerous, although it is a good vantage point over the Taiya Valley and the mountains opposite.

The trail above the viewpoint climbs less steeply and angles to the left (southwest) up the slope. It passes over huge rocks, many thickly carpeted with various lichens and mosses. Keep to the well-beaten pathway through these gardens, since they will not survive excessive trampling and such displays are rare.

A few minutes later the trail pauses on the lip of a huge rock which overlooks Lost Lake, a black pool trapped in a shallow bowl. The trail then drops steeply to the lake shore and its outflow. This may be crossed by a fallen log. Campsites will be found along the lake shore.

Grade forest
Distance 1.5 miles
Time 1.25 hours one way
Elevation gain 1400 feet ±
Trail condition poor
Trail characteristic forested mountain slopes
Access by car, 10.5 miles from Skagway
Administrative agency: no official maintenance; marked by private citizens

Blueberries

Visitors travel trails of Southeast Alaska, thankful for the scene, the feeling of beauty and aloneness, hopeful that it will remain that way. The unspoiled land is a resource to be used and reused, a resource whose recreational use still leaves Alaska as it was — the "lonesome land," loved and appreciated by those who have come to visit or live under conditions different from those they left.

Robert E. Howe, Superintendent
Glacier Bay National Monument

Naming geographic features implies man's "mastery" of the land, not his respect of it.

Charles Janda

. . . features that are unnamed . . . leave a flavor of the unexplored.
Bruce Paige

GLACIER BAY NATIONAL MONUMENT

Glacier Bay stands in icy aloofness 70 miles northwest of Juneau. Great snow-covered mountains soar upward to 15,000 feet, supporting vast ice fields that spill out radially as glaciers. Because of increasingly balmy climatic conditions, the glaciers are receding rapidly, opening up narrow, sheer-walled, ice-choked fjords. The magnificent scenery thus presenting itself is accessible to motorboats and, with the application of common sense, hand-propelled craft. However the greatness of Glacier Bay lies not only in its awesome scenery, but in its subtleties. In the upper reaches of the bay the first emissaries of the plant kingdom have seeded themselves and hold the rocks together in a web of roots so fragile one hardly dares breathe, much less walk, on them. Interstadial wood — remnants of ancient forests standing before the last ice age 3000 years ago — is discovered today on the beaches and river gravel beds. In some places, such as Nunatak Cove and Forest Creek in Muir Inlet, and Adams Inlet, it stands vertically as tree stumps. This ancient wood is combustible; visitors are asked not to light fires in the areas where it is found.

The complexity of the plant kingdom and its hold on the soils increase as the gap widens between the plants and the tidal glaciers, until at Bartlett Cove (Monument Headquarters), 50 miles from the tidal glaciers, there are young, parklike stands of Sitka spruce and hemlock. When Captain Vancouver sailed through Icy Straits in 1794, Bartlett Cove was covered with ice. As the delicate toehold of vegetation becomes more robust, it is like an invitation to the pioneers of the animal kingdom. A few brown bears roam a vast territory in the upper bay, mountain goats graze the sparse mountain slopes, and the voice of the wolf is sometimes heard from within the cottonwood and willow growths.

The vertical-walled fjords and coast are teeming with life. Gulls, puffins, and guillemots balance their eggs on ledges hundreds of feet above the inlet; tern colonies, occasionally harried by bald eagles, are found on rocky shorelines and islands, and kittiwakes nest in Tarr Inlet. Killer whales occasionally swim through in bands of 15 or so, and humpback whales blow fountains of fine spray and slap the water with their tails. Seals constantly encircle a kayak, their heads popping up like periscopes and their unblinking eyes agog with curiosity. Land otters are very occasionally observed plucking mussels off the rocks at low tide — they chew their meal with abandon and a noise resembling the crunching of potato chips. In Adams Inlet terns rise from the water in clouds, chased by parasitic jaegers, black birds similar to a seagull but in flight vaguely resembling a precocious crow! The pursuer stays within inches of the fleeing tern's tail, both birds performing a stunning aerial acrobatic display before the victim is forced to regurgitate its food. The jaeger deftly catches the tidbit in midair and disappears like a streak of black lightning.

Glacier Bay is a vast outdoor laboratory and an unforgettable learning experience for the sensitive person. Its remoteness, outstanding scenery, and wildlife make it a fitting candidate for National Park and wilderness status. The preliminary proposal by the National Park Service would declare land from tidewaters wilderness, except those areas on the southern periphery of the Monument. Adams, Hugh Miller, and Dundas Inlets would be included within wilderness classification, partly because of vast concentrations of nesting geese and ducks and other birds liable to suffer from the inroads of noisy outboards, and partly for the unique experience they offer to those prepared to rough it. Mining is presently in the exploratory stage and is causing minimal damage so far, but full-scale mining, a future possibility, would cause irrevocable changes to the environment. Development of this sort would call for open pit mining, the blasting of a tunnel under one of the largest glaciers, and ore-loading facilities on the outer coast. A phasing-out of all mining activity is included in the preliminary draft of the master plan for Glacier Bay, as policy for National Park status, but the plan requires

Glacier Bay

an act of Congress for implementation and therefore needs public support.

The best centers of access into Glacier Bay are Juneau and Sitka. Regular commercial flights are made from these cities to Gustavus during the summer, and charter flights and boats can be arranged from both cities. The nearest ferry service is from Juneau to Hoonah across Icy Straits, but hopefully a foot passenger ferry service will be introduced to Gustavus in the future.

Bartlett Cove, on the south end of the bay, is connected to Gustavus and the airstrip by 10 miles of road. No other roads into the bay are, or should be, planned. One therefore has to paddle one's own canoe, or charter a floatplane or boat. Restrictions may, and should, be put on air travel to certain areas because of disturbance to wildlife and loss of wilderness character. Water landings are currently allowed in most open bays. The same restrictions may also apply in the future to motor vessels for the same reasons.

The *Seacrest*, a tour boat, sails daily in the summer from Bartlett Cove up Muir Inlet; the boat will drop off anyone for an extra fee. Floatplane charters are available from Bartlett Cove, and carry at least three people depending on gear. Further inquiries regarding access should be made to the Superintendent, Glacier Bay National Monument, National Park Service, Box 1089, Juneau, Alaska 99801.

Camping is available on the beach at Bartlett Cove about a quarter of a mile south of the lodge.

Hikers and canoeists should check in at Bartlett Cove for the following reasons:

1. Park personnel may have local knowledge of the area, which can be of help logistically, aesthetically, and for reasons of safety (e.g., prevalent ice conditions in Muir Inlet, other campers in the area, Park Service patrol schedules, special hazards, etc.).

2. In case of emergencies or overdue parties, the Park Service must know where to start looking. Before a trip, preparation of a fairly accurate itinerary is extremely important.

3. Any guns taken into the National Monument must be sealed and registered at Park Headquarters. A State fishing license is required for fishing.

All boats, regardless of size, should stay clear of steep hillsides. Rolling and falling rocks are an extreme hazard, especially in Charpentier, Tidal, and Johns Hopkins Inlets and the eastern coastline between Beartrack Cove and Adams Inlet.

Avoid going ashore on bird rookeries during June and July. Birds are laying, incubating, and hatching and are disturbed by human presence during these months. Nesting success can be severely retarded merely by a casual walk.

All garbage should be carried out to Goose Cove or Bartlett Cove for proper disposal by authorities.

Most of the hikes described in this section are not "trails" but "ways." The freedom from thick brush and trees in the upper bay allows the pedestrian to use his or her imagination. The following, as well as the "routes" marked on my maps, are merely suggestions:

Bartlett Cove:
GB1 **Bartlett River (sightseeing)**
GB2 **Beach and Nature Walk (sightseeing)**
Map required: Juneau B-6 (1:63,360 series topographic).

Adams Inlet:
GB3 **Adams No. 1 (low-level)**
GB4 **Adams No. 2 (alpine)**
Map required: Juneau D-6.

Muir Inlet:
GB5 **Nunatak (alpine)**
GB6 **White Thunder Ridge (alpine)**
GB7 **Forest Creek (low-level)**
Maps required: Mount Fairweather D-1 and Skagway A-4.

Tidal Inlet (West Arm):
GB8 **Gloomy (alpine)**
Map required: Mount Fairweather D-2.

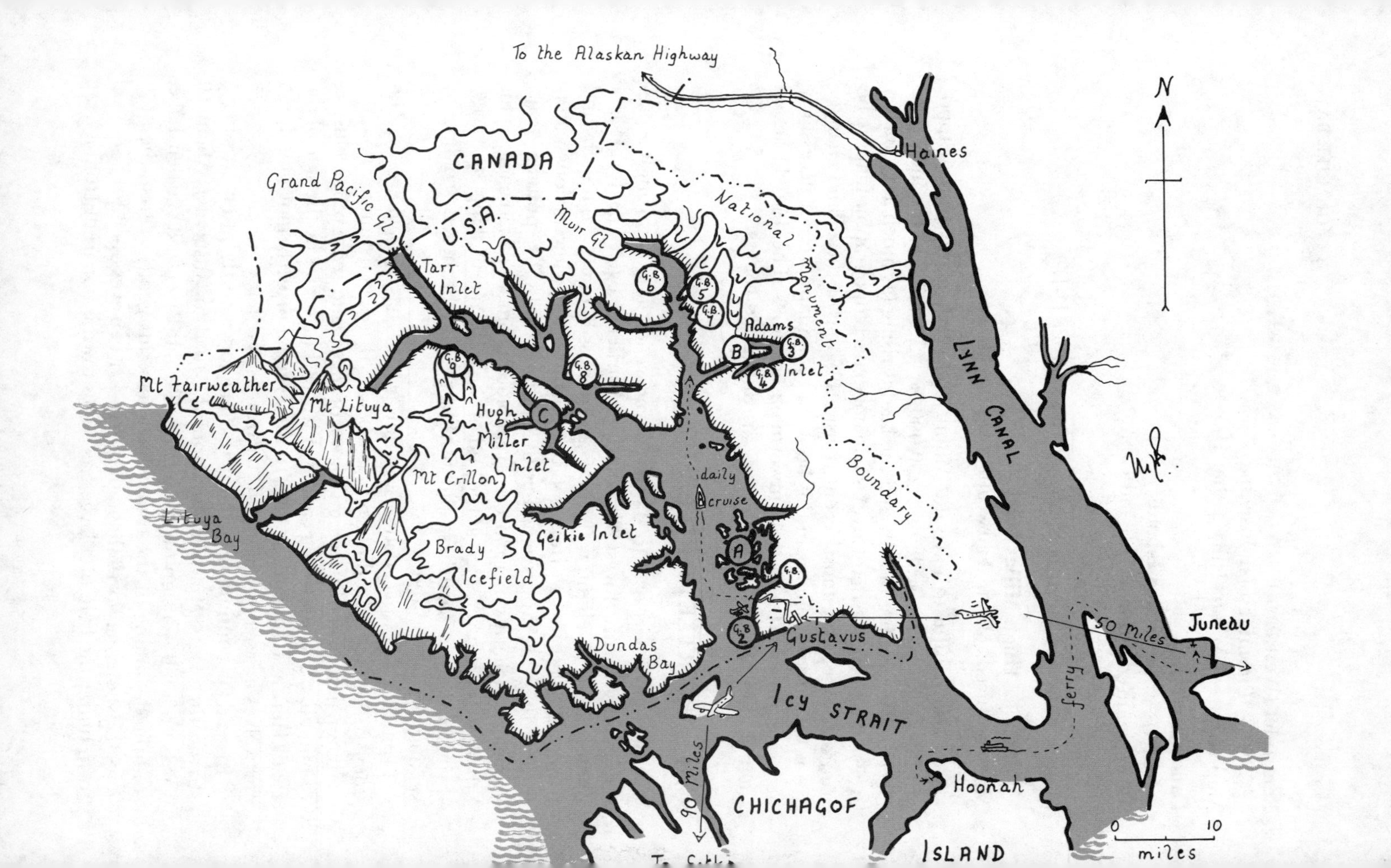

To the Alaskan Highway
N
Haines
CANADA
U.S.A.
Grand Pacific Gl
Muir Gl
National
Monument
Boundary
LYNN CANAL
Tarr
Inlet
G.B. 6
G.B. 5
G.B. 7
Adams
Inlet
B
G.B. 3
G.B. 4
G.B. 9
G.B. 8
Mt Fairweather
Mt Lituya
Hugh
Miller
Inlet
C
Mt Crillon
daily
cruise
Lituya
Bay
Geikie Inlet
Brady
Icefield
A
G.B. 1
G.B. 2
Gustavus
Dundas
Bay
50 Miles
Juneau
ferry
Icy STRAIT
90 Miles
Hoonah
CHICHAGOF
ISLAND
0
10
miles

Reid Inlet (West Arm):
GB9 **Ptarmigan (sightseeing)**
Map required: Mount Fairweather D-3.

Canoe Routes:
GB(A) **Beardslee Islands**
Maps required: Juneau B-6 and C-6.

GB(B) **Adams Inlet**
Maps required: Juneau D-6, Mount Fairweather D-1.

GB(C) **Hugh Miller Inlet**
Maps required: Mount Fairweather D-2 and C-2.

It is also helpful to have the Mount Fairweather and Juneau topographic series with a scale of 1:250,000, or 3.75 miles to the inch. The glaciers are receding rapidly and the land is rising (as much as 12 inches every 10 years in Bartlett Cove), so do not expect topographic maps to be accurate, except the most recent revisions. Some of these land changes are reflected in the maps in this book, but the maps are not necessarily accurate; they are taken from my own observations. The dotted lines on them do not reflect real trails; they are suggested routes.

GB1 BARTLETT RIVER

A pleasant, short trail to Bartlett River wends its way through a predominantly spruce forest surrounding Bartlett Cove. The forest is a photographer's delight, with fuzzy green moss hanging from limbs and trunks. Bartlett River offers good opportunities to view various waterfowl if they are approached with caution. Gadwalls, pintails, teals, shovelers, mallards, mergansers, great blue herons, and bald eagles, plus other birds are often seen at the end of the trail. Wrens, kinglets, varied thrushes, hermit thrushes, and warblers might be heard scolding or staking territory in the forest.

From Bartlett Cove Lodge walk toward the Lagoon, where the National Monument Headquarters is located. If it is midsummer note the Indian paintbrush of varying yellows, oranges, and reds, yellow clusters of mimulus, and white bog candle or leafy white orchis by the side of the road. Herons frequent the bay. In the evening or early morning, listen for wolves or coyotes calling in the Beardslee Islands.

Instead of continuing around the Lagoon, shortly after crossing a stream turn right at a road junction (the road to Gustavus). About 50 yards up a hill is a sign on the left for Bartlett River and Bartlett Lake, and the beginning of the trail, which descends gently at first, then follows the shoreline north through the trees. Keep eyes open for a squirrel town under the bole of a large tree. This town is apparent from a heap

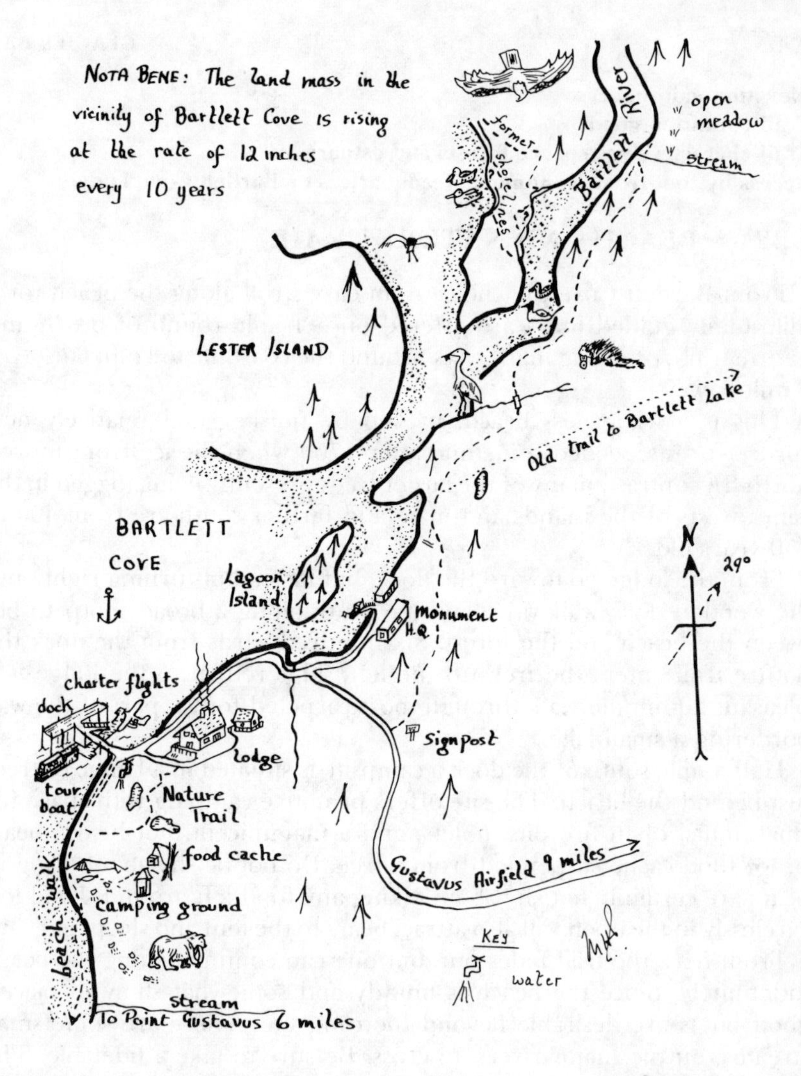

of cone husks studded with squirrel holes; the squirrels hoard good cones in the tunnels underground.

About half a mile from the road a footpath branches to the right up a steep bank. This goes to Bartlett Lake but is hard to follow since it is no longer maintained. Keep left; soon the Bartlett River trail crosses a small stream. A few more minutes of walking brings one to the river bank where a fresh, clear-running stream joins the larger river. The trail ends here but the river can be followed upstream for several miles. Brown or black bears occasionally visit the meadows at the trail end.

Grade sightseeing
Distance 1.5 miles (2.3 miles from Bartlett Cove Lodge)
Time 1 hour one way

Elevation gain none
Trail condition good
Trail characteristics spruce forests and estuary
Access by foot from Monument Headquarters or Bartlett Cove Lodge

GB2 BEACH AND NATURE TRAIL

From Bartlett Cove the choice is an easy stroll along the beach for a mile (daily guided tours are offered on a 1-mile round of beach and nature trail), or a long, hard walk around the coastline to Point Gustavus 7 miles away.

This is a wilderness beach, backed by muskeg and relatively new spruce forests, seeded sometime after 1760 when the ice front moved north. In contrast, many of the larger trees presently being logged in the rain forests of the islands and mainland farther south are from 400 to 750 years old.

From the lodge go toward the dock, but instead of turning right onto the wooden dock walkway, continue south along a broad footpath between the beach and the forest. Six hundred yards from the dock the nature trail enters the trees to the left. This return to the lodge is a pleasant 20-minute walk through moss-carpeted forest, part of the way bordering a small lake.

Half a mile south of the dock a campsite is situated in a fringe of trees just behind the beach. The site offers primitive camping with space for small tents, open fire pits, toilets, and a magnificent, but heavy, bear-proof food cache suspended from a tree. Do not be shy about using it; bears are certainly not shy about taking any food left around. Food left carelessly in the open will also attract bears to the tent and sleeping gear.

From here the trail fades out, but one can continue along the beach indefinitely. Since the beach is muddy and somewhat slimy in places, good boots are desirable beyond the campsite. There are some small streams, but no major rivers, to cross. Be sure to take a tidetable. The only time real difficulties may be encountered is during high tides, when it may be necessary to bypass the beach by walking through the forest bordering the shoreline. Watch for interstadial wood on the beach front.

Grade nature trail and campsite, sightseeing
South to Point Gustavus, low-level
Distance up to 7 miles
Time 1 hour round trip to campgrounds and nature trail
Beach to Point Gustavus 5-6 hours one way
Elevation gain none
Trail condition excellent; beach, no trail
Route characteristics beach, intertidal zone
Limitation high tide
Access by foot from Bartlett Cove

Moody Gorge, Adams No. 1 trail

GB3 ADAMS NO. 1

Wherever you go in Adams Inlet, you cannot go far wrong. I saw a gorge, from "mesa" country on the southwest side of the Inlet, and was so intrigued that the next day I set off in my kayak. It was more than a pleasant surprise — a deep, intimate gorge between the lower flanks of Berg Mountain, and the finest examples yet of standing interstadial trees.

The river flowing out of the gorge is born under the Girdle Glacier and drains into the northeast corner of Adams Inlet between Berg Creek and Granite Canyon. The beach is large and covered with shingle, and the landings are muddy. Probably the best landing is on the east side of the river, although this leaves much to be desired because of thick mud at low tide. The river is a fast-flowing glacial stream emerging from the gorge about 1.5 miles from the beach. The gorge is doubly blessed with character on cloudy days: the brackish, but gleaming river emerges from black, beetling crags where moisture glistens wickedly; the clouds boil and tumble over the canyon like steam coming from a cauldron. Goats step daintily down the mountain out of the mists, and the redpolls play in the willow. Gray-crowned rosy finches look uncommonly handsome on the ground, and the golden-crowned sparrow sings his haunting, sweet three-note song, "Oh dear me." The walk up the canyon has no marked trail, only goat trails, and goat families are sometimes seen on the shoreline.

Cross the river at the mouth, to the west side, then follow the river upstream across a large shingle outwash. Many gulls nest in the area in

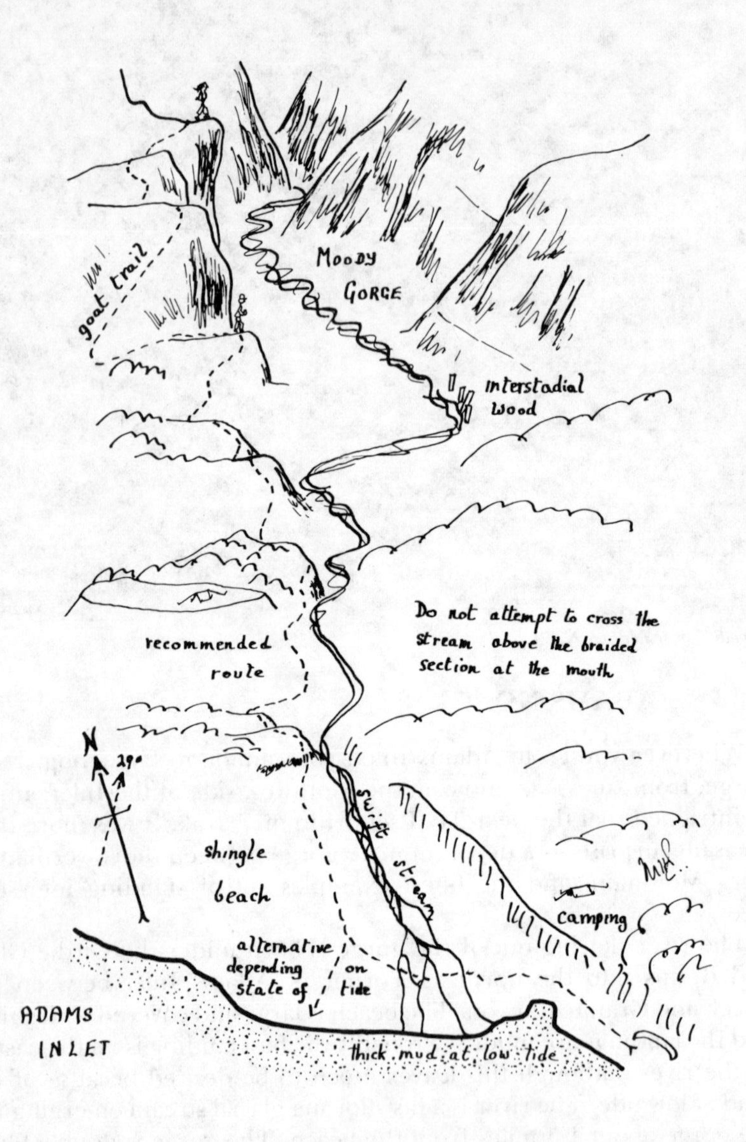

June and July and will not hesitate to initiate an aerial attack if they consider you too close. Follow the goat trail over the first rocks, staying close above the river. After passing over this, one finds another, higher 30-foot moraine directly ahead, and to its left, an attractive dryas-covered platform providing an ideal camping spot.

To find a way through encroaching brush, stay close to the river. A goat trail disappears into willow; follow this and the trail soon emerges above the river on a steep bank, then turns away around the edge of the mound. No further trouble with brush is encountered. A low viewpoint of the gorge is reached in approximately an hour and a quarter from the shoreline. A group of interstadial trees stand upright on the far side of the river bank. These remnants of an ancient forest were recently uncovered by the retreating ice.

From this point a goat trail leads up a steep bank, then traverses to the summit. Follow it and continue along the edge until a final viewpoint is reached 800–900 feet above sea level.

Use caution if the river is crossed up the canyon; it is a swiftly flowing glacial stream. The best crossings are found at the mouth.

Grade low-level
Distance 2.5 miles
Time 2 hours in, 1 hour out
Elevation gain 900 feet
Trail condition goat trails only
Route characteristics gorge; fine examples of interstadial wood
Access by tour or charter boat or floatplane to entrance of Adams Inlet; from there on by nonmotorized vessels except by special permission

GB4 ADAMS NO. 2

While camping in Adams Inlet I discovered some fascinating "mesa" country and deep gorges reminiscent on a small scale of the Chiquito Colorado Canyon, Arizona. Bank swallows use the gorge walls — steep banks of river sedimentation subject to severe gully erosion — as nesting towns. A wide, swift river, full of ice chunks, washes down from the fast-retreating Adams Glacier. This stream is dangerous to ford. If a crossing is made, however, a rope for belay should be used, or at the very

Mountains above Adams Glacier

least, a handline or linked hands. The hike is a cross-country adventure through open country and mesas to the glacier on the west side of the valley, with a choice of returning by the river.

Adams River is a large river and is unmistakable. It is busily building a huge, muddy delta on the south shore of the inlet, west of Tree Mountain. Adams Glacier is presently about 3.5 miles from the shoreline and 1000 feet above sea level.

Beach the boat west of the delta and walk back toward the river along the shoreline. If the high westerly route is taken (marked alternate 1 on the map), before reaching the river start climbing toward, and then into, a gorge lying under a dominant hill, 1565 feet high. Sometimes a stream flows out of the canyon. Farther up, the walls are delicately carved and fluted by wind and rain, with razor-sharp vertical edges. They are composed of aggregate, stratified gravels, sands, and clays and seem highly unstable.

When the gorge divides take the left fork and climb the bank at the head of the canyon. Traverse south across the hillside, over dryas-covered slopes, then drop into the next canyon. The side walls are loose, and trickles of gravel are seen and heard at times. Cross the stream at the bottom and climb out by the most convenient way.

Rough country is again traversed along the hill slope. Watch for goats on the mountain above and black ice on the slopes. The sharp, glacier-hung mountains above Adams Glacier dominate the southeast skyline. A good viewpoint and picnic spot is reached just before coming to another steep-walled canyon. Follow the upper lip of this canyon east down the hillside, then drop into a smaller gorge which will be apparent on the left. Follow it downhill — but watch for "quick mud" — until arriving at the dirty, silt-laden rearguard of the retreating glacier. An ice bridge was there in the summer of 1971, but things change rapidly. Keep descending until Adams River is reached about a quarter of a mile from the glacier. (See note above about crossing the river.)

For variety, return along the west side of the river (marked as alternate 2 on the map). In a mile there is a turbulent side stream, previously crossed in the canyon above. It requires a detour, taking one away from the main stream and across many mesas. Finally, rough country forces one back to the main riverbed, quite easily followed for about three-quarters of a mile. On the bank to the left note the thin, dry layers of humus between stratified gravel beds. These are remnants of an ancient interstadial forest floor and in places are as much as 15 feet below subsequent river or lake sediment.

The river then cuts inward into a steep bank on the west side, forcing a climb up the steep bank on the left. Stay fairly close to, but above, the river, until the worst of the gully-eroded mesas are circumnavigated. Then strike southwest across country, over small streams, through some

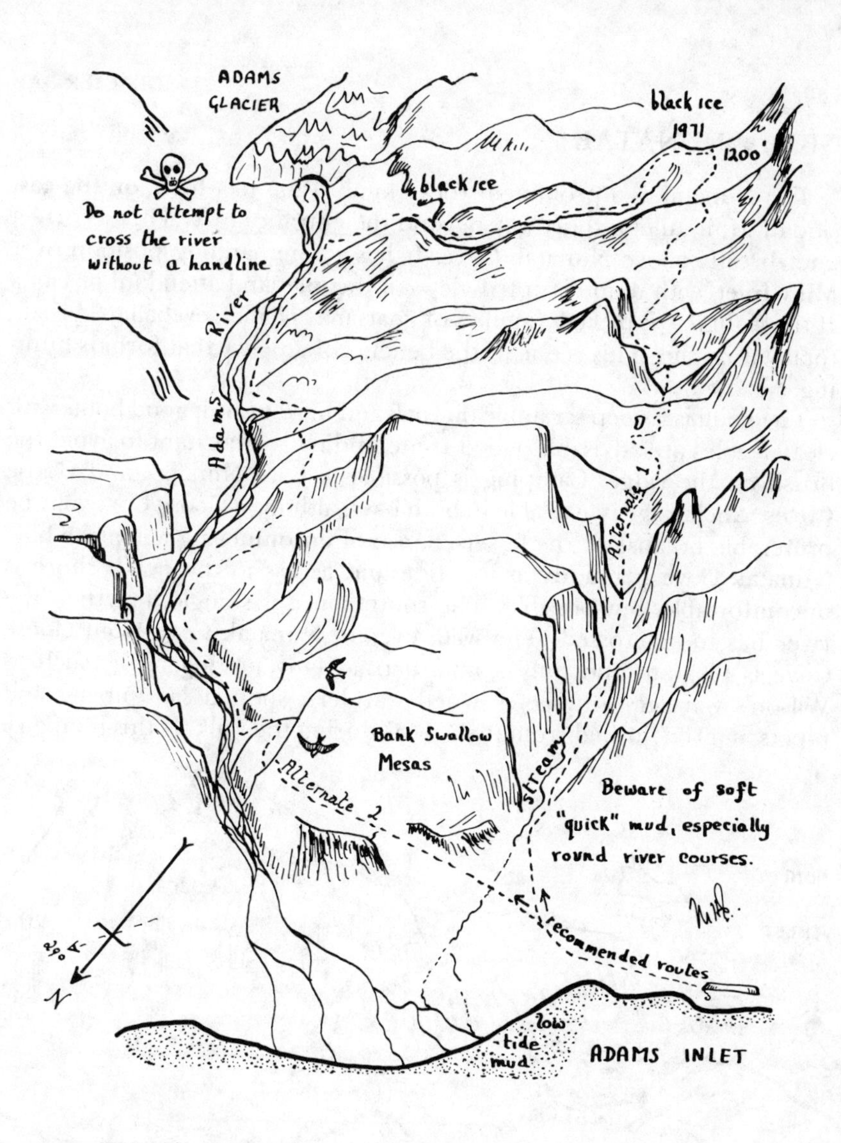

sparse brush to the beach. It will be a surprise to see how far one has climbed and how lovely the views are above Adams Inlet looking north. There are good camp spots about a mile from the beach.

Grade alpine
Distance 5 miles one way
Time 3 hours each way
Elevation gain 1500 feet by high route, 500 feet by low route
Trail condition no trail
Route characteristics open country, recent glacial recession of geologic interest
Access by boat into Adams Inlet

GB5 NUNATAK

The Nunatak is a prominent rocky knoll, 1205 feet high, on the east side of Muir Inlet a short way beyond the entrance to Wachussets Inlet and directly above Nunatak Cove. It has a commanding position over Muir Inlet, with uninterrupted views of the inlet and attendant glaciers. If the right day is picked, families of goats may be met, eyeball to eyeball, totally unafraid. This is one of the benefits of a policy that forbids hunting.

The knoll is a steep scramble on rock and hard gravel; good boots with cleated soles are advisable. Good route finding is important to avoid the brush on the ridge. Camping is possible in both Nunatak and Goose Coves. Anchorage is available in both bays, although Goose Cove may be preferable because of the lesser chance of encountering ice in the bay. Nunatak Cove is muddy at low tide and access to the north shore is uncomfortable, but possible. The south shore is shingle, but then the river has to be crossed. The walk over to Nunatak Cove from Goose Cove is pleasant and only a mile extra. Many nesting birds, such as Wilson's warblers, orange-crowned warblers, spotted sandpipers, and pipets, may be flushed from their nests during the walk. If this happens,

do not disturb the nest or tarry too long in the general area.

From the north end of Goose Cove walk up the small stream that enters the cove at this point. Climb out of its gully on the left about 300 yards upstream. Continue north cross-country, keeping to the left of some large ponds. Go between the smaller ponds ahead and be careful of "quick mud." A few yards north of the ponds a gully leads directly to the south beach of Nunatak Cove. This route seems to avoid the worst of the alder between the two coves, although it is thickening; check with local rangers before hiking. It takes about half an hour to cross the peninsula. Watch for examples of interstadial wood in Nunatak Cove.

Walk along the beach to the river, and follow the river upstream for about half a mile. It then widens and flows in a sweeping curve to the north. This is probably the best place to cross, but beware of "quick mud" on the far side. Almost immediately another stream is crossed. It is the last water; from here it is a steady climb to the ridge. Make for the steep part where the Nunatak rises in a series of rock steps above a brush-covered notch. When under the rock, traverse to the left, and a way can be found up steep loose scree by climbing from one ledge to another. The climb is somewhat exposed and nasty. To mark the way down a small stone cairn was built on top of the edge.

Follow the ridge upward, but stay to the right to keep clear of the densest brush. More scrambling may be needed to reach the summit, although the route is fairly obvious. Goats are often met in numbers up here, sometimes nonchalantly poised on the edge of sheer drops. About 2 hours after crossing the river the summit is reached, and its point is lofty and breathtaking, dropping off sheer on all sides. Signs of recent activity by a helicopter crew on top are due to an interest in molybdenum deposits within the depths of the Nunatak. Mining, if economically feasible and allowed, would involve stripping the surface terrain and in effect would level the Nunatak.

Grade alpine
Distance 2.7 miles one way from Goose Cove
Time 3 hours up, 2 hours down
Elevation gain 1350 feet
Trail condition no trail
Route characteristics open country, rock knoll over tidewaters
Access by boat or floatplane to Goose Cove or Nunatak Cove from Bartlett Cove, 45 miles south

GB6 WHITE THUNDER RIDGE

About 4 miles north of Goose Cove on the west side of Muir Inlet is Wolf Cove, a shallow bay often choked with ice floes. Camping is possible on both sides of the river on the dryas-covered banks within the bay.

White Thunder Ridge rises on the north side of the cove and runs northwest, forming cliffs directly over the head of Muir Inlet. The cliffs are bare of vegetation for the most part, except for occasional mats of dryas (mountain avens) and pockets of willow and cottonwood alive with small nesting birds in early summer.

The ridge itself is one of the finest accessible viewpoints in the entire National Monument, with a vertical face 600–1600 feet high directly over Muir Inlet. From its many "summits" are views of the inlet and glaciers, especially McBride and Riggs Glaciers. From Wolf Cove, the time taken to the bench mark (1196 feet altitude) on the third summit is about 2.5 hours. To go farther than this, if snow is not too deep, a full day is needed.

Only one small two-man tent can be pitched on a flat piece of ground above a small, tinkling stream directly below the ridge in Wolf Cove and about 30 feet above high tidewater. About 100 feet higher up is better camping space, and higher still an even better spot by some tarns. Watch out for soft mud. (From this general area a 20-minute scramble onto a 300-foot knob, directly over the inlet and bay, allows one to see the country from above. It makes an unforgettable early morning or late evening walk.)

Follow the stream up the valley to the head. Travel to the right to the second summit, about 700 feet above Muir Inlet and a brief, easy rock scramble. It looks very much more than this in altitude, but sheer drops make height deceptive. Two cairns mark the top, from which there are sweeping views of tidewater, mountains, and glaciers. Stay on the ridge, keeping to the right, and a short scramble leads down to some more inviting rocky pools. (Do not make the mistake of coming off the ridge to the left, unless the intention is to go to the two lakes about 200 feet below. One otherwise gets cliff-bound over a gully, and height has to be regained to cross over.) From here it is a simple climb up a steep slope onto the main ridge to a bench mark and viewpoint. Please do not disturb the resident ptarmigan.

It is possible to hike from here to the highest point of the ridge, about a mile and a quarter farther on and 1900 feet above sea level. This involves a descent of about 200 feet. Even in mid-June deep snow may linger, causing difficulties in reaching the highest point of the ridge, but on hot days meltwater trickles are a welcome fringe benefit.

For an easy return, head for the two small lakes tucked away like jewels under the second knob. Walk around the east shore of the second lake and climb to the ridge above to the southeast. Follow the ridge down to Wolf Cove or go over it and drop to the small stream where the day's walk started. Again, beware of soft mud around the lake shore.

Mounts Case and Wright from Wolf Cove

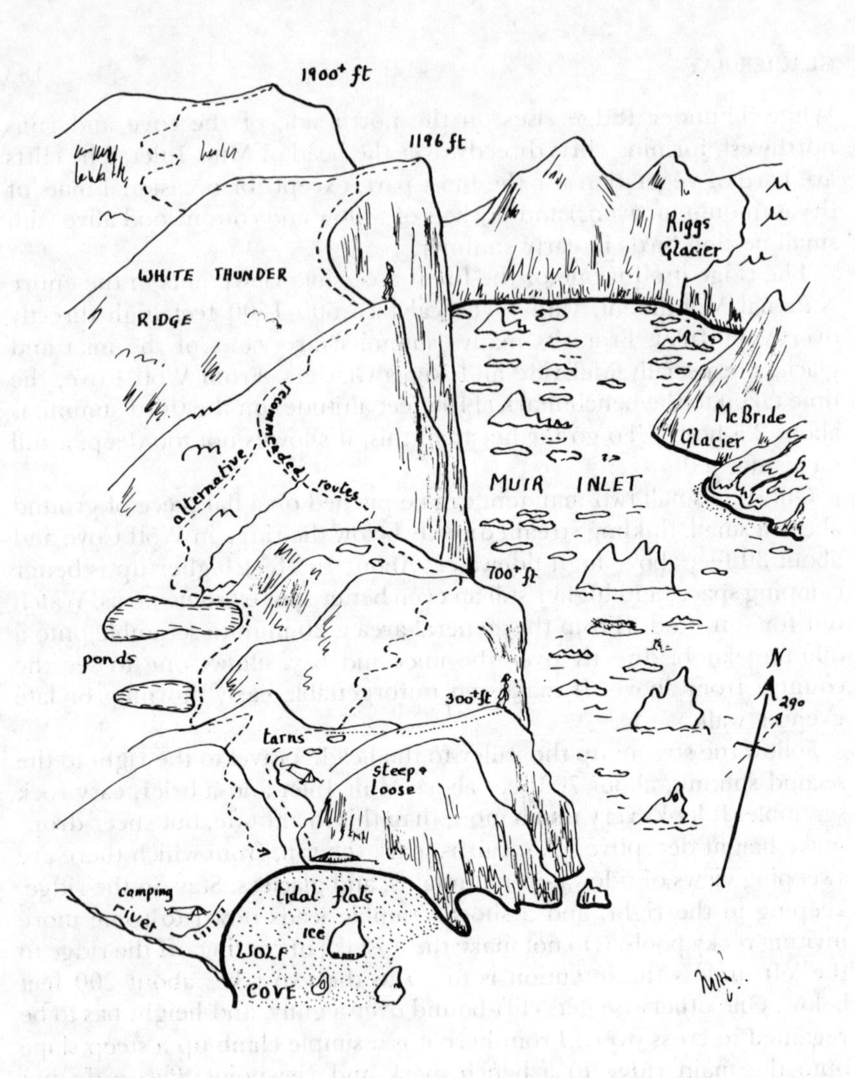

Grade alpine
Distance 2 miles to bench mark, 3.25 miles to 1900-foot summit
Time 2.5 hours up to bench mark, 1.5 hours down
Elevation gain 1500 feet to bench mark
Trail condition no trail
Route characteristics tidal cliffs
Access by boat to Wolf Cove, 50 miles north of Bartlett Cove

GB7 FOREST CREEK

Forest Creek flows into the east side of Muir Inlet on the north end of a long bay lying between the Klotz Hills and Goose Cove. A walk through more or less open country leads up the creek to a viewpoint of the rapidly receding Casement Glacier. Judging by wolf and brown bear tracks in evidence, this is a focal point of wildlife. The walk is not difficult, but it involves cross-country travel without a marked trail. Good boots, well-laced, are needed for deep bog holes, which are not apparent until a hiker falls into them.

From Goose Cove walk south along the beach for 2 miles. The beach and cove are sometimes a dazzling blue and white from stranded and still-floating icebergs. When the banks recede on the left and the beach widens, walk inland (east) toward the hills. A river flows underground close to tidewater but is found on the surface farther back. When confronted with a choice of valleys, take the right one; it goes east, then east-southeast. The river may be followed upstream to a "faery glen," where tranquil pools lie between constricting walls. Bright green equisetum (horsetail) is rampant, even under water.

Either follow the river closely upstream round its next bend, through groves of equisetum, or over the north bank to some ponds forming the headwaters of the stream. The mud up here can cause the loss of a boot in June or July. The country is wide open, with little vegetation on the

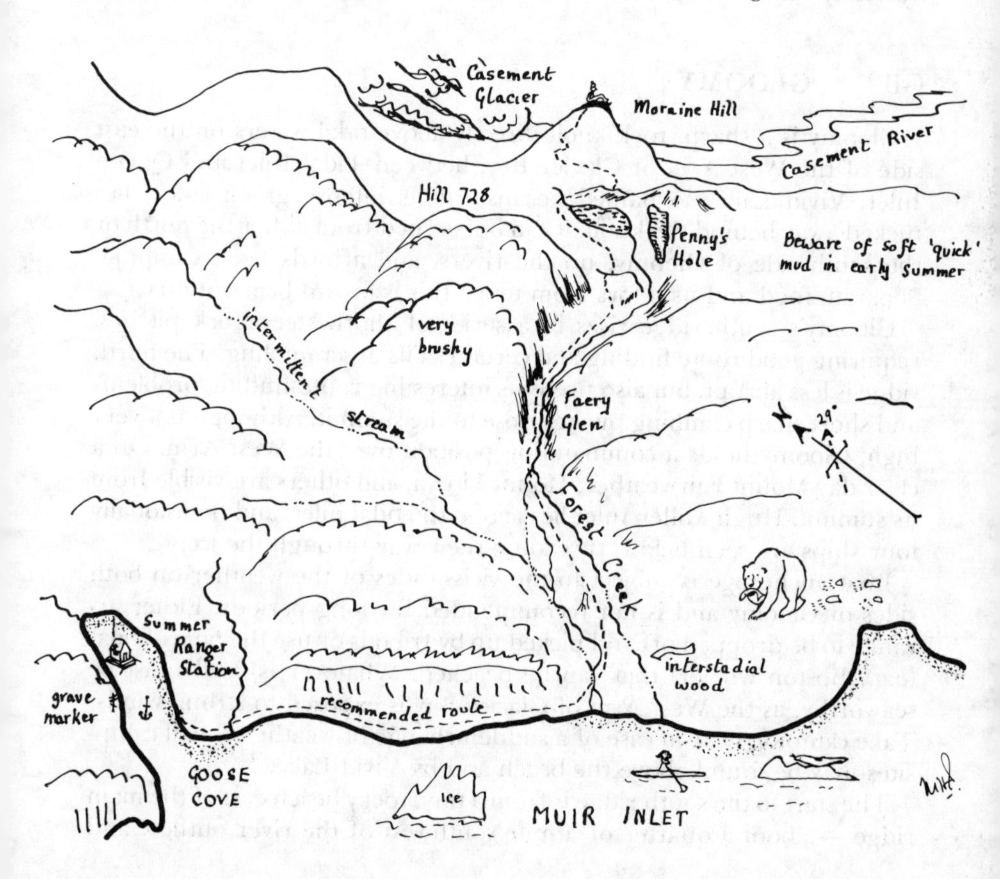

gravels deposited by ancient rivers and glacier. A steady climb ends on a prominent hill, about 100 feet high, half a mile northeast of the ponds. From here are open views of the entire Casement Valley and Glacier to Adams Inlet. According to the map, made from aerial surveys, this hill did not exist in 1948 and the land on which it stands was entirely under the glacier.

On the return do not attempt to climb Hill 728 to the west of the moraine hill; the views are not necessarily better, and the brush is daunting.

Grade low-level
Distance 5 miles from Goose Cove
Time 3.5 hours one way
Elevation gain 450+ feet
Trail condition no trail
Route characteristics: country recently opened by glacial recession; outstanding examples of interstadial wood
Access by boat or floatplane to Goose Cove, 50 miles north of Bartlett Cove

GB8 **GLOOMY**

Gloomy is a sharp, rock knoll directly above tidal waters on the east side of the West Arm of Glacier Bay, between Tidal Inlet and Queen Inlet. Vivid Lake, so named because of its intense green color, lies tucked away behind the knoll; it can be reached from either the north or the south side of Gloomy, up the rivers, and affords good camping. Separate food and its odors from tents; this is brown bear country.

Gloomy's south ridge rises in a series of short, steep rock pitches, requiring good route finding and certain skills in scrambling. The north ridge is less abrupt, but also presents interesting route-finding problems and short sharp climbing pitches close to the summit. Although not very high, Gloomy holds a commanding position over the West Arm. On a clear day Mount Fairweather, Mount Lituya, and others are visible from its summit. Hugh Miller Inlet lies across the tidal inlet, and occasionally tour ships are seen below, threading their way through the ice.

Boat anchorage is subject to the vicissitudes of the weather on both sides of Gloomy and is not recommended for long periods. Either arrange to be dropped off and picked up by friends or use the type of boat (e.g., Boston whaler) that can be beached. Whatever is used must be seaworthy, as the West Arm of Glacier Bay is exposed to strong winds. Take camping gear in case of a sudden change of weather. Small campsites may be found above the beach and by Vivid Lake.

The start to the south ridge is from a tiny, rocky beach east of the main ridge — about a quarter of a mile southwest of the river outflow and

Vivid Lake

south of Gloomy. A tiny stream tinkles into the bay. The main mountain rises above in irregular rocky leaps. Keeping the main ridge to the left climb up steep slopes smothered with a variety of wildflowers: cinquefoil, Indian paintbrush, lupine, and higher up, lush, circular carpets of campion and mats of mountain avens.

The stream course can be followed straight up, but it becomes steep. The slope briefly eases off, after about 400 feet of climbing, in alpine meadows covered with flowers. From here the entire mountain seems composed of cliffs, but climb steeply to a gully above, on the left of the meadows. This gives access to the ridge through a vulnerable spot under sheer bluffs forming the upper end of the lower ridge. If, instead of finding the gully, one continues in much the same direction as before, a route is possible up rotten, exposed rock. On the second alternative

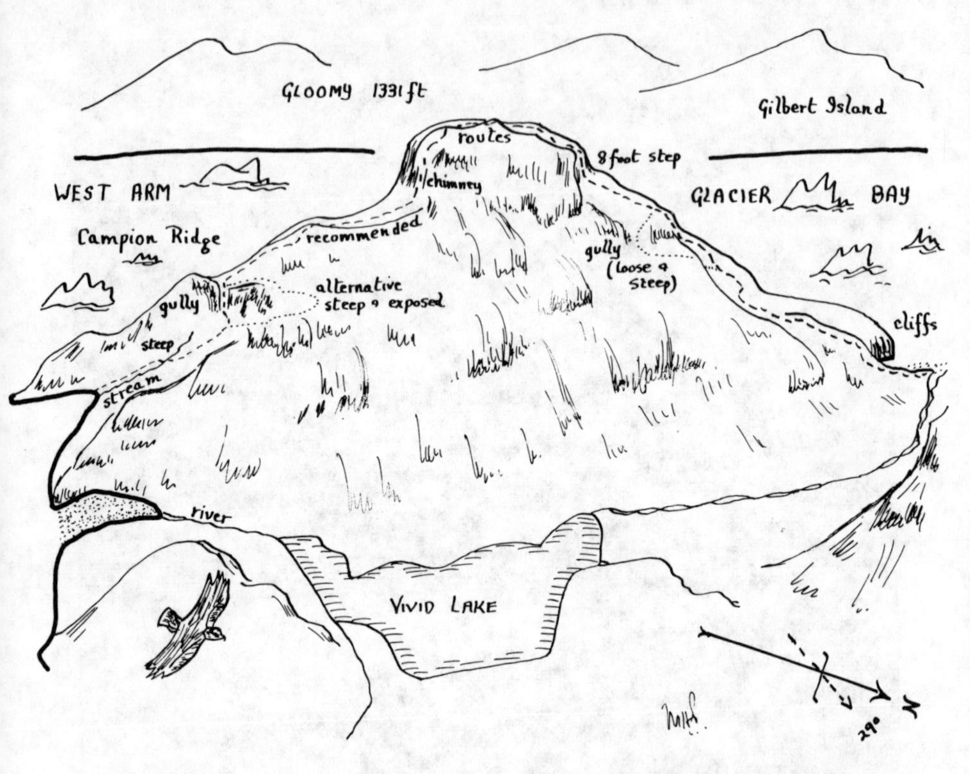

grassy ledges are reached first with commanding views over Vivid Lake. Then find a route on the rocks above, traversing to the left. Beware! The rock is loose, and there is a steep, unbroken drop below, even though the climbing is not technically difficult.

The two alternatives meet in a shingle depression between crags; the route is up an obvious open gully. This leads through a series of pleasant scrambling pitches, past carpets of dryas and campion to the summit ridge. After a succession of false summits, the summit knob will finally become visible, rising at least 80 perpendicular feet above a depression in the ridge. Observe it carefully to find its vulnerable point — a chimney about 20 feet high discernable on the right above a snow plume (present in mid-June). A scramble up the chimney gives direct access to the summit. Do not traverse to the left from the ridge unless serious climbing is contemplated.

The views from the summit are unlimited. To descend the north ridge, look carefully for a crack about 8 feet high, terminating on a broad ledge, a few yards north of the summit. (On the right of the crack is an overhang; a few feet to the left is another route down, requiring awkward exposed moves.) Below the crack, the ridge drops gently for a quarter of a mile, then abruptly as a step once more. Three of us, at this point, traversed to the right and descended a steep, rotten crack onto snow below. After seeing the ridge from below, however, we felt this to be a poor choice of route and suggest a scramble directly over the end of the ridge.

Until late June, expect snow on the slopes below. If hard it aids the descent by providing a series of glissades. Gravitate to the right, toward the river. One then has a choice of descending over exposed slabs or fighting brush, although neither alternative presents serious difficulties. But aim for the beach close to the river, since the ridge to the left ends in cliffs over the water.

Grade alpine; *experienced hikers only*
Distance of traverse 4 miles
Time 2.5 hours up; 1.5 hours down
Elevation gain 1331 feet
Trail condition no trail
Route characteristics rock knob, open over tidal waters; interesting route-finding problems, scrambling
Access by boat or floatplane, 40 miles north of Bartlett Cove

GB9 PTARMIGAN CREEK

A short, easy walk up Ptarmigan Creek starts from a crescent-shaped beach 3 miles west of Reid Inlet. An old miners' road goes up a hill from the east end of the beach (east of the river) to a cabin about a mile from and 500 feet above the beach. From the hill is a panoramic view of the mountains behind Russell Island and Tarr Inlet. For those who care to do their own route finding, the walk can be extended over a 1500-foot hill to the east of Reid Inlet, or onto a 3000-foot ridge both to the south and west of the cabin for views of Lamplugh Glacier.

Looking toward Tarr Inlet

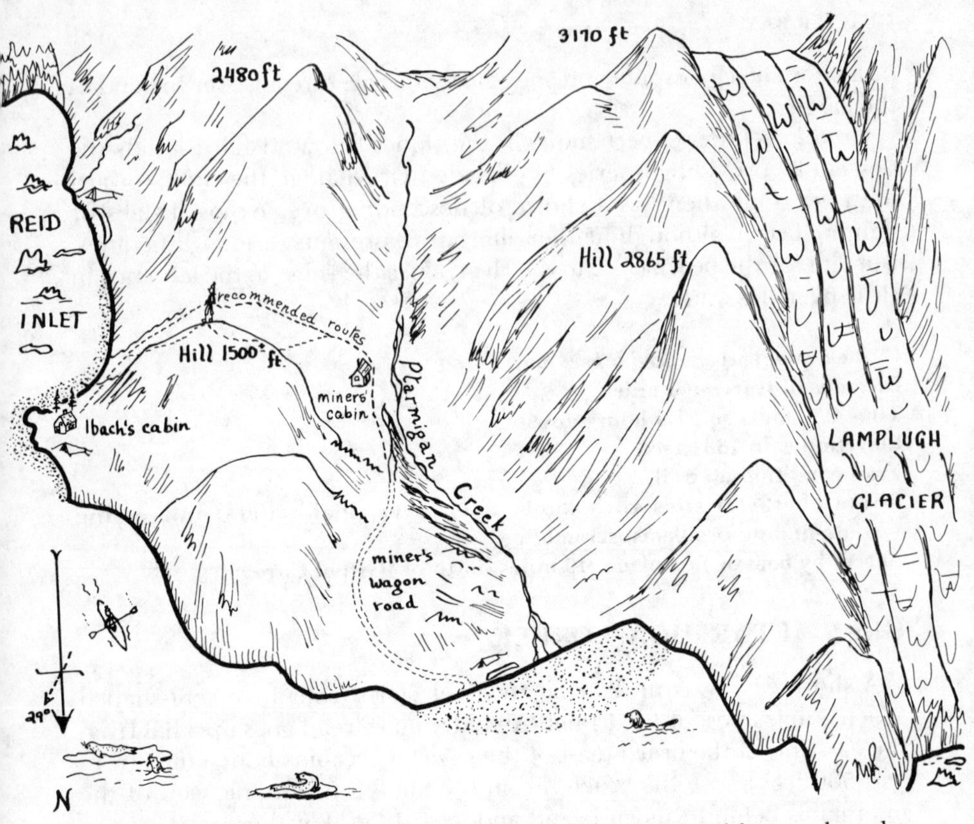

Beach the boat on the east side of Ptarmigan Creek. Either anchor the boat properly or bring it above the high water mark, otherwise my experience of the summer of 1970 might be repeated — an otter loosened the painter from under several rocks and allowed my kayak, moored below the high tide mark (sheer laziness on my part), to start drifting away on the rising tide. Even though recurrence of this incident is unlikely, all kayaks should be brought well above high tide for safekeeping.

The beach end of the road is marked by rusty, derelict equipment left by miners. The old road then climbs a hill around a wide curve to the left. After about 500 feet of climbing the road gets lost on the edge of a washed-out bank over the river. A small footpath can be followed behind the edge to a private cabin about 200 yards farther on. The cabin sits well above the river on slopes covered with dryas and sprinkled with willow and cottonwoods. Camping is good both here and on the beach.

An extension of the walk is to wander up the sparse willow-covered slopes of the hill east-southeast of the end of the road, following the line of the shore below. A climb of about 1500 feet brings one to the end of the ridge above Reid Inlet, with clear views in all directions. One can then drop down by steep slopes or down a gully to Reid Inlet. This makes a pleasant half-day hike in good weather, of 4-5 miles and 3.5-4 hours. A day pack with map and compass should be taken for any extension beyond the road.

Grade sightseeing
Distance 1.2 miles to miner's cabin
Time 30 minutes
Elevation gain 500 feet
Trail condition good
Trail characteristics open valley and beach
Access by boat or floatplane, 56 miles north of Bartlett Cove

CANOE ROUTES

The canoe "trails" described do not take the canoeist into thick ice, and on many routes no ice is seen. However, notes have been added on areas where encounters with ice floes can be expected (see page 206). The areas covered in these notes are recommended for experienced kayakers only, and the following precautions should be taken:

1. Wear warm woolen clothing or a wet suit. Water temperatures drop dramatically on glacial inlets and are sometimes barely above freezing.
2. Stay away from large icebergs. They have a habit of turning or falling apart without notice. The thunder of their motion is heard much of the time, day or night, in Muir Inlet, Johns Hopkins Inlet, etc. Ice laden with glacial silt may sink an inch or so below the surface of the water; also, an innocent-looking floe, with a sudden movement, can tip a kayak over.
3. Do not approach tidal glaciers within a quarter of a mile, even inactive ones such as Reid and Lamplugh Glaciers. They may jump to life when least expected, causing columns of ice to collapse into the inlet (especially at low tide when the ice below is undermined). This action, called "calving," can create waves in narrow inlets from 2 to 30 feet high, depending upon the distance from the glacier and the size of the iceberg created. Although waves over 5 feet high are rare, even small waves are capable of overturning kayaks, moored or free-floating and manned, and can also inundate gear placed on rocks close to the water's edge.

Beware of sudden, severe squalls close to glaciers on otherwise clear, calm days. These winds slam onto the water from a glacier without warning, causing momentary difficulties with small, hand-propelled craft.

4. Keep in mind that floating ice is continually on the move, and shifts with winds and tide. It may disperse out of an inlet and then return, closing off any escape route.

(Courtesy Glacier Bay National Monument)

5. Wildlife and photography enthusiasts, whose attention is periodically diverted from paddling, should note that unattended kayaks run on a collision course with floating ice in high winds. Since nine-tenths of floating ice is under water, it is not subject to the influence of winds as are kayaks.

6. Sturdy construction (e.g., fiberglass) is best because of the abrasive and shearing properties of floating ice. Take a repair kit along.

7. Because kayaks and cruise ships are not compatible in narrow inlets, kayakers are advised to obtain cruise ship schedules at Bartlett Cove before going into the bay, avoid steamer lanes (usually midbay), and always take the boats high on the beach when going ashore.

Trips on open waters (for example, those areas covered in Additional Area Information, page 206) are recommended only for kayaks and experienced kayakers. See the Introduction, page 30 for general information and precautions necessary on all canoe runs.

Take a Juneau tide table, and if intending to hike, take the U.S. Geological Survey topographic maps indicated for each area. Navigation charts may otherwise be taken, but these lack detail in most of the areas described. Those for Hugh Miller Inlet have been recently revised, and other charts of Glacier Bay are presently being updated because of a rapidly rising land mass that is causing marked changes in the Beardslee Islands, Adams Inlet, and other areas.

White water running is not included in these routes. The only swift currents encountered are through tidal narrows, where the strength of the current depends on the state of the tide, for example, the long entrance into Adams Inlet and the entrance into the "Inner Sanctum" of Hugh Miller Inlet. It is best to avoid narrow tidal passages within the Beardslee Islands shortly before and after low slack tides, because strong currents and shallow waters prevail.

GB(A) BEARDSLEE ISLANDS

A cluster of islands, whose waters are too shallow for large vessels and which are therefore relatively undisturbed, lies between Bartlett Cove and Beartrack Cove, 12 miles north. The inlets, lagoons, and parklike forests of these islands, the Beardslees, make enchanting canoeing.

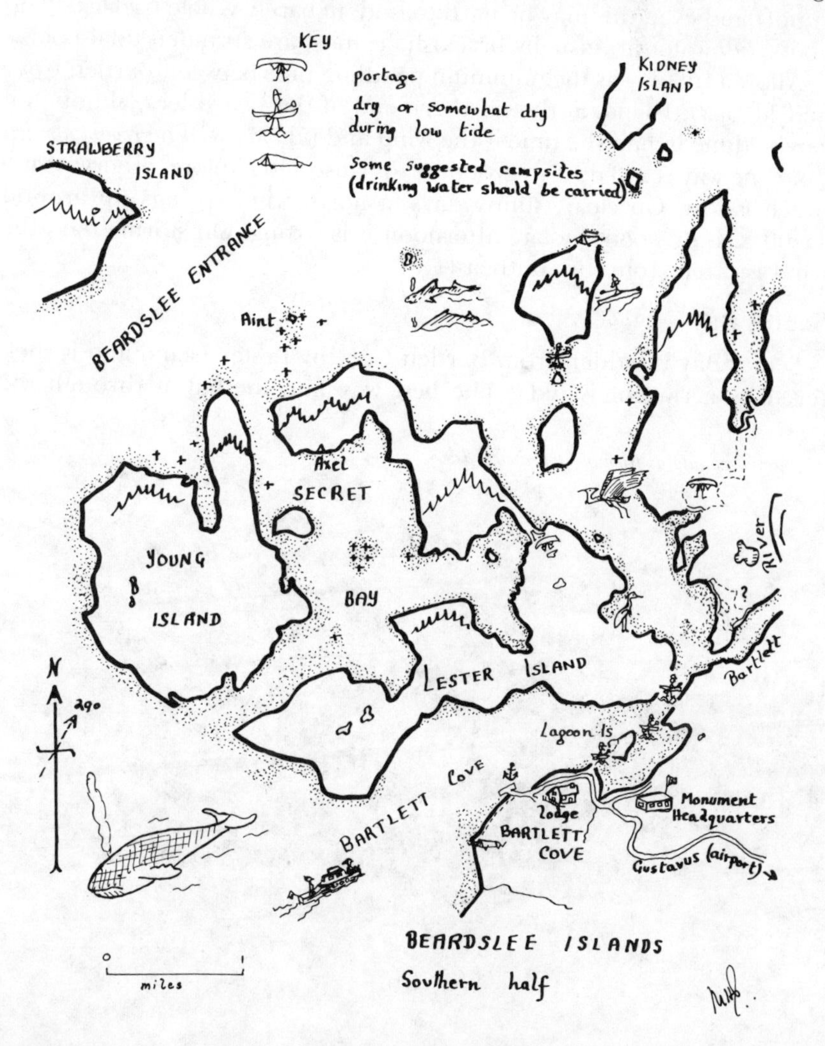

Campsites are almost uncountable along the shoreline, some with breathtaking views into the Upper Bay. The islands have their own variety of wilderness song. Coyotes cry in the late evenings and early mornings, the cries tossed back and forth from one island to another. Wolves howl, seemingly always in the distance. Loons yodel softly, one to the other, early in the morning in sheltered bays, and small-bird song fills the air during the day. The islands have their share of black bears; brown bears tend to stay on the mainland. But be warned; many apparent islands are now continuous with the mainland because of recent uplift.

The best drinking water is obtained from streams on the mainland. Water should be carried, since only the larger islands have surface runoff and even this may be hard to find, in barely visible trickles. Pools above tidewater are usually brackish, as most are stranded tidal pools.

Allow a full day as the minimum paddling time between Bartlett Cove and Flapjack Island, at the northern end of the Beardslees, although it can be done in half the time if the wind and tide allow. The *recommended* time one way is 2–3 days to give time to pause and explore, otherwise too much is lost. On clear, sunny days, a north wind springs up around 11:00 A.M. or noon; by late afternoon it is strong. On stormy days the wind is often from the southeast.

Secret Bay

Secret Bay is hidden from Bartlett Cove by Lester Island and is sheltered by a ring of islands. The best way into the bay is through the

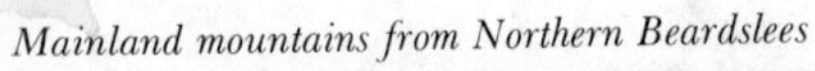

Mainland mountains from Northern Beardslees

western tidal narrows during periods of fair weather. The route follows the south shore of Lester Island and is exposed to most foul weather winds. To avoid difficulty with currents and shallows, plan to arrive at the narrows just before high tide. The current flows into Secret Bay on the incoming tide. Otherwise, go northeast through the tidal narrows between Lester Island and the mainland (see the section on Bartlett River for further details). Follow the east shoreline of Lester Island to the short "opening" into Secret Bay marked on the U.S.G.S. topographic maps. This "gut" is now a short portage even during high tides. Another passage at the northern end of the lagoon is getting shallower each year but is still open.

From Bartlett Cove dock into Secret Bay by the western passage is about 6 miles, and the eastern alternative, with short portage, is about 5 miles.

Bartlett River

Bartlett River mouth is about 2 miles northeast of Bartlett Cove Lagoon (National Monument Headquarters) and is reached through the narrows between Lester Island and the mainland. If possible, run on a high tide. The current is confusing and most dangerous on a strong ebb, especially where the current meets the main body of Bartlett Cove. The narrows are too shallow between mid- and low water for comfort. Canoeists should ask for advice at Bartlett Cove, where Park personnel can predict the severity of the current.

The Bartlett River flats and estuary are rich in birdlife (see the Bartlett River trail, GB1, for more details), but the land topography is confusing because of continuing uplift. Beware of the difficulty in perceiving the difference between tidal mud flats and solid land at low tide.

The long, thin tidal passage going north-south between the mainland and an unnamed island, marked on the U.S.G.S. topographic maps, no longer exists. It now makes an interesting walk and study of the floral and faunal development taking place.

Strawberry Island

About 1.5 miles of choppy tidal water separate Strawberry Island from the other islands. Beach camping is good; views northward are superb. On the island is an old fox farm, now rapidly falling apart from disuse.

Hutchins Bay

Bounded on the west by many islands, Hutchins Bay, especially along its mainland shoreline, is the best place within the Beardslees for good drinking water. The beach close to a stream east of the north tip of Kidney Island makes an adequate campsite. Another stream enters the

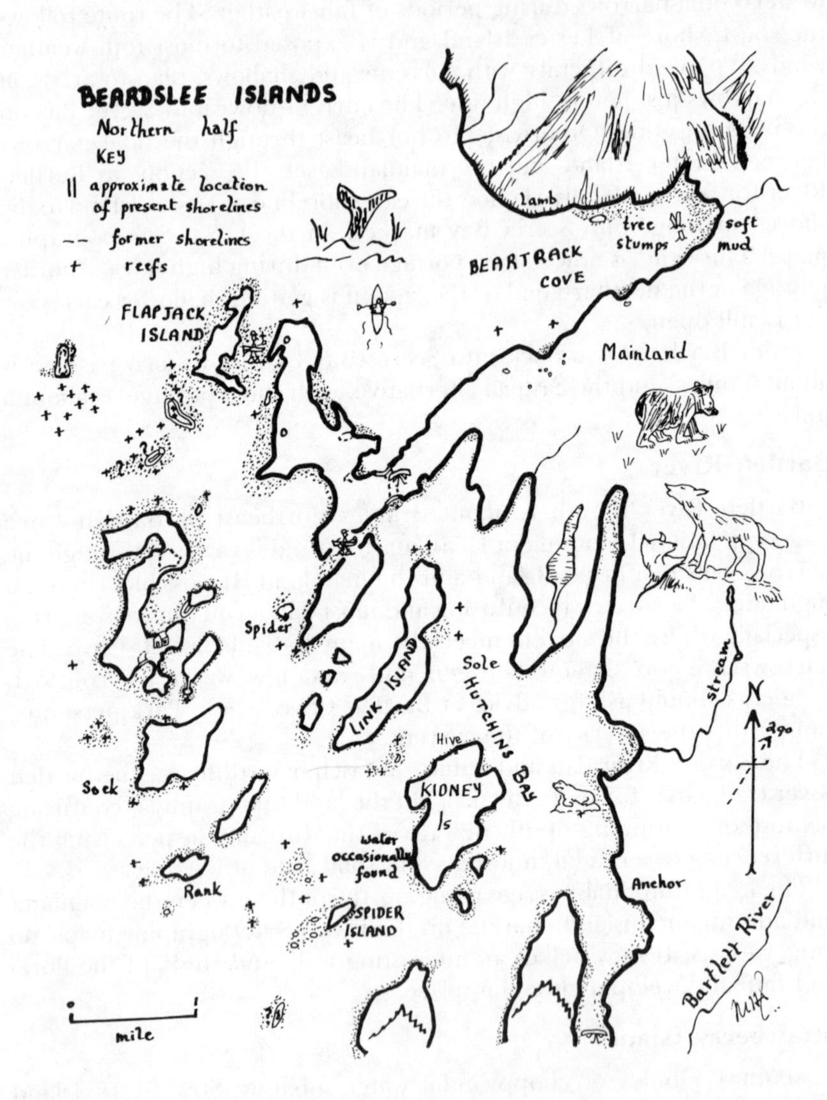

bay on the west side of a tidal finger, farther north. The unnamed island south of Kidney Island offers attractive but waterless camping.

Listen for seals and sea lions. Many are draped over rocks in the southern half of the bay; their barks and bellows can be heard for long distances over the water.

The "narrows" (now closed off at the southern end, due to uplift) going south from Hutchins Bay is a peaceful inlet about 2 miles long, lacking the strong tidal currents and eddies associated with a double-ended tidal passage. There is good shore camping here. Tiptoe through the kelp to the far (southern) end, since it is often visited by various forms of wildlife; kayakers have a chance to remain concealed at low tide.

A northern "passage" (marked as such on U.S.G.S. maps) between Hutchins Bay and Beartrack Cove is now permanently dry and requires a portage of about 50 yards. Stranded tidal pools along the portage contain brackish water. Another tidal passage southwest of this one, between two islands, is dry at low tide.

Western Islands

Islands, some large with parklike stands of spruce, many only rocks or mud banks with a flutter of birdlife, most unnamed, are scattered in a haphazard fashion west of Kidney and Link Islands. All are interesting. Most are dry. Camping is plentiful and varied. In the northern half, west of Link Island, is another old fox farm on what was once a collection of three islands, now merged into one.

Camping is superb on north and west shorelines. A small island south of the "Spider" bench mark offers attractive but waterless camping. Also the north shore of the fox farm "collection of islands" offers unparalleled sunsets behind a backdrop of 15,000-foot mountains, first flushed red then deepening to purple. If human presence in the area is sufficiently inconspicuous, it is sometimes possible to hear the songs of the coyote, loon, or wolf, under the brilliant skies of a dying sun.

If a smooth passage is preferred between Link Island and the outer islands on days of fresh northerly breezes, wait for low tide. Then protective mud flats surface southeast of Flapjack Island, creating calmer waters.

Beartrack Cove

The passage between Flapjack Island and the unnamed island to the east is dry at low tide. It is best to run through between mid- and high tides, unless one has the energy to portage the short distance or the time to wait for the water to rise.

For further information on Beartrack Cove see Additional Area Information, Beartrack Cove to Adams Inlet, page 209.

Distance Bartlett Cove to Flapjack Island, 12 miles
Paddling time one-half to 1 day
Recommended time 4 to 10 days island exploration
Camping: good beach camping many places; expect to find drinking water on the mainland and sometimes in small quantities on the larger islands
Terrain tidewater islands containing parklike stands of spruce
Tidetable and map: Juneau tide tables necessary. Because of a rapidly rising landform do not expect maps to be accurate
Access from Bartlett Cove, Monument Headquarters

Adams Inlet

GB(B) ADAMS INLET

Adams Inlet is a landlocked tidal lagoon located east of Muir Inlet and 35 miles north of Bartlett Cove. John Muir, founder of the Sierra Club and its first president, built a cabin on a point just south of the entrance to Adams Inlet in July 1890, then spent many summers there. At that time the ice front was approximately 1 mile farther north, and Adams Inlet existed as an ice field. Geologic change, manifest usually through ancient evidence and deduced by logic, is seen here in the life span of one person. Adams Glacier is now hard to find, several miles from the southern shore. The tidal bay, isolated and ringed by mountains, is changing further in character through rapid uplift and river and glacial sedimentation. Thus the bay becomes shallower by the year. The shoreline is muddy, and low tide pebble beaches are rare.

Thousands of water birds nest in the vicinity. Harlequin ducks, scoters, and mergansers often congregate in the narrows en masse, the scoters happily riding the currents backwards in a long file. In late June, flightless Canada geese in their annual moult squabble in groups of several hundred within the sanctuary of the bay. Terns, harried by jaegers, rise off the narrows in a white, whirling snowstorm of screaming birds. Loons reach out across the water with their weird, warbling cries. Mountain goats come to the beaches in families. A road advocated by the State of Alaska and the Juneau Chamber of Commerce would make hollow mockery of Adams' wild splendor; its greatness lies not just in its scenery, but in its wildlife.

See page 175 regarding access to Adams Inlet from Bartlett Cove. Those interested in paddling from Bartlett Cove, see page 209, Beartrack Cove to Adams Inlet, and page 193, Beardslee Islands.

Narrows

Access into Adams Inlet is through a 6.5-mile-long tidal narrows. Plan to run in on an incoming tide with a bird guide at hand, and binoculars and camera close by. Paddling is a matter of staying close inshore, keeping the nose straight, and staying out of eddies, unless closer observation of wildlife is desired. Care should be taken if the shore is forsaken for the central current — it is very rapid at times, especially during big tides. Also, Ripple Rock, situated about halfway in, slightly closer to the south shore, is a hazard to those who wander away from the shoreline or cross

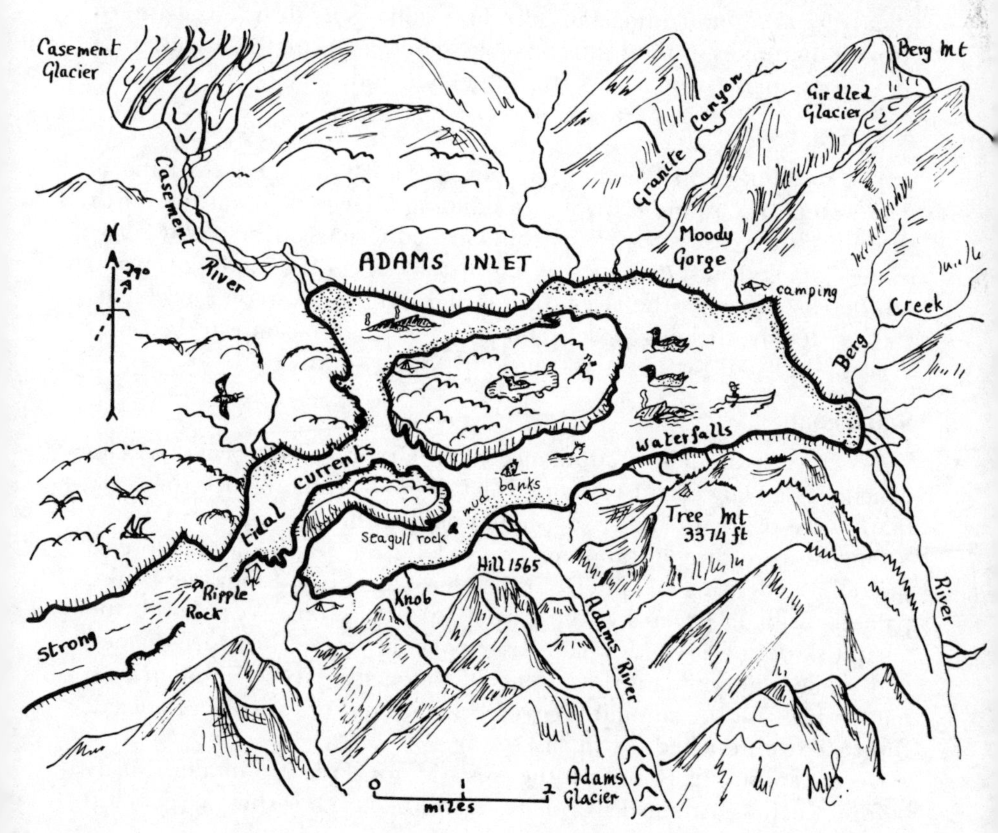

the narrows prematurely. *Do not cross the narrows until the rock is safely passed*, or its position accurately determined. Allow 2.5-3 hours to reach Central Island.

Campsites are found close to Ripple Rock on both sides of the narrows. One is on a promontory on the north shore (the presence of fresh water is doubtful), and the other on dryas-covered meadows on the south shore. Beach the canoes on the west side of a small peninsula for the latter campsite. The beach is awkward on the far side and shelves steeply at low tide. The same general area is accessible to camping after circumnavigating a long peninsula, one of the eastern portals of Adams Inlet Narrows.

Northwest

The shoreline has shelving banks covered with brush. Casement River runs into the bay and has a large muddy delta. A good campsite is located on the northwest corner of Central Island, on a flat, dryas-covered meadow protected by a scattering of cottonwood and willow and above a steeply shelved beach. A stream runs by from the center of the island. Landing and unpacking are best done at high tide because of copious quantities of mud. It is possible to find goats on the island, since they occasionally swim across from the mainland.

Northeast

The coastline is undramatic, but the views in all directions are superb. The waters of Granite Canyon are building a large delta on the north shore. Farther east is the river from Girdled Glacier, overshadowed by some shapely peaks. (See Adams No. 1 trail, GB3.) If a landing is made on the east shore of the river during high tide (to overcome problems with a steeply shelving beach and mud) a perfect campsite becomes available on a large, flat, dryas meadow facing southwest.

Southeast

Berg Creek and a large, unnamed river have joined to form one delta which has advanced into Adams Inlet about 1.5 miles since the 1948 maps were printed. The rivers should be worth exploring on foot.

Only uncomfortable camping exists along the south shore. Close to the delta and rising steeply from the shore are gullied moraine banks, painted brilliant green by thin carpets of equisetum. Westbound, the abrupt slopes of Tree Mountain rise above tidewater. They are seamed and gullied and contain their share of waterfalls. Tree Mountain is so named because the summit is covered with trees, the vestige of ancient forests left untouched by the last ice age.

Good camping is found on the west side of Tree Mountain, shortly before reaching Adams River delta. Here the beach is shingle (pebbles) and the top of the bank is level in places. Ground cover is mountain avens (dryas), and there are willow and cottonwood trees; a small stream runs under the west edge of the bank. From here, open country, split by deeply eroded banks ("mesas") of sedimentary gravels, is worth exploring. For interest stay close to the river; for ease of walking stay back from the river, on the underskirts of Tree Mountain. Watch for nesting bank swallows. (For a hike through the "mesas" on the west bank of the river, see Adams No. 2 trail, GB4.)

Adams River is difficult and dangerous to cross on foot. The braided section of the delta would probably be the easiest and safest place to cross, but it is wisest to paddle around the delta.

Southwest

Central Island has a shingle beach on the south side, and one or two possible campsites (without water) if a high bank is climbed. The island is thickly covered with brush, but from the south side a fairly open route leads to the lake in the center.

Beyond Adams River delta (considerably larger than the 1948 maps indicate) westbound, are many good campsites on dryas platforms, with small streams handy. A walk onto a prominent, 600-foot knoll, 2 miles southwest of Adams River, gives commanding views over Adams Inlet to Muir Inlet. Under the knoll there is a fine camp spot by a small stream. Overshadowing the entire area is Mount Case and other, unnamed, glacier-hung peaks, 5000 feet high.

Additional camping is found at the head of the westernmost bay, although mud is encountered in quantity at low tide. The unnamed river entering the inlet at this point can be traced into its gorge; the west bank is easier to follow. Smaller campsites may be found on the peninsula that forms the northern boundary of the bay, but most are without water. The narrow neck of the peninsula makes a good place to observe happenings in the entrance narrows. To avoid an expanse of mud, beach the kayak at the north end of the tidal flats at the head of the bay, directly under the peninsula.

Distance: tidal narrows, 6.5 miles
Inlet, east-west, 7 miles
Inlet, north-south, 2 miles
Recommended length of stay: 3 to 4 days
Camping: many good campsites, especially on southwest shoreline
Route characteristics: landlocked tidal inlet noted for birds and other wildlife; under wilderness designation
Limitations: ingress and egress dependent on tides; mud along the shoreline
Tide table: Juneau tide tables essential
Access: by boat or floatplane to entrance of narrows, 35 miles north of Bartlett Cove; in good weather, paddle from Bartlett Cove

GB(C) HUGH MILLER INLET

The entrance into Hugh Miller Inlet is 36 miles northwest of Bartlett Cove on the southwest side of the West Arm. Like Adams Inlet, it is rich in wildlife, with hundreds of nesting land and water birds, and humpback whales, porpoises, seals, and killer whales in deeper waters; but it is unlike Adams in that its total attraction is not within a tight geographic area. Hugh Miller's tidal inlets splay outward like tentacles, probing into hidden mountain recesses and chasing vanishing glaciers up valleys.

Again dryas (mountain avens) is the faithful soil-binder, mat-former, and plant pioneer. Although much of the countryside is open, facilitating exploration on foot, willow and cottonwood are becoming established — the forerunner of giant forests of the future. Snow lingers late and is sometimes on the ground until mid-June.

A Park Service draft proposal for Glacier Bay makes Hugh Miller Inlet (and Adams Inlet and Dundas Bay) off limits to motor craft, allowing access only to hand-propelled craft beyond Blue Mouse Cove. Restrictions on motor-powered access into the inner bay (marked "Inner

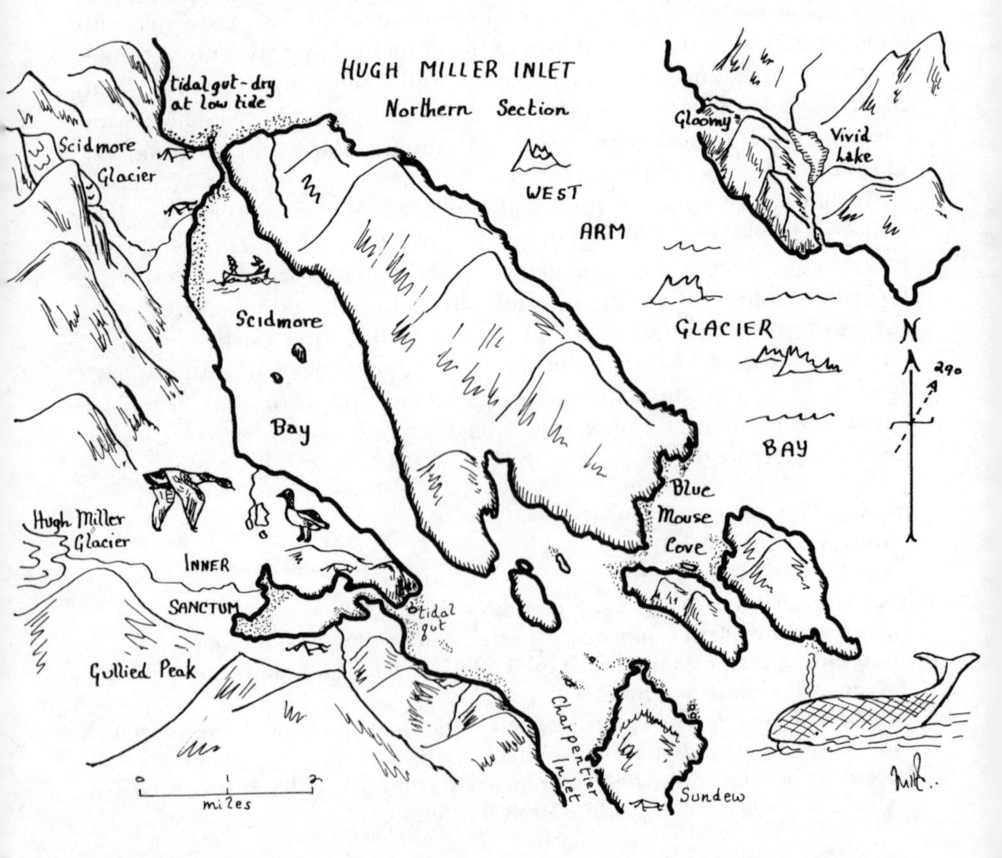

Inner Sanctum, Hugh Miller Inlet

Sanctum" on the map) are presently in force because of disturbance to nesting geese. Check with the National Park Service at Bartlett Cove before going into Hugh Miller Inlet.

Entrance

A large area south of Gilbert Island, taking in Blue Mouse Cove, a sprinkling of islands and rocks within the entrance, and the peninsula

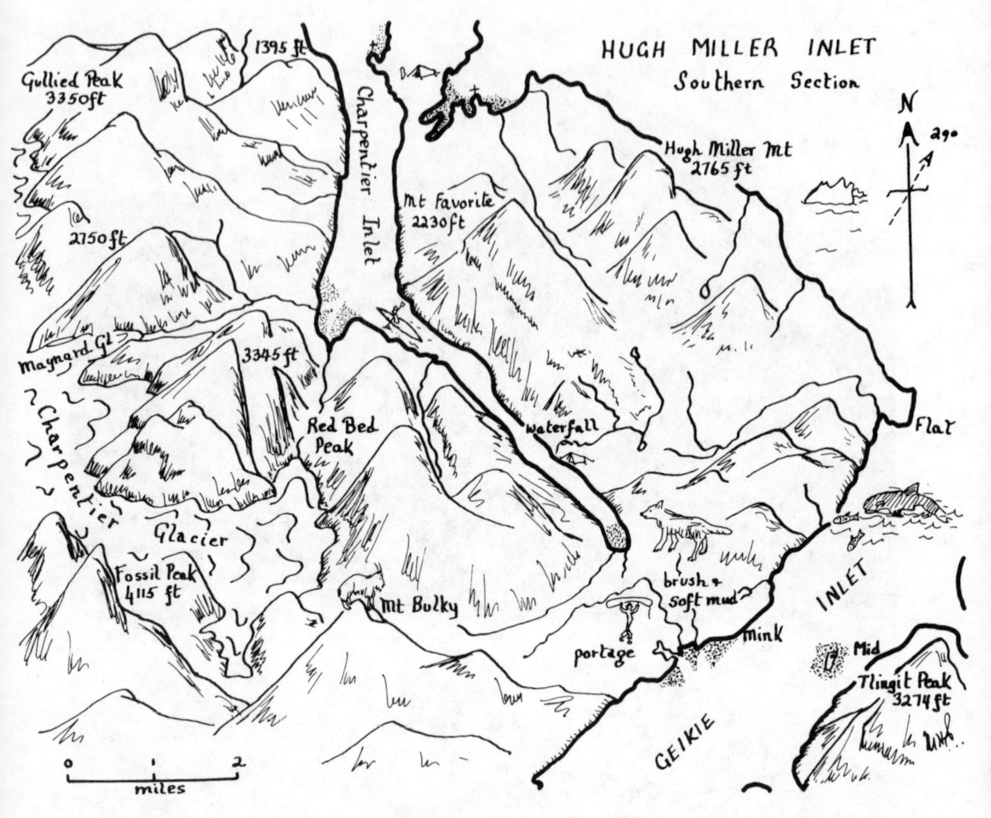

guarding the opening into Charpentier Inlet, make up the portals of Hugh Miller Inlet.

Campsites abound all around the entrance. Some rocks northwest of the unnamed peninsula mentioned above make a good vantage point for watching passing sea life. Be sure the rock of your choice is not one that will be submerged by high tides. Carry drinking water from the mainland. Pleasant camping is found at Sundew (see map).

Scidmore Bay

A landlocked tidal bay, 5 miles long, lies west of Gilbert Island. At its north end, serpentine narrows make a high tide exit into the West Arm possible. Dry at low and mid-tide, they should be run on the ebbing tide northbound within 2 hours of high slack. Two sources of fresh water are found along the west shore of a bay located at the northern end of the narrows. Camping is good behind the shoreline.

The southern end of the narrows has no streams, and water has to be carried some distance except during spring runoff in May and June. Flat camping areas are extensive in the area. More campsites, with fresh water from runoff, are available along the west shore of Scidmore Bay.

In the center of the bay are two rocky islands supporting a variety of birdlife. Two and a quarter miles northwest of the bay entrance, on the west shoreline, a stream can be followed south to some lakes, or over a 150-foot hill to overlook the Inner Sanctum and Scidmore Bay. The terrain is open to extensive views in all directions. From here one can descend into the inner bay. Be very careful not to disturb nesting geese, and be wary of soft mud encountered during and shortly after snow melt.

Inner Sanctum

A small, shrinking, inner tidal bay lies hidden behind a high pebble bank. Access is through a tidal gut no more than 0.8 mile long which does not run dry and has a strong current between slack tides. The best time to enter the bay is on an incoming tide; exit should be timed to coincide with the ebb tide. Canoes can be walked through if time is important and the tides are wrong.

The Inner Sanctum harbors a great variety of nesting geese and ducks. Overnight camping is highly recommended for small groups, but be very careful not to disturb any nesting grounds. The southern shore has high, flat benches and streams, the northern shore plenty of flat, dryas platforms with water only during spring snow runoff (until mid- or late June). The west end is composed of mud flats and a glacial river, and teems with birdlife.

Charpentier Inlet

Charpentier Inlet points a long, skinny finger at Geikie Inlet, 9.5 miles from its entrance. Its knuckle forms a wide valley, containing the glacial outwash of the severely shrunken Charpentier Glacier, 4 miles south of the entrance. From here the inlet extends 4 miles southeast through a steep-sided channel with many waterfalls and eroded gullies. A small campsite is found on the north shore, 1.3 miles from the end, under a waterfall. Watch for wolves and wolf tracks.

At the far end of the inlet a walk or portage to Geikie Inlet is possible, 1.5 miles across a narrow neck of land. At first the way is open over an outwash plain, crossing a stream flowing into Charpentier Inlet from the south; but when a stream system is encountered running southeast into Geikie Inlet, there is soft mud and the beginnings of thick brush.

Distance: 9.5 miles from entrance to north end of Scidmore Bay
9 miles to south end of Charpentier Inlet
6.25 miles to west end of Inner Sanctum
Time 4–5 days minimum
Route characteristics many tidal inlets, noted for birds and other wildlife; designated wilderness
Access by charter boat or floatplane to Blue Mouse Cove, 36 miles northwest of Bartlett Cove

GLACIER BAY: ADDITIONAL AREA INFORMATION

WEST ARM

Hugh Miller Inlet to Reid Inlet

U.S.G.S. topographical maps required: Mount Fairweather 1:63,360 series D-2, D-3.

This pleasant, rocky coastline, exposed to southeast storm winds, has lots of small, rocky bays good for camping. There are one or two small caves above the beach about halfway — one with a built-in shower! A very snug little cove lies just beyond the caves, northbound. There is a fairly large bay just south of Reid Inlet headland with lots of sea birds and good camping. Watch for nesting cormorants on the cliffs. Little ice activity is found along the coast until Reid Inlet is reached. Paddling time from Scidmore Bay narrows (Hugh Miller Inlet) to Reid Inlet is 3–4 hours.

Reid Inlet

This is a pleasant bay with a somewhat inactive, receding glacier at its head. It is filled with ice floes. There are beautiful camping spots for small tents on the north shore close to the glacier. Good camping is also found at the northern entrance to the bay. Permission should be obtained before using Ibach's cabin here (see GB9, Ptarmigan Creek map).

Reid Inlet to Johns Hopkins Inlet

U.S.G.S. topographical maps required: Mount Fairweather, D-3, D-4.

A rocky coastline, with a good beach and good camping at Ptarmigan (see GB9, Ptarmigan Creek) extends north. Otherwise sheltered coves and bays are scarce and the coastline is exposed to foul-weather southeasterly winds. On clear, sunny days beware of sudden squalls off Lamplugh Glacier. The glacier is not too active but does calve occasionally, especially at low tide. Lamplugh is photogenically superb in late afternoon, with shafts of sunlight filtering through towering seracs against the black backdrop of an immense mountain. From Lamplugh Glacier westbound, the scenery becomes decidedly vertical, and more ice is encountered as the corner into Johns Hopkins Inlet is turned.

A tight little cove, facing northwest and having a small stream, makes a perfect small-tent camp spot. To be found just before one turns the last corner and sights Johns Hopkins Glacier, this is the last horizontal camp-

Reid Glacier

site on the south side of Johns Hopkins Inlet. Allow 5–6 hours for this paddle.

Johns Hopkins Inlet

Johns Hopkins is a vertical-walled fjord, chock-full of ice and containing an active glacier. At first sight the glacier appears to be only 2 miles distant, but in actual fact it is 9 miles away. Uncomfortable camping, not recommended for canoeists, is found under Kashoto Glacier; anything farther in from here is vertical.

The same is true of the north shore except for the Topeka Outwash, a large alluvial fan on the apex of the northern curve, 10 miles northeast of the glacier. Warning: the streams in Johns Hopkins Inlet contain small amounts of arsenic! Many streams go underground before reaching tidal waters, so search for camping on foot behind the shoreline. I camped on the fan for one night without being poisoned!

The hazards of paddling in Johns Hopkins Inlet are shifting ice, rising winds, glacial action, and unstable hillsides. Take all of these factors into consideration before paddling far beyond the entrance of the fjord. A paddle in thick ice within the narrow confines of the fjord is not recommended, especially when the weather is in doubt. (Bad weather is often forecast by high, thin cloudiness, or a thin, translucent veil over the sun, but these signs are not necessarily infallible.)

An early morning paddle within the opening of Johns Hopkins Inlet before the winds rise should not be missed, as the fjord is loaded with dangling icefalls and dominated by 13,000- to 15,000-foot glacier-hung peaks. On clear days it is photogenically best before 9 or 10 A.M., before winds ruffle the calm surface.

The ice is covered with seals, terns, gulls, and pigeon guillemots. Black oyster catchers nest along the shoreline, and porpoises are friendly. The inlet is very noisy, even at night, with the crash of falling ice, the vertical walls acting as amplifiers. Land-based mammals are apparently rare here.

Tarr Inlet

U.S.G.S. topographical maps required: Mount Fairweather D-3; Skagway A-6.

Not as spectacular as Johns Hopkins Inlet until Margerie Glacier is reached, Tarr Inlet is open to foul-weather south winds and northerly gales; there is little shoreline shelter en route. Campsites abound along the shoreline. Heavy ice is not usually encountered until within 4–5 miles of Margerie Glacier. Margerie Glacier is truly splendid: its terminus,

Kayaking in ice, Johns Hopkins (Manya Wik)

almost 160 feet high, is the ice overflow from Mount Fairweather and Mount Quincy Adams, 15,300 and 13,650 feet, respectively. Do not approach within a mile of the terminus; this one is active and seracs are ready to fall any minute. Even at a mile a telephoto lens is barely necessary, except perhaps a 90-mm lens. Kittiwakes nest on the south side of the glacier.

Grand Pacific Glacier is less active but should be treated with respect. Allow at least 8 hours paddling form Johns Hopkins Inlet to Grand Pacific Glacier.

EAST SHORELINE

Beartrack Cove to Adams Inlet

U.S.G.S. topographical maps required: Juneau C-6; Mount Fairweather C-1 (optional), D-1. Also see page 193, Beardslee Islands, northern half, GB(A).

Beartrack Cove is open to those northerly winds rising about 11 A.M. on clear, sunny days. Good camping is found on the south shore. Where the river meets the bay there are snags and thick, thick mud. Do not attempt to walk up any of the steep mud banks found here. Avoid the head of the bay altogether on strong or rising northerlies, as the snags and deadheads (logs under water) become a death trap. Otherwise, the bay is beautiful. There is also good camping in the grass at the head of the bay. This is noted black bear habitat, so keep food well separated from camping gear and boats. Brown bears are seldom seen. Watch for coyotes and wolves.

North of Beartrack Cove a beautiful coastline has steep, wooded slopes. Good camping is found at York Creek, a torrent hurtling straight from the mountains into tidewaters. Again this is bear country; their tracks are often seen along the shoreline. A bell is not of much use against the roar of the torrent, so go warily through any brush when collecting water.

The coastline is highly exposed to all winds until Spokane and Sandy Coves are reached. A solid wall of rock reaches skyward shortly before Spokane Cove. Watch for cormorants, guillemots, and gulls nesting on the rocks. There are also many bald eagles. Keep well away from the cliffs while paddling past.

There are plenty of good campsites in Spokane and Sandy Coves. An especially attractive, but waterless, spot is on a high-tide island called "Dance" (bench mark) on the map. Watch for puffins around the islands north of Sandy cove. Swainson's, hermit, and varied thrushes are heard in the woods in early summer. Swainson's thrush has a bubbling upward song, and the hermit thrush sings the first few bars of Beethoven's 8th Symphony!

Keep watching for puffins on the northbound journey. The coastline becomes vertical once more, with streams dashing onto the rocks below. The cheerful chatter of wrens is sometimes heard from the rock walls. More cormorants, guillemots, and gulls inhabit the sheer walls; marbled and Kittlitz's murrelets ride the waves and fish under the cliffs. Goats use suction pads within sharp-edged hoofs to maintain their hold on nearly vertical rock walls as they descend to the littoral zone.

Garforth Island has idyllic campsites on both the north and south ends. Every stretch of beach is jealously guarded by black oyster catchers, who do not hesitate to attack any unwanted intruder. The rest of the island is owned by crows, whose noisy meetings are held nights and mornings. Goat families are so numerous on Mount Wright opposite that they resemble a rash of moving white dots.

The first icebergs of any size are usually met in this area, many of them dumped on the beach at high tide. The beach front flattens out around Muir Point and into Adams Inlet. There is plenty of camping on dryas-covered banks close to three major rivers and many smaller streams. Allow at least 3 days from Beartrack Cove to Adams Inlet. Distance is about 27 miles if bays and coves are explored.

Muir Inlet (northbound)

U.S.G.S. topographical maps required: Mount Fairweather D-1; Skagway A-4, A-3.

Northbound from Adams Inlet, the pleasant, rocky coast of the Klotz Hills is passed first, dominated to the south by Mount Case and Mount Wright. It is exposed to all winds. Ice begins to be met in quantity. There are at least two cozy little coves, one a perfect picnic site or small-tent campsite, and a small stream. Watch for mountain goats along the shoreline.

Huge liners and private pleasure craft sail into the inlet. Be prepared for bow and stern waves off the larger vessels.

Next on the northbound route is a 7-mile-long beach already claimed by brown bears and liberally sprinkled with interstadial wood. Northerlies and westerly winds off the glaciers are bad here. Wachussets Inlet sometimes acts as a funnel. If the winds become too strong, it is probably best to get out and walk, or to avoid them by arriving before noon on clear, sunny days.

The entrance to Wachussets Inlet is on the west side of Muir Inlet. Since the area was mapped in 1948, Wachussets Glacier has receded at least 6 miles. The inlet now presents a raw landscape with dryas, equisetum, willow, and cottonwood returning gradually and holding the bare soil together in patches. There is plenty of camping along the shoreline, although drinking water may have to be carried. Parasitic jaegers extend their range into Wachussets Inlet.

North of the long beach on the east shoreline is Goose Cove. It is relatively ice-free and is used as a summer ranger camp. (See GB7, Forest Creek, and GB5, Nunatak, for more detail.) Camping is good on the south shore of the bay, with fresh water available. Nesting ptarmigans abound, and seals and their pups are common in icy waters and riding on ice floes; otters occasionally play and feed in the cove.

Sealers Island has a tern colony on the west shore and many nesting glaucous-wing and herring gulls — please do not disturb. Exquisitely carved ice floes get hung up on the northern side of the island. Many of these are held together more by faith than anything else and are likely to shatter before one's eyes.

From here to Muir Glacier the bay becomes noisy. Ice booms, crashes, and roars day and night. Lost seal pups bawl for their mothers, a heart-rending sound very hard to get used to. The glaciers shudder, moan, and churn inside as if in troubled sleep. Their ice walls come crashing down, setting up miniature tidal waves; terns scream in front of the towering walls.

Nunatak Cove has standing interstadial trees. A firm, pebble beach fronts the south side, but mud borders the northern shore. Icebergs often make Nunatak Cove their port of call.

On the west side of Muir Inlet is Wolf Cove (see GB6, White Thunder Ridge). Camping is good in the cove, but the mud is still present in lesser quantities, and ice is thickly strewn across the beach. Northbound from here the western shoreline becomes vertical. Hundreds of seals ride the floes and swim in the waters. The east shoreline is relatively friendly if the ice floes will permit access. McBride Glacier has retreated onto dry land but remains a pretty glacier, especially when seen from White Thunder Ridge opposite.

The same warnings apply for upper Muir Inlet as for Johns Hopkins Inlet (see page 207). Small camps on rock platforms are possible close to Riggs and Muir Glaciers, but beware of places exposed to rockfall from above and waves caused by glacial calving. Muir Glacier is now about 3 miles around the corner behind White Thunder Ridge, or 5 miles west of Riggs Glacier, and is shrinking rapidly. *Do not get cut off by shifting ice.* Allow 2–3 days paddling time one way. Shoreline distance from Adams Inlet to Riggs Glacier is about 18 miles. Ice permitting, the *Seacrest* (daily tour boat from Bartlett Cove) sails to Riggs Glacier.

WEST CHICHAGOF COASTAL CANOE RUN

Almost 50 miles north of Sitka, a portion of the west coast of Chichagof Island splinters into thousands of smaller islands and islets. Shattered remnants lie scattered out to sea as surf-washed rocks and skerries, caught within a net of kelp, forming a barrier against Pacific swells. Here is the home of the sea lion and the fortress of the recently transplanted sea otter. Behind the protective vanguard of islands, sheltered tidal backwaters build a web of landlocked waterways inviting exploration by inquisitive canoeists. From tidewater, great virgin rain forests march upward to the graceful peaks that shape the backbone of the west wing of Chichagof Island.

Thus travelers can paddle in sheltered lagoons by whiskered giant spruce, at arm's length from the mighty Pacific, and, in the same instant, through the back door glimpse a pod of sea lions in the furious surf or sea otters belly-up adrift in the kelp beds. Such tableaux may be captured within Mirror Harbor, the Myriad Islands, and those islands running south to Piehle Passage. Beyond the spindrift, hidden inlets and bays advance at high water into tall, whispering spruce, beckoning the curious to follow. Larger interconnecting bays concealed behind narrow tidal gates assert themselves to the base of the mountains.

In these features this wild, unspoiled country is unique. Yet at the same time West Chichagof is typical of Southeast Alaska: like a dense, green cloud, stately Alaskan rain forests cover the ground from alpine altitudes to shoreline, occasionally interspersed with open muskeg containing sparsely scattered lodgepole pine, small peat pools, and a ground cover of grasses, heaths, Labrador tea, and a minuscule, pink pincushion named sundew. The forests are composed of giant, old-growth Sitka spruce and hemlock, which, in combination with the total saltwater and freshwater environment, give support and cover to a rich variety of wildlife on the beaches, in the water, and in the air.

An unobtrusive kayaker may observe for a brief moment a bald eagle soaring on extended wings, using thermals to gain height and delicate adjustments of the body to maintain equilibrium; he may be able to watch a playful mink or otter hunting or scavenging the shoreline or be startled by the sharp three- to five-note whistled warning of the greater yellowlegs, a sound that, once heard, is never forgotten. Brown bears frequent salmon streams in late summer or browse in the intertidal zone; and shy, but curious Sitka black-tailed deer and fawns hover nervously on the edge of the forest. Dabbling and probing in quiet backwaters are

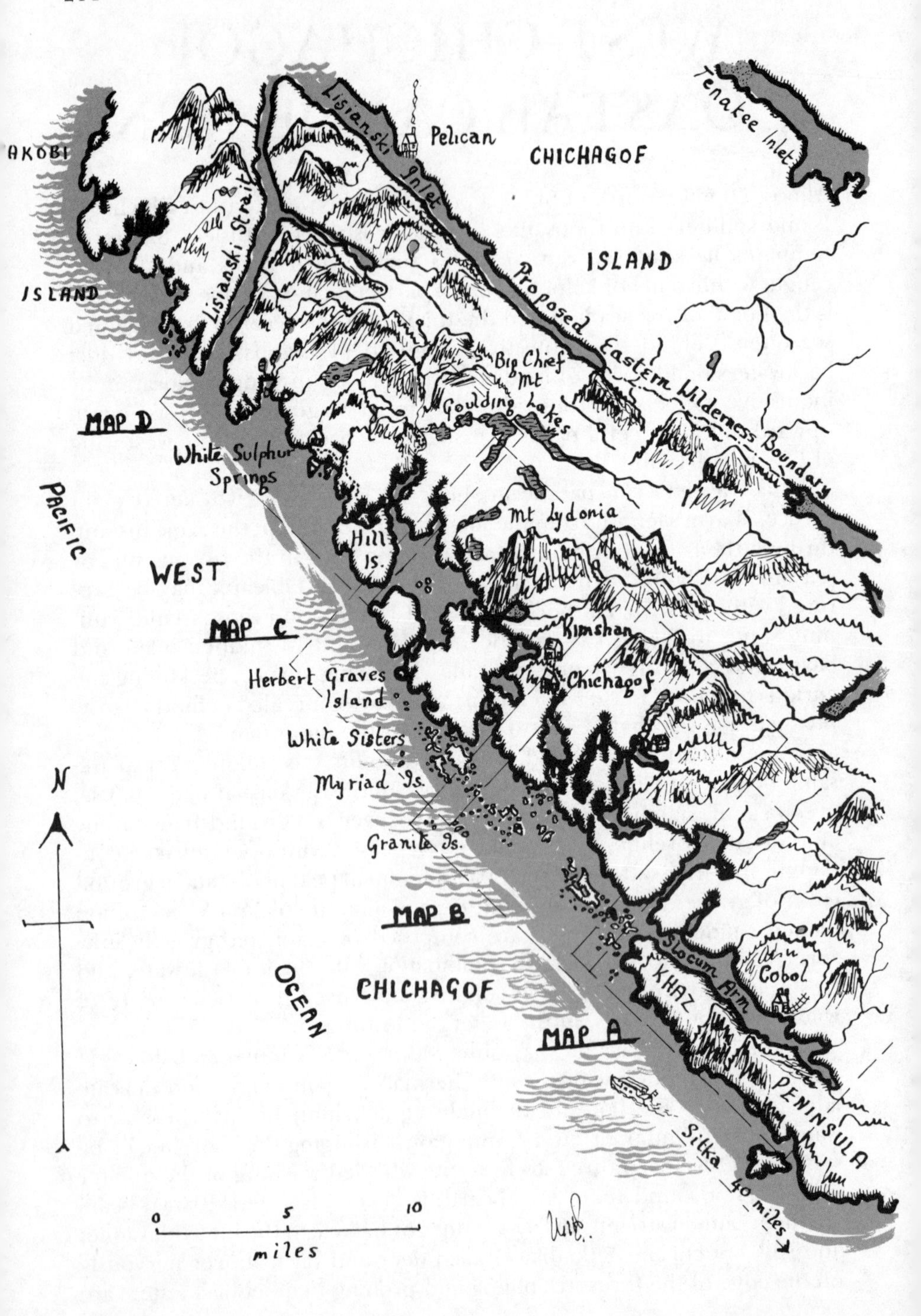

Tenakee Inlet
Lisianski Inlet
Pelican
CHICHAGOF
ISLAND
YAKOBI
ISLAND
Lisianski Strait
Proposed Eastern Wilderness Boundary
Big Chief Mt
Goulding Lakes
MAP D
White Sulphur Springs
PACIFIC
Mt Lydonia
Hill Is.
WEST
MAP C
Kimshan
Chichagof
Herbert Graves Island
White Sisters
N
Myriad Is.
Granite Is.
MAP B
OCEAN
CHICHAGOF
Slocum Arm
KHAZ
Cobol
MAP A
PENINSULA
Sitka 40 miles
0
5
10
miles

shore birds, great blue herons, and surface-feeding ducks, such as green-wing teals, mallards, and pintails; Canada geese inhabit tidal marshes and freshwater lakes, and occasionally trumpeter and whistling swans visit the tidal zones.

West Chichagof Island is public land administered by the U.S. Forest Service and, like Admiralty Island, is under threat of clear-cut logging. The Sitka Conservation Society has submitted a Wilderness Proposal for West Chichagof and Yakobi Islands to the U.S. Forest Service.

The best starting point for the West Chicagof coastline is Sitka. Charter flights can be arranged with Eagle Air or Channel Flying. Special arrangements will have to be made for canoes. Foldboats are advisable for ease of stowing aboard aircraft. Boat charters can be arranged through Jack Calvin, P. O. Box 97; Chuck Johnstone, P. O. Box 316; and Ben Forbes, P. O. Box 557; all Sitka, Alaska 99835. Estimate 3–4 days boat charter to reach the debarkation and pickup points, with return to Sitka. Weather permitting, flights to West Chichagof take 40–60 minutes. If a party is relying on a floatplane rendezvous at the conclusion of their tour, they should take extra rations in case the flight is delayed by bad weather.
take extra rations in case the flight is delayed by bad weather.

Two U.S. Forest Service cabins, one on Goulding Lakes and the other at White Sulphur Springs, a few miles south of Lisianski Strait, can be reserved through the Sitka Ranger District, U.S. Forest Service, Sitka, Alaska 99835. Please leave all cabins in better condition than they were found and replenish any wood used. Some old buildings with weatherproof roofs still stand in the ghost towns of Cobol, Chichagof, and Kimshan, which grew during a gold mining era in the early 1900s and were abandoned during World War II.

Camping spots can be found almost anywhere along the beaches, and only places of special interest are mentioned. The tides are 7–8 feet in height — much smaller than at Ketchikan and Juneau, where tides range in height from 17–19 feet. But do not be fooled by a robust floral growth in the intertidal zones: despite appearances these areas are subject to periodic saltwater inundation. (See also Introduction, page 22.)

During mid- and late summer, camp on promontories exposed to breezes, since insects such as mosquitoes, "no-see-ums," and white socks can become a serious nuisance in windless, sheltered tidal inlets. Drinking water is rarely unavailable, except on small islands. But since some of the better campsites are isolated from running water, have enough drinking water on hand to last until the next day (dishes and cans can of course be washed in salt water).

Beware of sudden squalls on strong westerlies and northwesterlies. Black Bay seems especially prone to these winds; they bounce over Herbert Graves Island and land flat-handed on the bay waters. Sea fog from

Chichagof in earlier days

the west is frequently encountered but is sometimes forced off the water, or blocked altogether, by the mountains and larger islands. Slocum Arm, Klag Bay, and Kimshan Cove are often clear and sunny when visibility is poor or nil in Ogden Passage, Piehle Passage, or Mirror Harbor. Fog is commonly the precursor of good weather, and when it dissipates an unveiling takes place: the peaks gradually divest themselves of their veils, allowing them to lap around their feet for a short time before they disappear altogether. The spectacle calls for a camera.

To paddle the 30 miles of coastline, allow at least 2 weeks, although more time would be desirable. It is possible to see portions of the coast in less time. Detailed maps or nautical charts and compass are absolutely necessary. If intending to hike, U.S.G.S. topographic maps, 1:63,360 series, should be carried. The topographic quadrangles required are:

Slocum Arm and Ford Arm: Sitka B-6 and C-6
Piehle Passage, Sister Lake, Kimshan, and Portlock Harbor: Sitka C-7
Goulding Harbor and Lakes, Pelican and Mirror Harbor: Sitka D-7
White Sulphur Springs trail: Sitka D-7 and D-8
White Sulphur Springs, Lisianski Strait, and part of Yakobi Island: Sitka D-8

The smaller scale 1:250,000 Sitka series would also be helpful to enable one to see the whole area at a glance. Sitka tide tables are essential. The required charts can be obtained locally in Sitka or Juneau:

West coast of Chichagof Island to Khaz Bay, No. 8280
Cape Edward to Lisianski Strait, No. 8258
Yakobi Island to Lisianski Strait, No. 8260

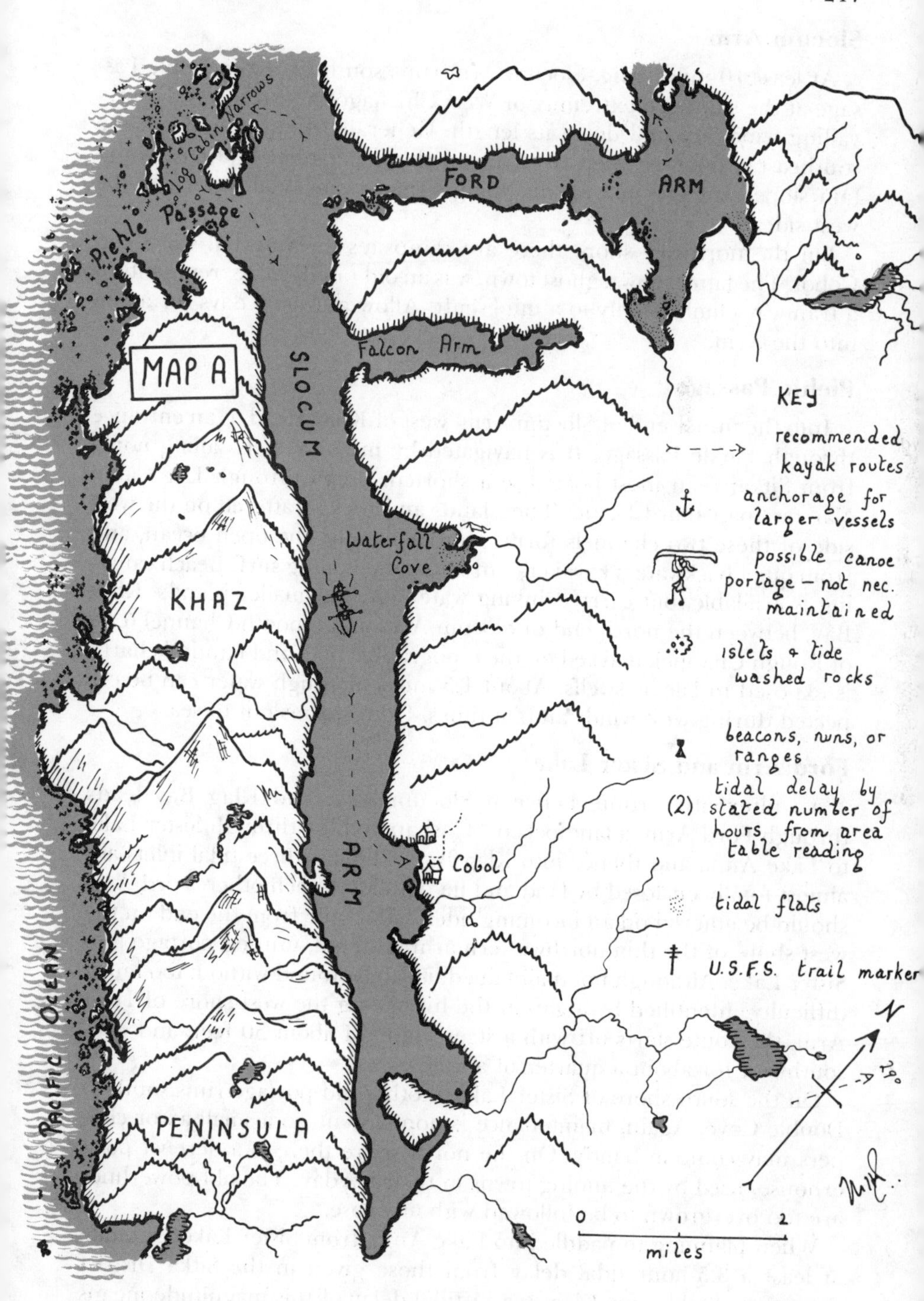
Log Cabin Narrows
Piehle Passage
FORD
ARM
Falcon Arm
MAP A
SLOCUM
ARM
Waterfall Cove
KHAZ
PENINSULA
Cobol
PACIFIC OCEAN
KEY
recommended kayak routes
anchorage for larger vessels
possible canoe portage - not nec. maintained
islets & tide washed rocks
beacons, runs, or ranges
(2) tidal delay by stated number of hours from area table reading
tidal flats
U.S.F.S. trail marker
N
29°
0
1
2
miles

Slocum Arm

At least 10 miles long, Slocum Arm runs southeast from Piehle Passage at the southern extremity of West Chichagof and receives the prevailing winds up and down its length. Generally these come from the southeast in poor weather, from the north during good weather. Mountain slopes are precipitous, dropping straight into tidal waters on the west side.

On the northeast shore there are campsites in Waterfall Cove and Cobol. The latter, now a ghost town, was an old family mine; remnants of a tramway climb steeply to a mineshaft. Allow at least 2 days for a trip into the Arm.

Piehle Passage

Into the upper end of Slocum Arm, west of Khaz Head, is an entrance through Piehle Passage. It is navigated by motor vessels sailing north from Sitka; then most boats use a shortcut north through Log Cabin Narrows past Baird Island. The islands and rocks scattered on the west side of these two channels form a buffer against the open ocean, and from quiet backwaters kayakers can watch the boiling surf. Beach camping is available, but carry drinking water for the smaller islands. Khaz Bay, between the north end of Slocum Arm and Smooth Channel (east of Rough Channel, marked on the topographic map and nautical chart), is exposed to Pacific swells. About 1.5 miles of rough water can be expected during west winds and, at times, from storms out to sea.

Ford Arm and Sister Lake

An alternative route between Slocum Arm and Klag Bay leads through Ford Arm, a landlocked "T"-shaped inlet, through Sister Lake to Lake Anna and thence into Klag Bay. The last three tidal inlets are almost totally enclosed by land and lie parallel to each other. Ford Arm should be entered on an incoming tide; half a mile from the end on the west shore of the thin northwestern arm is an old, unused portage into Sister Lake. Although not maintained, it can be found without too much difficulty. Identified by a gap in the hills along the west shore of Ford Arm, the route starts off with a steep climb of about 50 feet, and goes southwest for about a quarter of a mile.

On the south shore of Sister Lake another old portage runs south to Double Cove. Again, maintenance is nonexistent, so a small ax or clippers may come in handy. On the north shore there is a derelict powerhouse, used by the mining towns in their heyday. The old powerlines are too overgrown to be followed with any ease.

When planning to paddle into Lake Anna from Sister Lake, estimate at least a 3.5-hour tidal delay from those given in the Sitka District correctional tables for Klag Bay. A tidal delay of this magnitude means that for the first 3 hours after low slack in Klag Bay, the tide is incoming in Klag Bay and Lake Anna, while it is still outgoing from Sister Lake. The narrows from Sister Lake to Lake Anna can only be run with the tide or during slack, because of strong currents.

The narrows between Lake Anna and Klag Bay are not as critical, but those from Klag Bay into open sea can only be paddled with the tide or during slack. Consequently, once out of Sister Lake, one should plan an overnight stopover in Lake Anna or Klag Bay to better synchronize travel with the tides. An overnight camp in Klag Bay is, in any case, highly recommended.

Klag Bay and Lake Anna

Ingress into Klag Bay can either be made from Smooth Channel through The Gate into Elbow Passage, or by weaving between the islands of choice into Elbow Passage, west of The Gate. A range (a navigational aid for fishing boats, etc.) is placed within The Gate. Canoes may have more latitude than powerboats with choice of routes, but they have less choice of timing. The best time to navigate the narrows is with the tide or

Klag Bay and Doolth Mountain

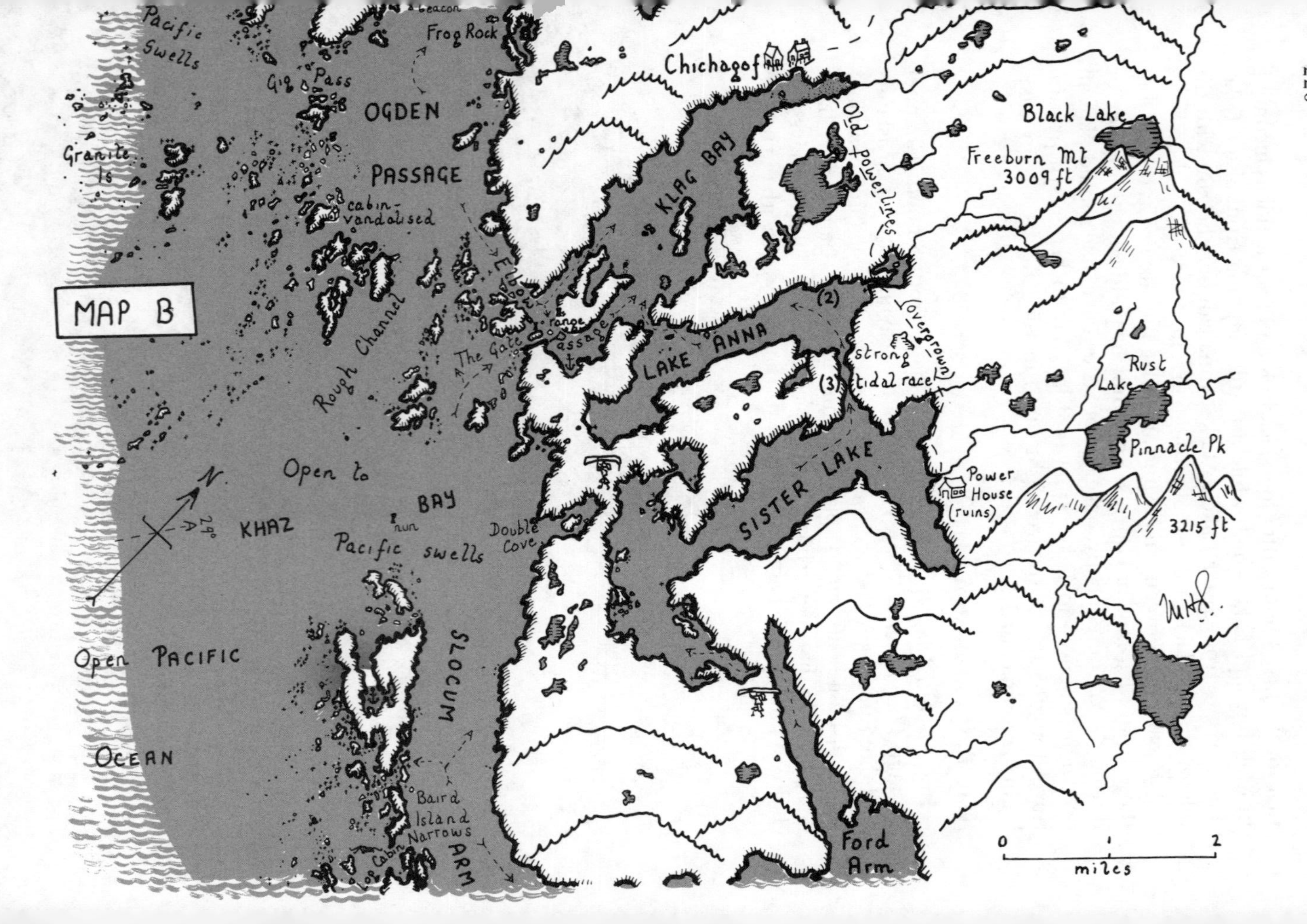

MAP B
Pacific Swells
Granite Is
Gig Pass
OGDEN PASSAGE
Frog Rock
cabin-vandalised
Rough Channel
Elbow
Orange Passage
The Gate
Open to KHAZ BAY
Pacific swells
Double Cove
Open PACIFIC OCEAN
SLOCUM ARM
Baird Island Narrows
Cabin
Chichagof
KLAG BAY
Old powerlines
Black Lake
Freeburn Mt
3009 ft
LAKE ANNA
(2)
(3)
strong tidal race
(overgrown)
SISTER LAKE
Rust Lake
Pinnacle Pk
3215 ft
Power House (ruins)
Ford Arm
N.
29°
0
1
2
miles

during slack. Choose flood tide to gain entrance into Klag Bay and ebb flow for the return.

Those running east into Elbow Passage from Ogden Passage will find a choice of two short narrows at the west entrance. The south passage is wider and less awkward, with fewer rock snags and less kelp; it is certainly the better choice in fog. Both channels have strong currents between slack waters. One mile farther east, canoe voyageurs can go on either side of Klag Island, but the west channel is rocky and contains masses of kelp.

Klag Bay is more populated than the other inner tidal bays, with occasional visits from fishing boats and floatplanes. The shoreline and islands are liberally sprinkled with campsites on the edge of the trees. Visible at the head of the bay is the ghost town of Chichagof, now in the middle stages of decay; many buildings are tumbledown, but some still stand. An old powerline route over the northeast shoulder of Doolth Mountain, to Kimshan Cove, is overgrown in places and hard to follow.

The passage between Klag Bay and Lake Anna is short and can be paddled against the current during the early stages of the tide. Lake Anna is less frequented than Klag Bay and offers more seclusion. A grave marker stands on a small island half a mile north of the entrance from Klag Bay. Both inlets are ringed by peaks of 3000 feet or so — Doolth Mountain to the northwest and Freeburn Mountain, Pinnacle Peak, and Flat Top to the north and east.

Myriad Islands

These islands, rocks, and reefs are populated with an abundance of land- and sea-based wildlife. Beach camping is available, although some smaller islands may not have drinking water. Larger islands, such as Herbert Graves Island, have streams to the beaches, even during dry periods. The Myriad Islands abut directly onto open Pacific waters and here is their charm: kayakers can camp on lee shores and walk across the island to the surf-exposed beach on the far side.

Access is by paddling across Ogden Passage or island-hopping (far more interesting) from The Gate and Smooth Channel. One of the larger islands south of Gig Pass had a good cabin, now made uninhabitable by vandals. The miniature rain forest stands on the islands are park-like, with tall trees and thick, moss-covered floor. Eagles, ravens, deer, mice, and seals are friendly; beachcombing reaps its own special rewards for the addict. It is doubtful if these small islands are within brown bear range.

Estimate a full day to explore the islands between Smooth Channel and the Myriad Islands west of Tawak Passage. Straight distance is about 7.5 miles, but it is easily doubled with detours. Overnight camping on the islands is recommended.

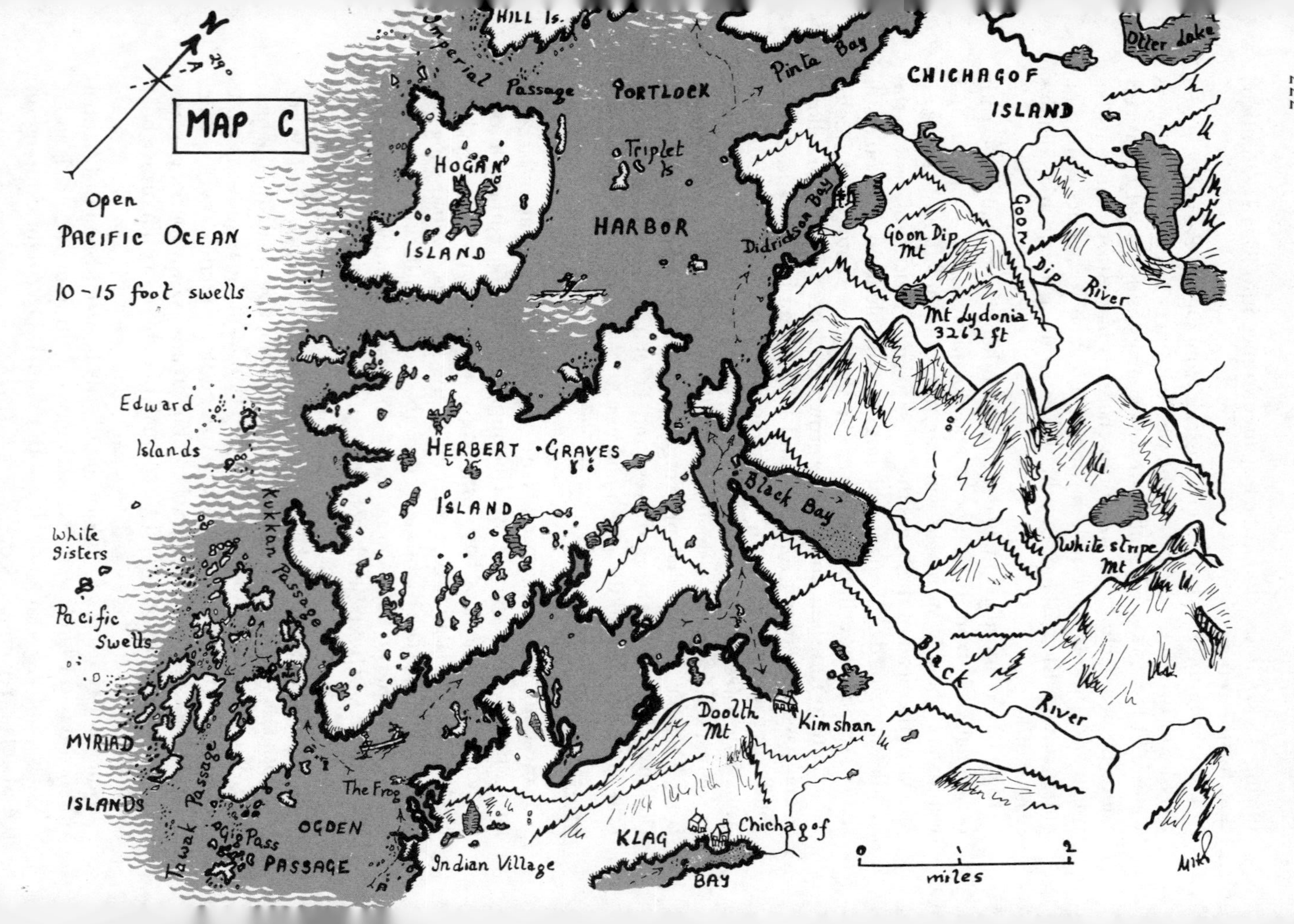
MAP C
Open
PACIFIC OCEAN
10-15 foot swells
Edward
Islands
White
Sisters
Pacific
Swells
MYRIAD
ISLANDS
Tawak Passage
Gig Pass
OGDEN
PASSAGE
HILL Is.
Imperial
Passage
HOGAN
ISLAND
PORTLOCK
Triplet
Is
HARBOR
HERBERT GRAVES
ISLAND
Kukkan Passage
The Frog
Indian Village
KLAG
BAY
Chichagof
Doolth
Mt
Kimshan
Black Bay
Black River
White stripe
Mt
Mt Lydonia
3262 ft
Goon Dip
Mt
Goon Dip River
Didrickson Bay
Pinta Bay
CHICHAGOF
ISLAND
Otter Lake
0
1
2
miles

Kimshan

Kimshan Cove and Black Bay

If any place could be considered the heart of West Chichagof, it would be Kimshan Cove and its namesake, the ghost town of Kimshan overshadowed by Doolth Mountain and the shapely line of Mount Lydonia. It is approximately halfway up the coast from Cobol to Lisianski Strait. On both sides of the narrows south of Kimshan are many secret, hidden passages only a canoeist or kayaker would find. Some contain secluded waterfalls and interesting moss-covered rock formations. Deer haunt the beaches, and salmon plane atop the tidal waters in late July and August.

Those paddling north through Ogden Passage might find Indian Village. One tumbledown cabin, long abandoned, set on a bank above a clear stream, and a patch of wild iris (quite a rarity in these parts), are all that remain to be seen. Be cautious of the steps; the wood is rotten and threatens to give way before too long. North of the village is Frog Rock, an intriguing "geobiologic" landmark.

Kimshan is a forlorn huddle of old houses along the shore. Behind are the remains of a mine with thick, brush-covered slash covering the north shoulder of Doolth Mountain. Wander a short way up the hill for a view of the cove and Surveyor Passage, but expect to be soon bogged down in brush.

When exploring the coastline, do not expect the maps to be precisely accurate since the topography is undergoing gradual change. For example, Frits Island now has a pebble isthmus connecting it to the shore of Kimshan Cove.

Black Bay is a pleasant surprise. It is totally dominated by Mount Lydonia, and two sentinel islands guard the entrance into the bay. The entrance is about 2.5 miles from Kimshan, reached by a paddle through Surveyor Passage, where winds and tide sometimes combine to either help or seriously frustrate the canoeist. Even when paddling *with* the tide, it is possible to be blown backwards by a strong northerly wind funnelling through the passage. The ebb tide runs north.

The southern tip of Lydonia Island has room for camping above the beach, in the open or in the trees, depending upon one's preference. The point provides beaching on two sides, thus ensuring a sheltered beach at all times. Drinking water should be obtained from Herbert Graves Island, the opposite shoreline.

Portlock Harbor

Situated north of Surveyor Passage, Portlock Harbor is a large back-water bay, sheltered from Pacific swells by three islands: Hill, Hogan, and Herbert Graves.

From the east side of Didrickson Bay a short, well-marked trail climbs over a 100-foot hill to Didrickson Lake. The trail beginning is indicated by a Forest Service diamond-shaped marker, standing on the shore about 1 mile north of the bay's entrance. Farther north is Pinta Bay, with its long, wooded shoreline. Triplet Islands, Lock Island, and small

Mount Lydonia from Surveyor Passage

In Portlock Harbor

islets along both east and west shorelines of Portlock Harbor have interesting and photogenic rock formations.

Mileage from Lydonia Island to Goulding Harbor can vary from 5 straight miles to 12 miles if the two eastern bays are explored, and 7.5 miles if the west shoreline is traveled.

Goulding Harbor — Goulding Lakes foot trail

There is nothing stark about the scenery around Goulding Harbor. It is soft, with plush forested slopes and an intrinsic charm that is hard to define. Perhaps it is the light on the water, or the way the bay insinuates itself inland by a progression of bays and headlands.

The inlet is 2.6 miles long (if the bays are not counted) and runs northeast from the north end of Portlock Harbor. Camping is to be found above the beaches; be sure you *are* above the beach! (This is the land of the yellow cinquefoil, where, despite appearances, periodic saltwater inundations occur; see page 215). Choose islands or headlands in late summer, to stay within the breeze zone and out of the fly zone.

A Forest Service diamond-shaped trail marker is visible at the head of the bay, indicating the beginning of a 1.25-mile trail to Goulding Lakes. A few yards behind the marker is a shelter of sorts in the trees. It is rudely constructed and would only be considered for emergency use.

A wet pathway, requiring rubber boots, starts from the marker and travels uphill, north through tall trees then emerges in a meadow where

YAKOBI ISLAND
MAP D
Lisianski Strait
Long paddle to Elfin Cove
Canoe Pass
2294 ft
CHICHAGOF ISLAND
River
Stranger
Pinnacle Peak
Swells from 10 - 15 feet
Islas Bay
"Porcupine" Islands
Lake Elfendahl
Stop River
North Mt 1848'
White Sulphur Springs
F.S. cabin
Lake Morris
Open PACIFIC OCEAN
Bertha Bay
Sea Level Slough
Falls creek
Mt Crowther 2847'
Big Swells
N
Dry Pass
Big Chief Mt 3050±'
Mt Douglas
TRAIL
Goulding Lakes
Goulding Hbr
Hill Island
Otter Lake
Pinta Bay
Portlock Harbor
miles

careful watch is needed for tree blazes before the path plunges back into trees. An old tramroad is followed next into a second muskeg. In the open, the route travels the west shore of a lily pond, whose waters on calm days faithfully reflect the graceful line of Big Chief Mountain. Once more in the trees, the trail climbs to about 100 feet above sea level, coming close to some roaring falls where the Goulding River descends almost directly from the lake above. Next the trail turns right (east) to cross a tributary by a log bridge, then climbs steeply up the opposite bank and traverses right toward the falls. Goulding River is followed to Goulding Lake, the trail ending by the lake shore after a steep descent. Prior to this, a division in paths may create mild confusion on a short stretch of muskeg. The two paths run parallel, however, and as long as the river is followed the lake is found without trouble. A rowboat is furnished by the Forest Service for general use and should be left as it is found.

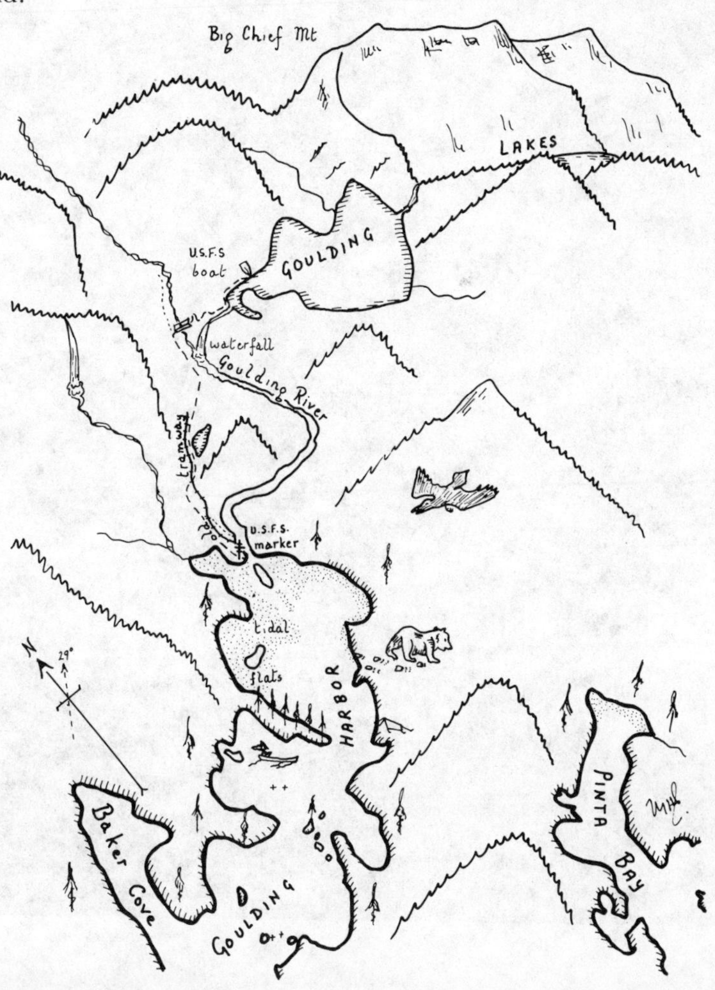

Those interested in entering the Goulding Lakes system farther east can portage canoes to the trailhead. A short steep climb up some falls leads one to a second lake; another portage may be necessary to gain access into Otter Lake. A Forest Service cabin is located on the north shore of Otter Lake, but arrangements should be made first before its use is planned.

The trail from Goulding Harbor to the first Goulding Lake takes 35–40 minutes to walk one way. Do not worry if, on the return after crossing the last muskeg, you wander onto an old miner's trail heading south. This leads to the west bank of Goulding River, 200 yards upstream from the Forest Service marker, and is practically parallel to the Forest Service trail.

Dry Pass

A solemn passageway, overshadowed by spruce and hemlock, reaches west from the entrance to Goulding Harbor into a wide backwater separated from the Pacific by a narrow band of land. At the southwest end a narrow passage called Dry Pass leads through the surf to the Pacific Ocean. From here there is a choice: either travel through the pass and paddle northbound along the coast to Mirror Harbor and White Sulphur Springs, or cache the boats and walk the 4.5 miles overland. (See foot trail description for White Sulphur Springs, this page.) Choice is difficult as the routes offer different perspectives. The character of the coastline is changed. It is now open to Pacific swells, has rocky headlands and bays providing fleeting shelter, and is studded with small islands, surf-washed rocks, and kelp beds. Behind the coast are open muskeg and shapely peaks.

Parties choosing Dry Pass must be highly skilled kayakers. Although it can be negotiated at almost any stage of the tide, one must watch for rocks and running surf. It is advisable to walk the shoreline first or to camp in the immediate vicinity and observe the pass at different stages of the tide. Once outside, kayakers are subject to the vicissitudes of open ocean. Stay together, and watch for changes in the weather.

Large boats can be anchored at the northern end of the quiet backwater, northeast of Dry Pass and north of an unnamed island. The trail to White Sulphur Springs starts here.

Foot trail from Dry Pass to White Sulphur Springs

The trail to White Sulphur Springs follows the shoreline north through spruce and hemlock forest and open country. In places it is not maintained by the Forest Service and is hard to find (although im-

Big Chief Mountain

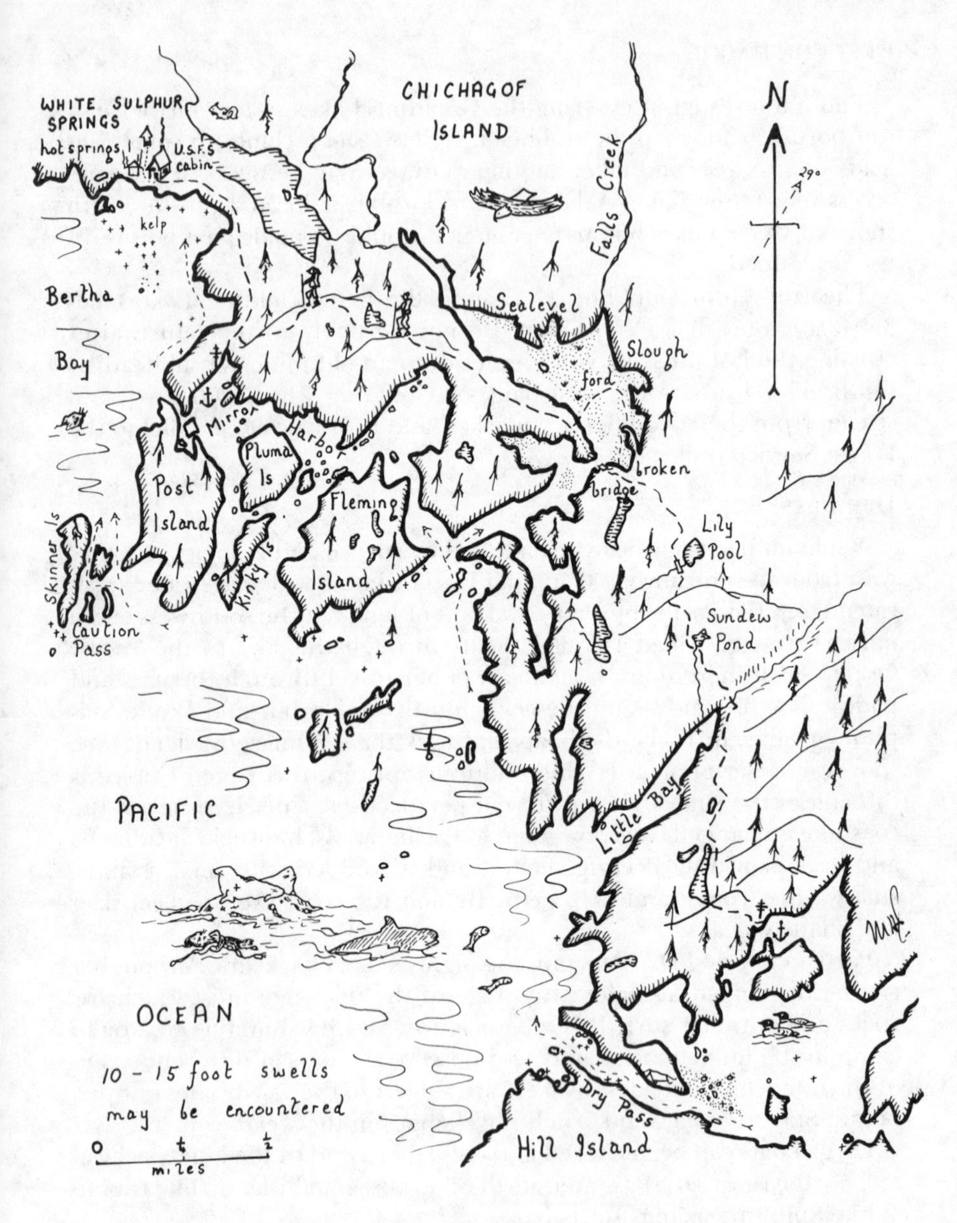

provements by the Sitka Group of the Sierra Club have helped). However, if map, compass, and common sense are used, the trail should not be lost for long. The last mile, well-trodden, begins in Mirror Harbor. Most large-boat owners, fishermen, etc., prefer to anchor in Mirror Harbor and walk this last section to the Forest Service cabin.

Hikers should plan to arrive at Sea Level Slough (a tidal inlet about halfway to White Sulphur Springs) between mid- and low tide. A footbridge across the slough was destroyed some years ago and needs restoration. With overnight gear about 1.5 hours are needed to reach the slough.

If canoes or kayaks are left at the trailhead, remember that this is bear habitat. Do not leave food, and be sure there are no fishy odors in the vicinity of the boats. Large vessels can anchor opposite the U.S. Forest Service trail marker (anchorage mentioned previously under Dry Pass). The trail marker requires repainting and is hard to see from the shore; it faces east on a small promontory opposite an unnamed island 0.6 miles northeast of Dry Pass.

The trail climbs gently at first, going west, then north, as it drops to a lily pond. (On the return the trail is confusing at the top of the hill, but keep right, continuing downward to reach the beach.) It then winds north through trees, past another pond, until Little Bay is reached in approximately a mile. In this section Pacific surf can be heard in the distance.

Little Bay is a narrow, steep-sided tidal inlet permitting tantalizing glimpses out to sea. The trail crosses the stream at its head and climbs uphill through muskeg to another lily pond rimmed with masses of spatulate sundew (*Drosera angelica*) growing in the middle of the trail. The path then dips up and down through open country, never exceeding 150 feet or so above sea level. Again, it passes muskeg pools covered with lilies and surrounded by the tiny, more common sundew (*Drosera rotundifolia*) with tiny, spiked leaves shaped like tennis rackets. At this point the conical peak of North Mountain comes into view and the route is dominated by Mount Douglas to the east.

Finally the path drops to Sea Level Slough, a landlocked tidal inlet frequented by bears. Be sure to have a bell, whistle, or can full of pebbles. Even at low tide a walk upstream is necessary to avoid deep wading or possibly a swim. Choose the widest spot for crossing the main stream. A subsidiary stream, on the far shore, does not usually present a problem.

Once more the trail climbs out of the trees into open country, for unsurpassed view of coastline, islands, and ocean. The path can be lost when it crosses open country, but it continues west over the summit of a 100-foot hill, veering southwest as it drops to Mirror Harbor. A hundred yards before reaching the beach it joins the well-beaten path for its last mile and follows the shoreline to White Sulphur Springs. (For further description of the hot springs and cabin, see page 232).

MIRROR HARBOR AND WHITE SULPHUR SPRINGS

Canoe Trail for Skilled Kayakers *Only*

When traveling northbound, kayakers going "outside" into open ocean can explore the islands and inlets of the coastline. Mirror Harbor has sheltered anchorage for larger vessels. The trail marker for the last mile of trail to White Sulphur Springs is visible on the shore in the West Arm north of Post Island. (For further description, see White Sulphur Springs foot trail.)

Kayakers paddling farther north might find partially sheltered passage through Caution Pass en route to Bertha Bay, but they must be prepared for slop and cross chop. In Bertha Bay the shoreline is exposed to Pacific swell and kelp is considerable, but the momentum of the running surf is dampened by many rocks guarding the beach.

A Forest Service cabin and bathhouse (White Sulphur Springs) are located on the north shore of Bertha Bay. The cabin is in good condition and has bunks for eight people, a table, a cooking and heating stove, and wood. Basic cooking utensils are furnished. Water is supplied by a small creek flowing from a peat pool a few yards west of the cabin, or it can be collected from the roof during rains. The water should be boiled before drinking. Please register with the U.S. Forest Service before using the cabin and leave it in good condition.

The area's main attraction is a hot sulphur spring next to the cabin. Although it has recently been enclosed in a bathhouse, it is still possible to sit in the hot springs and watch the Pacific rollers boil over the rocks and disintegrate on the beach.

Kayakers who decide to end their trip at White Sulphur Springs can arrange to be picked up in Mirror Harbor or Dry Pass by boat or plane, weather permitting.

North to Lisianski Strait

Those desiring to go on to Pelican or Elfin Cove have a long paddle ahead. Pelican is approximately 25 miles and Elfin Cove 40 miles from White Sulphur Springs. Exposed waters are encountered through Islas Bay, although a portage might be tried behind Point Urey (marked on map D). Its possibilities or limitations are unknown to the author. The channel through Canoe Pass is dry at most stages of the tide, except high.

Lisianski Strait funnels the wind and could be a longer paddle than expected. Good camping is to be found just south of Stag Bay on Yakobi Island, the west shore of the Strait. In 1969 a group of kayakers from Seattle paddled the West Chichagof coast from Slocum Arm and elected to continue to Elfin Cove. I am indebted to them for the extra data gathered over and above my own experiences.

Limitation: for experienced groups only
Distance 32 air miles from Slocum Arm to Lisianski Strait
Time: allow at least 4–5 days to see any portion of West Chichagof; allow at least 2 weeks for total distance

Characteristics wilderness, open seas, sheltered tidal inlets; mountainous coastline with sea and land wildlife
Access by charter boat or floatplane, 50 miles north of Sitka
Facilities: U.S. Forest Service cabins available at White Sulphur Springs and Goulding Lakes
Includes Goulding Lake foot trail and White Sulphur Springs foot trail

Some useful small-boat anchorages:

1. Log Cabin Narrows, northern end
2. Khaz Bay, 1.2 miles southeast of Deuce Island, at the end of a long inlet (almost bisecting a large island)
3. Elbow Passage, at the "point of the elbow" in the most southeasterly bay
4. Kukkan Passage, 1 mile north-northwest of "Snipe," a beacon marked on the U.S.G.S. topographical map and nautical charts; the anchorage is enclosed within an island forming the southwest boundary of Kukkan Passage
5. Dry Pass; start of White Sulphur Springs trail
6. Mirror Harbor, West Arm

Eagle

ADMIRALTY ISLAND CANOE TRAVERSE

Currently under threat of extensive clear-cut logging, Admiralty Island is still wilderness without massive interference of roads, men, machines, and noise. Logging incursions in its past were minor and miniature compared with the practices of today. Admiralty's splendor is still primitive. Virgin rain forests still mantle it; distinctive peaks rise, still unscarred; its population of brown bears still roam in their natural habitiat, free from harassment. How long will this last? Heaven help us if this — the last untouched major island of the archipelago — falls victim to the violence and ravishment of modern industry. What will we have left to show our children?

What is Admiralty Island? It is Chutsinu (Killisnoo), Home of the Alaska Brown Bear. They live in harmony with their environment, foraging for roots, skunk cabbage, and rodents in the spring, fishing for returning salmon in the streams close to tidewater in later summer. They roam far and wide during the summer, sometimes foraging on the beaches or working their way through berry patches high on the mountainside. They generally stay away from man — if left alone.

Admiralty Island is the habitat of the bald eagle. Magnificent birds, with a wing span of over 6 feet, they soar on rising thermals and in minutes glide from the shoreline over the highest mountains. Bald eagles nest in the largest and oldest trees, preferring those with a thick, bushy crown and secondary branches radiating outward like the spokes of a wheel. Such trees are rare.

Admiralty is the abode of its deer, who graze high and undisturbed in the summer, escaping in winter through tall trees to the beaches in search of limited forage. Access to the beach through heavy forest cover is essential to their survival in deep snow.

What is Admiralty Island? It is forests — great spruce and hemlocks that spread a burst of branches at their crowns and allow the light to filter through to cast a delicate glow on the moss-covered ground. It is rivers and stream riffles, overshadowed by ancient hemlocks splashed red with fungi and hung with moss and insects that shortly become prey for feeding salmon and trout below. It is the sunlight shafting between giants to ensnare in a halo of light the gaudy iridescence of a dragonfly in flight; it is the grey, steel-like quality of tidal waters before a storm. It is the evening rainstorm sweeping across deeply forested hills, each fold of the hills a masterpiece in itself shown stark against its companion by long trailers of rain, each fold a different shade of purple.

(R. T. Wallen)

What is Admiralty Island? It is the sum of its parts: from the smallest trembling whisker on the inquisitive face of a marten to the glorious alpenglow cast by a dying sun on its highest rock summits; from a nuthatch upside down on a mammoth spruce, 850 years old, to the whispering tide of trees quivering in breezes and shaking in tempestuous gales, flowing over hills and through dells, everlastingly changing in depths of color and mood.

This is Admiralty Island. To strip her of her trees is to strip the Mona Lisa of her paints for the price they will bring. This priceless masterpiece, once destroyed, cannot be recreated. It would become a lingering memory in the minds of those who loved Admiralty Island for its own sake, like the features of a loved one gone before his time. What legacy do we want to give our children?

A little south of the geographic center of the island a sprinkling of lakes is strung like a diamond bracelet connecting east with west through a natural break in the mountainous backbone. These lakes are connected by short, recently rehabilitated trails, making possible a canoe portage across the island from Mole Harbor to Mitchell Bay. Many years ago, the U.S. Forest Service, the administrative agency for the island, built three-sided shelters in strategic spots on almost all of the lakes; most are still in good condition, although their porous roofs dictate careful placement of sleeping bags when rain threatens. Though neither mosquito- nor bearproof, they make pleasant open campsites and give shelter if needed. A smoky fire sometimes helps to keep away mosquitoes, no-see-ums, white socks, and other flying insects; bears can be thwarted by hanging food from a distant tree. (For further notes on bears, see Introduction, page 17.)

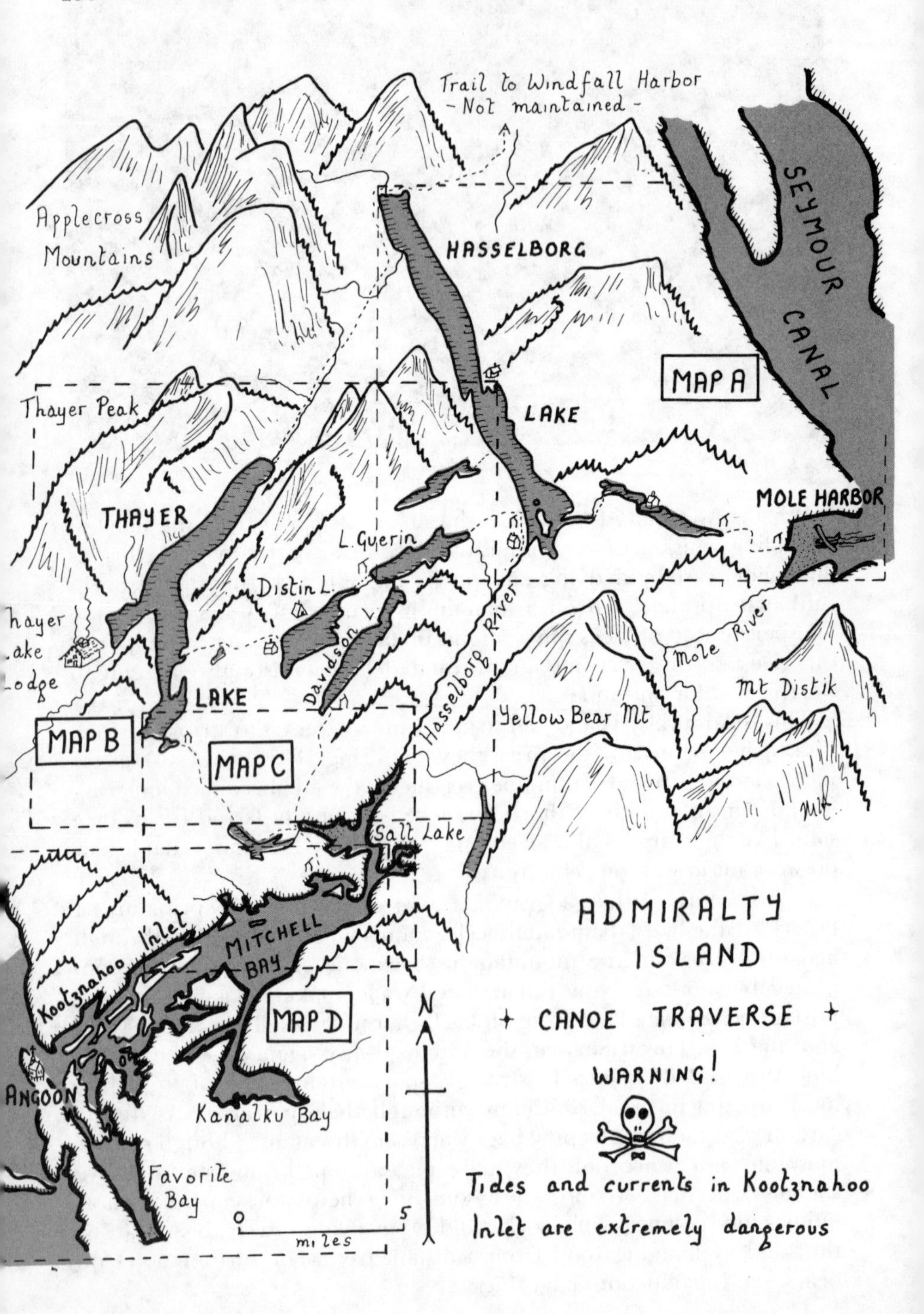

Trail to Windfall Harbor
-Not maintained-
Applecross
Mountains
HASSELBORG
SEYMOUR
CANAL
MAP A
LAKE
Thayer Peak
THAYER
MOLE HARBOR
L. Guerin
Distin L.
Davidson L.
Hasselborg River
Mole River
Mt Distik
hayer
ake
odge
LAKE
Yellow Bear Mt
MAP B
MAP C
Salt Lake
ADMIRALTY
ISLAND
Inlet
MITCHELL
BAY
Kootznahoo
MAP D
N
+ CANOE TRAVERSE +
WARNING!
ANGOON
Kanalku Bay
Favorite
Bay
0
5
miles
Tides and currents in Kootznahoo
Inlet are extremely dangerous

More sophisticated cabins — the closed-door variety, with plywood bunks, cooking and heating stoves, and rowboats — have been built by the Forest Service at many of the lakes. Register for use of these cabins c/o Forest Service, Chatham Ranger District, Box 1049, Juneau, Alaska 99801. (For further information, see Introduction, page 15.) Hasselborg Lake, the largest lake, has three such cabins and one usable shelter; Thayer Lake has two shelters and a lodge built with local materials — and a great deal of imagination!

Boats are available for public use at the cabins and at most trailheads. After use, please return them to the starting point and stow them upside down well above lake level. If not brought out of the lake by late-season users, the boats may be damaged by ice, will fill with rainwater and sink, or be lost when the lake waters rise during the spring runoff. Unfortunately most of the boats are too heavy for one person to handle alone.

The Tlingit village of Angoon lies on Admiralty Island's west coast at the west extremity of the beautiful and breathtaking — but extremely treacherous — waters of Kootznahoo Inlet.

The center of this relatively undisturbed wilderness is about 50 miles south of Juneau and 55 miles northeast of Sitka. Without any side trips, a canoe traverse of Admiralty Island through the Lake district is about 32 miles. It requires a minimum of 6 days for a strong party to do the shortest, though not necessarily the best, route through Davidson Lake to Mitchell Bay. For a leisurely trip and time to explore the larger lakes and Mitchell Bay, a tidal inlet, plan on being out at least 10 days. Only experienced kayakers should attempt the run from Mitchell Bay to Angoon, where even the backwaters south of Kootznahoo Inlet are often turbulent. The northern passage of Kootznahoo Inlet itself should be avoided at all costs. Angoon has no overnight accommodations for visitors, but food may be purchased.

Charter flights are available from Juneau, Sitka, or Petersburg to Admiralty Island. Special arrangements have to be made for non-foldboats. Channel Flying (Juneau), Eagle Air (Sitka), and, less often, Island Air (Petersburg) fly into the Admiralty lake district. Southeast Skyway (Juneau) has the mail run into Angoon and will make request stops at places between.

I have described the crossing of Admiralty Island from east to west, but it can be done either way. Those going through Thayer Lake can use the radiotelephone at Thayer Lake Lodge for emergencies. Bob and Edith Nelson are the builders, owners, and managers of the lodge. Their call letters are KWA 78; R.C.A. marine telephone call times are 9:00 A.M. and 6:00 P.M., between June 1 and mid-September.

Maps needed for the traverse are the 1:63,360 topographic series, Sitka C-1 and C-2. If you are going on to Angoon, Sitka B-2 is also needed. For an overall picture of the area it is helpful to have the smaller-scale 1:250,000 topographic series, Sitka map.

If desired, nautical charts for tidal inlets may be included: Mole Harbor No. 8228 and Kootznahoo No. 8247. If planning to explore tidal inlets, take a Juneau tidetable, which can be obtained in almost any marine sporting goods store in the larger towns.

Note: The bracketed numbers in the text refer to the areas marked by the circled numbers on the maps.

MOLE HARBOR TO LAKE ALEXANDER
(1 day, 2 days optional)

[1] Either land at Mole Harbor, where there is a shelter, and explore the coast with canoes for the first day, or fly directly to Lake Alexander, where there is a Forest Service cabin, and walk the trail to the beach, thus avoiding the first long portage.

The trail west from the beach at Mole Harbor to Lake Alexander is about 2.5 miles long and climbs from sea level to 600 feet. If starting at Mole Harbor, plan to arrive at high tide, because wide mud flats stretch on some lower tides as far as three-quarters of a mile. The tidal flats are alive with small waders: sandpipers, yellowlegs, dowitchers, plovers, etc., bay and sea ducks, and many of the tern-like Bonaparte's gulls. A couple of great blue herons hold court on the mud flats, and brown bears frequent the estuary, especially in July and August when salmon start their pilgrimage up the river.

Part of Mole River and the old Hasselborg homestead are on private land.

About three-quarters of a mile north of Mole River, an old Forest Service sign marks the beginning of the trail to Lake Alexander. A few yards behind the sign is an open shelter. The trail is in fairly good condition but will soon be overgrown if not kept brushed. It climbs steadily uphill for 1.5 miles, first passing through woods, then through stretches of muskeg, and back into trees again. Deep, steep-sided ditches were once crossed by two bridges, now broken; one crossing is a particularly miserable struggle with a canoe. From then on the trail is good and drops gently down to the lake, 349 feet above sea level. Another open shelter stands at the west end of the trail.

If you are going in the opposite direction it may be difficult to find the beginning of the unmarked trail. Go to the most easterly point of Lake Alexander and look for the shelter hidden in trees. It is separated from the lake by tall grass and a windfall. Eastbound, the trail starts from the shelter.

If canoes are to be portaged, allow at least half a day for the trail; otherwise it is only a little over an hour's walk. If two trips are made, first

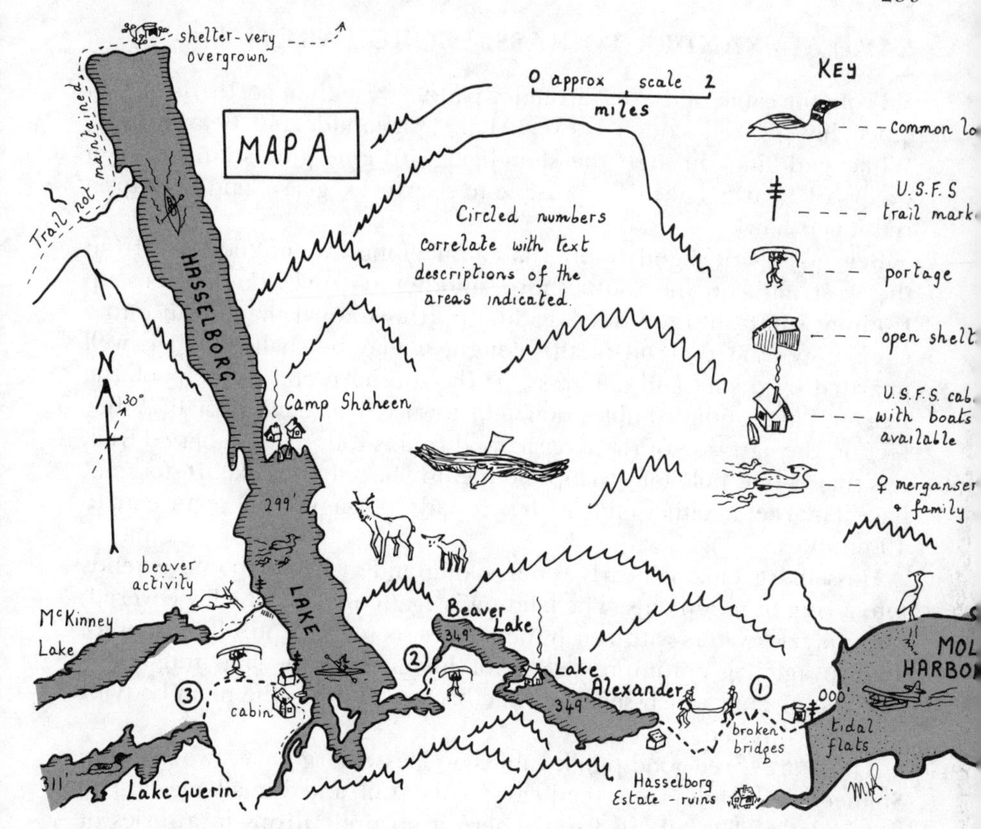

with pack and belongings and then with canoe, the trail mileage is multiplied threefold. If using this method (I found it to be satisfactory) *be sure to leave no food around the canoe* while you are gone, and hang food from a high limb when the pack is left at the far end. Carry food in your pockets; you will be tired and hungry by the time you pick up the canoe or kayak on the second lap.

A 30- to 40-minute paddle is made westward up Lake Alexander before the Forest Service cabin is sighted. It is 1.5 miles from the trailhead on a prominent knoll at the far end of the lake on the northwest side.

Pairs of loons might be seen and heard yodeling across the water. If one is quiet, the chance is good they will investigate a canoe or kayak, sometimes approaching within a few feet. A marten, who considers himself an honorary resident of the cabin, will no doubt be ready for any handout offered.

The total mileage from beach to cabin is 4 miles or 9 miles, depending on the method of portage used. Most parties should allow a full day for a portage this far.

LAKE ALEXANDER TO HASSELBORG LAKE (1 day)

From the cabin on Lake Alexander paddle west, then north, through a quiet, lily-covered slough between Lake Alexander and Beaver Lake. While paddling through the slough, before emerging into the open waters of Beaver Lake, it is possible to see ducks, geese, and perhaps a red-tailed hawk.

Beaver Lake is slightly more than a mile long. About 200 yards from the west end, on the south shore, another narrow slough opens up running south into the trees. Paddle up this toward the entrance to a circular pool at the end of the slough; it may be shallow and is well guarded by rushes and tall grass. At the southern end of the pool, the Beaver Lake outlet tumbles downhill toward Hasselborg Lake. A few feet on the east side of the river a good trail is found. [2] A blazed trail, less than a half mile long, drops 50 feet to Hasselborg Lake. It does not have a marker at either end. With two loads, portaging will require up to 40 minutes.

Hasselborg Lake is nearly 9 miles long and at its north end extends into a ring of mountains. The landing is again one of those lily-covered, tranquil backwaters with which these lakes seem so plentifully endowed. The voyageur is not impressed by the hugeness of the lake until a narrow spit of land which separates the backwater from the main body of the lake is passed.

There are three good public cabins on Hasselborg Lake: two at Camp Shaheen, 4.25 miles from the Beaver Lake trail, and a small one close to the outlet of Hasselborg River where it abruptly drops in a series of rapids at the southwestern end of the lake. This is 1.75 miles and about an hour's paddling time from the trail. Approximately 0.3 mile north of the small cabin the trail to Lake Guerin begins, the next leg of the traverse across the island. It is well marked on the shoreline and is easily spotted from the lake. Back from Hasselborg Lake shore is an open shelter. At the north end of the lake another open shelter is found only after a fight through heavy brush and windfalls. A trail once traversed north around Hasselborg Lake, going from Thayer Lake to Windfall Harbor, but after 30 years of neglect it is practically obliterated.

If you meet anyone they will likely be amazed to see you. Most people fly in from Juneau for a weekend of fishing, and it seldom occurs to them that there is another means of access, despite the fact that Alan Hasselborg, the first person to come here regularly, traveled via the lakes from Mole Harbor in the early 1900s.

If there is time, explore the shore, where an occasional deer and fawn or beaver and otter might be spotted, and paddle into inlets that penetrate the mountains in the northern part.

Morning and evening, red-throated loons shatter the silence with their banshee wails, but they will not permit a close approach as will their cousins, the common loons. Mergansers, sometimes with as many as 11 young in tow, are often seen giving diving lessons in secluded areas of the lake.

From Camp Shaheen, a leisurely paddle to the north end of the lake and return should take half a day. About the same length of time is required for the southern portion.

HASSELBORG LAKE TO DISTIN LAKE (1–2 days)

The trail from Hasselborg Lake to Lake Guerin is about 1.7 miles long and in good condition since it was cleared in the summer of 1971. [3] It is not marked from the Lake Guerin, or west, side, but at the northeast corner of the lake the trailhead is identified by a shed in its death throes.

The trail climbs gently 200–300 feet above the lakes before gradually dropping again to Lake Guerin, 12 feet higher than Hasselborg Lake. It stays within forest most of the time except for one spot. There are two or

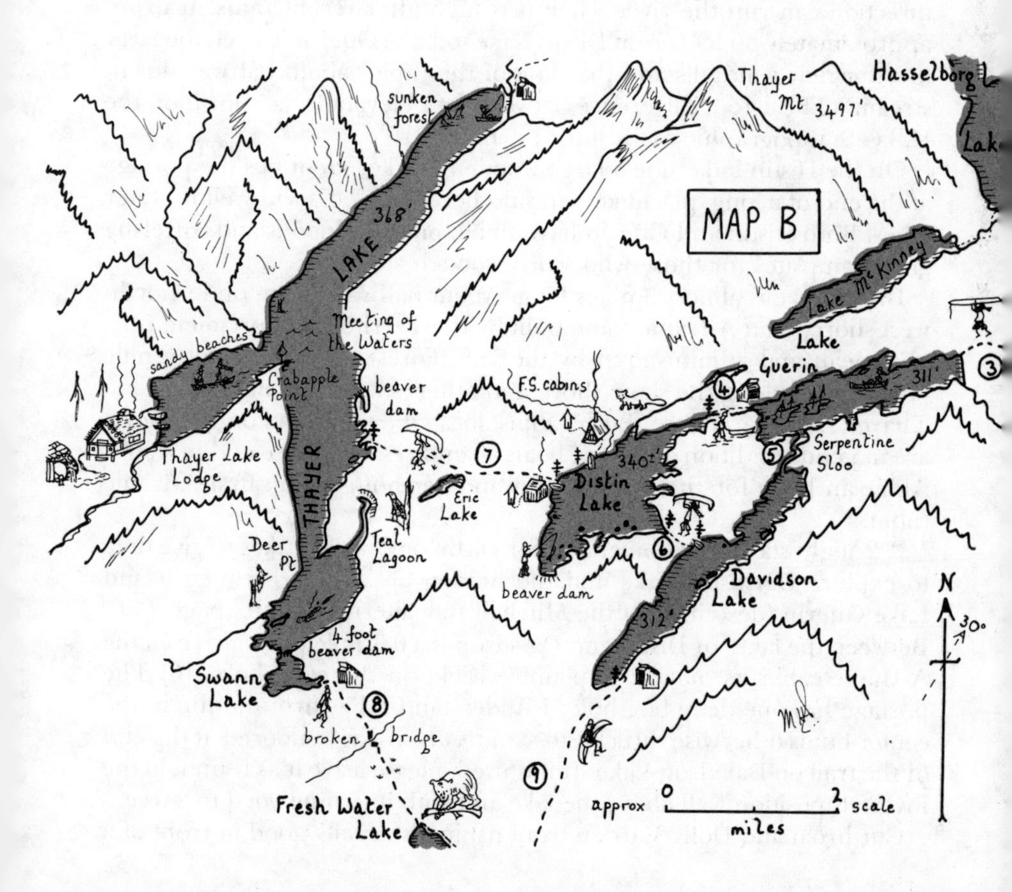

three wet places where skunk cabbage constitutes the undergrowth, and some small stream crossings which are not particularly difficult to portage. The only rough going could be through an inevitable reoccurrence of windfalls. To complete the traverse between the two lakes allow at least 3.5 hours for two portages.

A little over an hour is required to paddle Lake Guerin's 2.5-mile length. On its northwestern corner is an open shelter located close to the stream inflow from Distin Lake. The high alpine ridges of Thayer Mountain overshadow Lake Guerin to the north. To the south, Yellow Bear Mountain, Botany Peak, and Mount Distin take on distinctive shapes, separated from the lake by a collection of deeply forested knolls in the foreground.

A night can be spent in the shelter, which has a pleasant outlook over the lake toward distant mountains, or one may go on to Distin Lake. A short half-mile portage is made over a trail presently in good condition except at one point where the bank has fallen away. [4] The canoe can be towed from about halfway upstream. Those coming in the opposite direction can run the river when it is high after recent rains. It drops approximately 30 feet from Distin Lake to Lake Guerin. Check the river first for new windfalls and the state of the rapids about halfway downstream. (The 1-foot difference between lake elevations as shown on the U.S.G.S. topographic maps must be incorrect!)

On the Distin Lake side a large wooden marker identifies the portage at the end of a long, placid lagoon smothered in places with yellow water lillies. Both Distin and Guerin have small, pine-studded islands offering good campsites for those who scorn wooden shelters.

Distin Lake is almost 3 miles long. About halfway down, on its northwest shore, is an A-frame cabin built by the Territorial Sportsmen, Inc., of Juneau and administered by the U.S. Forest Service. About a mile farther west along the same shore is another, smaller cabin. The trail to Thayer Lake starts here. Both cabins, located by markers on the shore, are in good condition and have boats — and resident mice and martens. Allow an hour for the portage and another hour to the first A-frame cabin.

A 2-night stay is recommended for Distin or Guerin Lakes to give time to explore Davidson Lake and the hidden lily slough between it and Lake Guerin (described in the Mitchell Bay alternate route, page 249). Between the lakes of Distin and Davidson is a 0.3-mile portage; from the A-frame cabin its marker is plainly visible on the east shore. [6] The portage has one deep bog hole; I understand it has firm footing in the center but is otherwise difficult to avoid. A rowboat is moored at the end of the trail on Davidson Lake. If it is used, please leave it as found, in the inverted position well above the lake and with its painter tied to a tree.

Cutthroat and Dolly Varden trout fishing is usually good in front of a beaver dam at the southernmost point of Distin Lake, as well as in a small lake, locally called Eric Lake, on the trail to Thayer Lake.

DISTIN LAKE TO THAYER LAKE (1 day, 2 days optional)

The trail to Thayer Lake is 3.2 miles long, and extremely beautiful. The U.S.G.S. topographic maps show the trail incorrectly. It travels west-northwest and climbs to no more than 300 feet above Distin and Thayer Lakes, or 600 feet above sea level. [7] Recently it was cleared and marked, but it is boggy in places with many deep holes which are difficult to avoid. The trail winds through old-growth forest, past skunk cabbage patches, across one or two small streams, and through muskeg meadows, white with the narrow-leafed cotton grass, or bog cotton, as summer wanes.

The trail starts from the more southerly of the two cabins on Distin Lake. It climbs gently at first but later loses height many times through small hollows and swales; consequently the overall elevation gain is minimal. After approximately 2 miles it passes the end of a long, small lake (Eric Lake) half hidden in trees. Next the path traverses the hillside and gently drops to Thayer Lake. If doing two portages, estimate 5–6 hours between the two lakes. Since the trail was last cleared a couple of windfalls have occurred; expect more. At the Thayer Lake end of the trail there are no shelters, but the trail is marked by a diamond-shaped marker on the shore.

Thayer Lake has three radiating arms: a 3.6-mile north arm northeast; another 3.6-mile arm running south to a beaver dam and Swann Lake; and a 1.8-mile west arm extending southwest. The trail ends a third of the way down on the east side of the south arm.

Two open shelters are situated on the extremities of the south and north arms. Access to the south shelter is over a 4-foot beaver dam into the southern toe of Thayer Lake, known locally as Swann Lake. (The shelter is at the start of a trail to Fresh Water Lake, the next leg in the journey to Mitchell Bay.) Thayer Lake Lodge stands at the head of the west arm. Paddling time from the trailhead to either shelter is approximately 1.5–2 hours; to the lodge, about 1 hour.

There are abundant camping spots along the shore of the south arm of Thayer Lake, which has sandy beaches and tall lodgepole pines growing along its edge. Shallow spots have been marked with homemade buoys, but keep careful watch for snags in the water. Some snags are seeded with lichens, mosses, tall grass, ferns, and small flowers, and look like miniature gardens, often reflected in the dark lake waters. Some are used by nesting mew gulls to escape land predators. So many trees have sunk to the bottom of the lake as deadfalls that they resemble a sunken forest, especially in the north arm. Late in the year many logs

Thayer Lake Lodge

and upright trees in the woods are splashed with orange and sulphur-colored bracket fungi.

The northern end of the lake penetrates the Applecross Mountains (marked on the Admiralty Island area map), especially attractive when reflected in the clear, unruffled waters of the lake on windless days. The southern arm emerges from the mountains and has a variety of placid lagoons and secluded backwaters, sandy beaches, and a riot of shoreline flowers in August. Monkshood, dogwood, swamp gentian, fringed Grass of Parnassus, and fleabane are all fairly common. The west arm has similar attractions, with the Thayer River, the lake's main outflow, a quarter of a mile south of the lodge. On stormy days a rough spot will be encountered just off Crabapple Point, where the three arms meet and the waters churn violently.

Good lake fishing is to be found close to rivers and streams. Pan-size cutthroat and Dolly Varden trout are abundant.

THAYER LAKE TO MITCHELL BAY (1–2 days)

Paddle to the far end of the south arm of Thayer Lake and follow the south shore until a beaver dam is sighted behind a deadhead (a fallen log in the water). Go behind the log and beach the canoe on the left bank (it is a little easier to climb the dam on this side). Once over the dam, paddle along the eastern shoreline of Swann Lake until the open shelter is in view. Pond lillies bar the way, then tall grass, but a channel with a sharp right bend should be found shortly before reaching the bank. Do not get out prematurely; the water is deeper than it looks despite the grass. A fairly obvious path can be followed through boggy ground to the shelter. One watery hole is deep and wide but can be jumped if nothing awkward is carried. Good luck!

The shelter has a rudely constructed bunk made by the Nelsons many years ago when they were reconnoitering Thayer Lake as a possible site for a lodge. [8] The shelter is in poor condition, and I cannot vouch for the waterproof quality of the roof.

The well-marked trail takes off immediately behind the shelter, east for the first few yards, then generally southeast. Although recently rehabilitated, it is wet and boggy in patches. It is 2.8 miles to Fresh Water Lake, with a few short hills, mostly near the start. It loses almost 400 feet elevation to 20 feet above sea level. Allow 4–5 hours for a double portage, 2–3 hours for a single portage.

The trail is wet for the first few hundred yards, then climbs a short hill which is steep for canoe carrying. It wanders downhill and crosses two small stream systems, the second one an awkward gully badly in need of bridge repair. The trail is pleasant as it meanders through old-growth forest to emerge into a couple of small muskeg meadows. The route is marked, but not too clearly for those with canoes or kayaks balanced on head or shoulders. Be sure the next marker can be seen before commit-

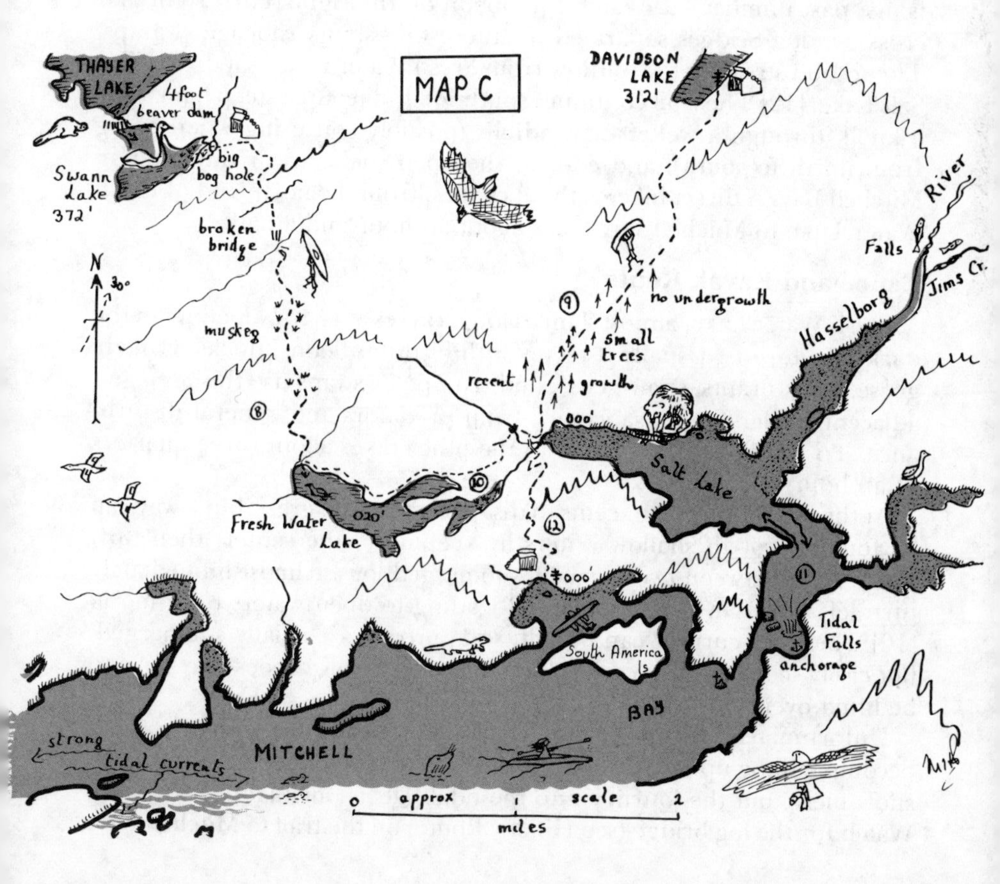

ting yourself to a long march into the unknown! Shortly before reaching the lake the path drops sharply to a stream, which is crossed before it drains into Fresh Water Lake. If the portage takes longer than expected, camp can be made on level ground by the lakeside and close to the stream. Other alternatives are discussed later.

Hikers' Route

Although it is not too well marked at first, the trail continues along the northeast side of Fresh Water Lake to within 100 yards of the tidal flats. It is 2.2 miles to the junction of the Lake Davidson trail; this is not signposted and can be confusing.

[10] Before reaching the junction the trail follows the north arm of Fresh Water Lake through pleasant woods before plunging into thick summer growth to make a sharp right turn onto a log. Another log crosses a cascading stream, and before reaching the junction the trail continues for 0.2 mile through more summer growth. Each tenth of a mile is numbered on red tree blazes from Thayer Lake, and the junction is just past number 49. Watch for ribbon on the right. Turn right and cross two log bridges separated by interesting skunk cabbage swamps. The second stream is the outflow from Fresh Water Lake as it drains into Salt Lake. [12] The trail continues south for 1 mile, up a steep bank over a knoll, through a welter of windfalls (possibly confusing when going from north to south), and ends at the open shelter near tidewater in Mitchell Bay. A direct hike, without canoes, from the north end of Fresh Water Lake to Mitchell Bay takes about an hour and a half.

Canoe and Kayak Route

Fresh Water Lake, almost 2 miles long, carves a narrow opening in the dark rain forests. Usually it teems with birdlife. Loons, ducks, Canada geese, black brants, snow geese, and trumpeter swans use this area and adjacent tidelands as a sanctuary from predators and general disturbance. To paddle from one end to the other takes about three-quarters of an hour.

At the far end the lake seems to disappear into tall grass, but a way can be found through shallow waters by keeping to the center; then turn sharp right between two partially submerged logs. Almost immediately turn left down an obvious channel leading to open waters once more. [10] The river current can be felt, so approach a partially submerged, but easily seen, log with care. When the water is low canoes may have to be lifted over.

Unfortunately the river is too shallow for clear runs without canoes becoming hung up on gravel bars (except after prolonged rain or during snow melt), but the journey into the tidal flats is only about 200 yards. Watch for the log bridge (see Hikers' Route) on the trail to Mitchell Bay;

Mitchell Bay

approach it cautiously since headroom between the stream and the bridge is no more than 12 or 18 inches. (I walked my kayak through both ways.)

MITCHELL BAY

The trip from Thayer Lake to Mitchell Bay will take 2 days for most parties with canoes (allowing time for exploration of the Hasselborg River to the falls a few hundred yards above Jims Creek). At least 5 extra hours are necessary to paddle from the head of Fresh Water Lake, through Salt Lake, and over The Falls (tidal) into Mitchell Bay to the shelter. Timing is dependent on tides (see below). Either leave the canoes at the bridge and backpack with overnight gear on the trail to Mitchell Bay, bringing the canoes over the next day, or camp at Salt Lake. Good spots are found along Hasselborg River, where encounters with bears should be anticipated during the salmon runs in August and September. Or camp directly above The Falls flowing into Mitchell Bay. If canoes are left overnight, *leave no food* close to them and be sure *no fishy odor* remains on them. Nothing attracts bears faster than fish, and they can make short work of a canoe or kayak.

The river into Salt Lake is shallow when the tide is low. Canoes have to be towed, sometimes through soft mud. Once in Salt Lake the effort is worth it — things start opening up after the narrow confines of the forest. Straight ahead the graceful form of Yellow Bear Mountain dominates the horizon; overhead skeins of ducks and geese may be seen in spring and fall.

The distance between the tidal flats and The Falls is about 2.5 miles; paddling time is about an hour, depending on tides, etc. Mitchell Bay tides are quoted at 1 hour and 25 minutes after the Juneau tides in the district correctional table, but those in Salt Lake above The Falls may be from 15 to 30 minutes later than in Mitchell Bay. This is guesswork, as a 15-minute time lag between Mitchell Bay high tide and high slack at The Falls was noted when the waterfalls disappeared for a brief period.

On an outgoing tide The Falls may be run by kayak, but study them first as they change in depth and speed from one stage of the tide to the next. If desired, canoes can be lined or portaged along the east bank of The Falls or through one of a couple of alternate channels west of The Falls. [11] The outgoing tide will carry the canoeist from here into Mitchell Bay. The north shore can be followed around Kluchman Rock, the site of a cross that commemorates the drowning of two members of an Angoon family. A passage then runs behind South America Island into a sheltered bay. Both a shelter (with a leaky roof) and a trail marker are visible from the water. The shelter is attractively located within the secluded bay.

Mitchell Bay is a large, landlocked body of water with interesting sandstone formations, narrow tidal lagoons, and a variety of bird- and

Fallen tree and reflections, Lake Guerin

sealife. Do not attempt to go into the deep and narrow northern part of Kootznahoo Inlet. Beyond Hemlock Point (marked on the U.S.G.S. topographical map) it acts like a vacuum cleaner on an outgoing tide, sucking anything that floats into the narrows. Between high and low slack water this is a seething cauldron of white water with waterfalls and whirlpools; even powerboats stay away during these periods.

West to East Route

Arrange to take canoes into Salt Lake on an incoming tide. If headed to Thayer Lake after paddling to the westernmost point of the tidal flats, take the left river fork, upstream, and go under the bridge to Fresh Water Lake. If headed for Davidson Lake, take the right fork and start portaging boats from the right bank before the bridge is reached. Turn right for the Davidson Lake trail going north then northeast; it soon starts to climb.

LAKE GUERIN TO MITCHELL BAY

(shorter alternative; 1–2 days)

If time is limited, the route from Lake Guerin bypassing Thayer and Distin Lakes through Davidson Lake, to Mitchell Bay, is shorter. This route lacks much of the interest and beauty of the trails to Thayer Lake, but it is a useful shortcut.

Follow the southern shore of Lake Guerin for 2 miles to a narrow inlet stretching south. [5] It is not easy to see and seems to disappear in long grass and encroaching trees. This is due to a sharp turn to the right, then left, that adds to its charm. Canoes probably will have to be lifted over a shallow gravel bar about a foot high and against a gentle current. (Contrary to the same heights shown on the topographic maps for both lakes, this would indicate that Davidson Lake is a foot higher than Lake Guerin.) These Serpentine Narrows, choked with yellow water lillies and attracting many species of waterfowl, open into Davidson Lake, creating a narrow wedge in the deeply forested countryside.

Davidson Lake is 3.6 miles long; at its south end is a shelter. A rowboat and Forest Service marker for a short portage to Distin Lake are located roughly halfway down on the northwest shore. (See Hasselborg Lake to Distin Lake, page 241.)

From the shelter at the south end a 3.4-mile trail climbs over the end of a 500-foot ridge (rising 200 feet above Davidson Lake), then drops gently to tidewater at Salt Lake in the upper end of Mitchell Bay. [9] It was recently cleared and marked and is currently in good condition. For part of the way the forest is somber and almost sullen, lacking undergrowth, life, and the sparkle found in the virgin forests of the other trails.

About halfway, the trail runs through an open patch of small trees no taller than 12 feet, then enters into what is apparently second-growth forest composed of slender trees tossed around by williwaws into huge mounds of fallen timber. Records show that in the late 1880s part of the forest in the vicinity of Salt Lake was burned after a fire started at a Tlingit fish camp near the mouth of the Hasselborg River. In places the havoc is so great the trail has had to be rerouted.

Slightly over 3 miles from Davidson Lake the trail descends into a valley containing a rapid stream. Canoes can be launched immediately, since about 50 yards downstream it joins the river flowing from Fresh Water Lake to Salt Lake.

Hikers should keep a sharp lookout for the Mitchell Bay trail (generally marked with ribbon) that branches to the left (southeast) as soon as the stream is reached. (If the turn is missed it is possible to end up at Thayer Lake 5 miles farther north!) Almost immediately this trail crosses two bridges, over the stream and river outflows from Fresh Water Lake. (For further details on this area, hikers see Thayer Lake to Mitchell Bay, page 246, and canoeists refer to Mitchell Bay, page 247.)

Allow 3–4 hours for the portage to Salt Lake or 5–6 hours for two portages.

MITCHELL BAY TO ANGOON
(experienced kayakers only; 1 day)

Parties toughened to wilderness travel and skilled in handling a kayak may want to go on to the Tlingit Indian village of Angoon. Arrange to arrive there on the day of the flight pickup or be prepared to camp close by; overnight accommodations are not available in the village. Flights can be arranged by telephone from Angoon or from the Southeast Skyways office a mile southeast of town. Extra groceries can be purchased in the local village store.

Do not attempt Kootznahoo Inlet, the long northwestern narrows reaching into Stillwater Anchorage (a misnomer!); these narrows allow too little time during slack water to run through safely. Even large powerboats avoid this channel during ebb or flood tides.

On an *incoming tide* a confused web of back passages can be negotiated, east to west, until one becomes temporarily "locked" inside an unnamed bay 1.5 miles east of Angoon. (All current directions are reversed on the outgoing tide.) Every outlet is barred by tidal falls or rapids until the tide turns. One then has 30–40 minutes of manageable waters, between slack water and a strong rip, to reach Angoon or Favorite Bay 2 miles south. Do not tarry too long, since slack lasts only a few minutes and currents are strong and treacherous once they start. Small waterfalls occur

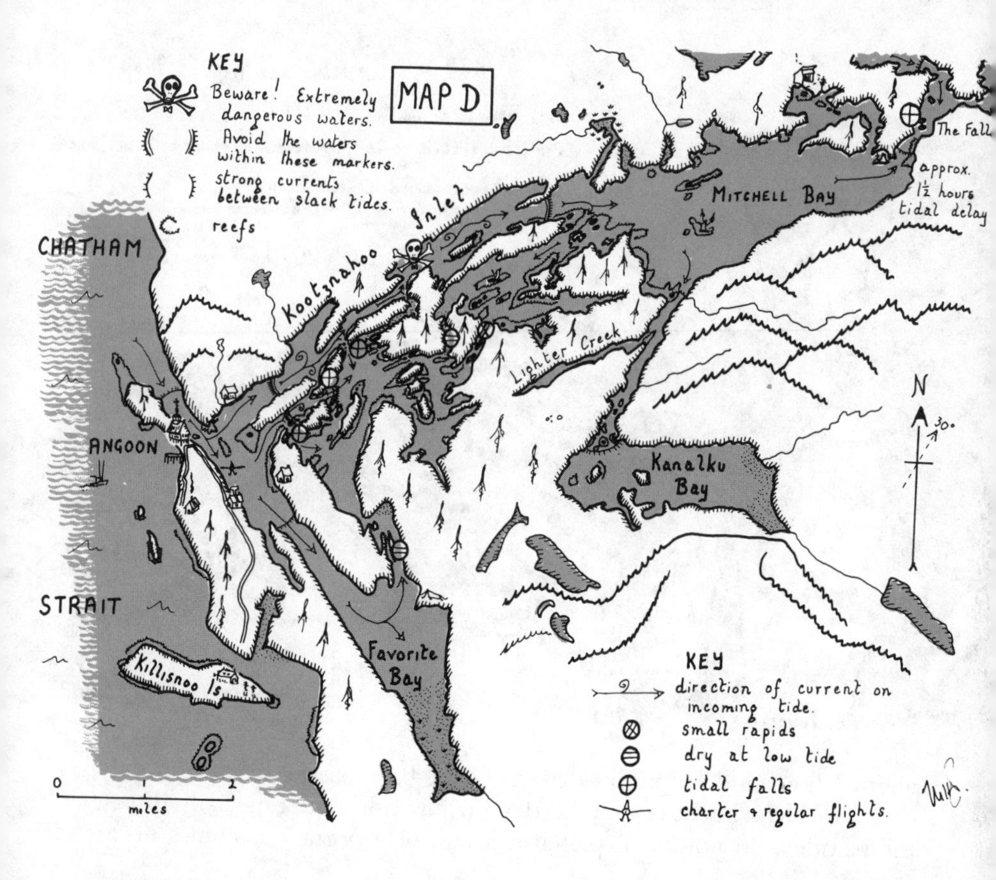

around the reefs east of the village, and a nun (unlighted buoy) anchored on the edge of the channel is sucked under water when the current regains strength.

Yet, for those wise in the ways of the wilderness and expert with a kayak, this is a journey not to be missed. Landlocked tidal bays and quiet backwaters, liberally sprinkled with forested islands and tidal rocks, open up in all directions. Bald eagles come low and flap leisurely through the trees; gulls and terns form a wild, screaming mob over the reefs and rock islets. Some of the tidal passages are so narrow they cannot be seen until one is in them, the trees almost touching overhead. Most fascinating of all, these placid lagoons are separated from the main channel by islands, and at the openings white water spills out as tidal falls or rapids. Despite the closeness to town, these backwaters are rarely, if ever, visited because they are accessible only during high and low slack. Map and compass are essential since one can become lost long enough to miss the tide to Angoon. Camping should be possible above the beach on the islands.

Use the Juneau tidetables and the correctional tables for Mitchell Bay. The tidal delay in the final backwater bay 1.5 miles east of Angoon is

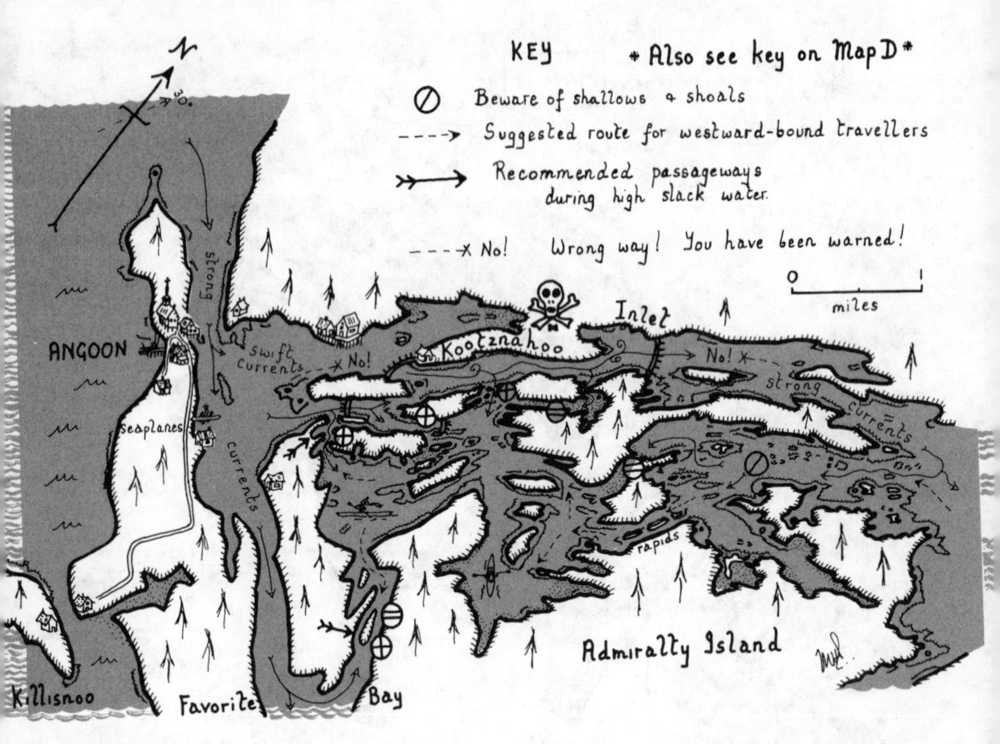

about 1 hour and 15 minutes. Many of the back passages (including the one into Favorite Bay) may be dry on low tide and especially during minus tides; do not be surprised if a wait or a portage becomes necessary.

Not allowing for distractions en route, the run from the east end of Mitchell Bay to Angoon or Favorite Bay takes about 4 hours, but to be sure of catching the tides start at least 4 hours before high slack. The total distance is about 10 miles.

Paddle west across Mitchell Bay (about an hour) and enter the tidal channel east of South Point (marked on the U.S.G.S. topographical map), going southwest. If the tide is incoming, its current will flow in the same direction (i.e., southwest) toward the inner bays south of Kootznahoo Inlet. Beware of rocky shallows. Proceed south, then take the western passage of a double channel going southwest. The passages are separated from each other by thin islands and reefs (marked "rapids" on the enlarged Angoon map, this page). Expect shallows and minor rapids through both passages. A way can then be threaded through the islands southwest then northwest to a backwater bay 2.5 miles northeast of Angoon; the bay is separated from Kootznahoo Inlet by islands and two tidal falls and rapids, one to the northwest and the larger on the southwest corner (each marked with a ⊕ on both maps).

Continue southwest into a larger, enclosed, hidden bay (marked on the enlarged Angoon map by an enthusiastic female paddler heading west-southwest) by threading through small islands once more. Then either paddle on south to Favorite Bay or find a tiny passage at the western end of the bay where it opens into the main channel behind Channel Point. These routes can only be used for escape at high slack when white waters have been transformed into a deceptive calm, a calm lasting only a few minutes before the tide turns.

Watch for seals and sea lions in the kelp on the way over to Angoon. Ravens use Village Rock, north of the small inner harbor, as their soapbox. Their curses and catcalls can be heard from the center of town. Good camping spots will be found in Favorite Bay, especially on the northwest shore.

Distance Mole Harbor to Mitchell Bay, about 32 miles
Time 6- 10-day traverse
Trail condition good
Terrain unspoiled rain forests, lakes encircled by mountains, tidal bays
Access by floatplane or charter boat from Juneau, Petersburg, or Sitka, 50–60 miles distant
Facilities: U.S. Forest Service cabins and shelters on most lakes

Angoon

ADDENDUM: SOME ADDITIONAL TRAILS

KETCHIKAN: REVILLAGIGEDO ISLAND

Information on trails marked with * included courtesy of Forest Service, South Tongass National Forest.

Naha

Eighteen air miles north of Ketchikan. Access by floatplane or boat. Trail is 6.3 miles from Naha Bay to Heckman Lake, and is boardwalk for the first 2 miles. Good steelhead fishing and Forest Service cabins are available on Naha River, Jordon and Heckman Lakes.

Tritan Trek (apply to SEAMA for further details)

1. Blue Lake to White River. For access, see K1 and K2. No trail; route is about 10 miles long, alpine in character. Overnight equipment needed. The route extends along the ridge north of Blue Lake, over John Mountain, to White River on George Inlet. Terrain is wild and unspoiled and views are superb.
2. White River to Harriet Hunt Lake. Foot access from Ketchikan, or boat access to an anchorage 8 miles north of Beaver Falls, to the east end of trail. Forest Highway 39 from Ward Cove and Ward Lake (see K4) affords car access to Harriet Hunt Lake at the west end of trail. The terrain is mainly muskeg, or bog, with minor changes in elevation. Poor trail, requiring corduroy for much of its length, 3 miles long.
3. Harriet Hunt Lake to Lunch Creek. Starts 16 road miles north of Ketchikan at Harriet Hunt Lake, and ends at Lunch Creek, 20 road miles north of Ketchikan. No trail; route 8 miles long, marked by SEAMA, takes one over alpine ridges 2500+ feet high, westward to Lunch Creek and Settler's Cove at the end of the North Tongass Highway. Good alpine camping and open views of Clarence Strait, surrounding islands, and mainland.

Mahoney Mountain

Access by a service road above Beaver Falls (see K3). Go along lower road around the shores of Lower Silvis Lake to end of road. Climb the wooded ridge on the northwest side of the damaged powerhouse. May find a tagged route. Alpine in character, it connects with the Blue Lake to White River section of Tritan Trek. Camping spots may be found in Upper Mahoney Basin within unspoiled alpine setting.

Mahoney Creek trail*

From George Inlet to Mahoney Lake, 0.5 miles; entrance to trail marked with a beach trail marker. Salmon fishing in the stream is prohibited; fishing is permitted in Mahoney Lake. Access to trail is by boat 5 miles north of Beaver Falls. Trail is in poor condition.

Talbot Lake trail (Ward Creek trail)

Access by road past Ward Lake (see K4) to Connell Lake Dam. Trail, almost 4 miles long, goes north and meets the road to Harriet Hunt Lake. The trail is in good condition, has little elevation change. A three-sided shelter is located on the northeast shore of Talbot Lake about halfway in.

Gokachin Lakes canoe trail*

Twenty air miles east-northeast of Ketchikan at the head of Thorne Arm. Round trip is 13 miles from Fish Creek to Gokachin Lakes to Big Lake and return to Thorne Arm. Three-mile portage to Mesa Lake, first 2.5 miles along established trail with natural but fair tread; well brushed. Last 0.5 mile needs marking and brushing along the creek to Mesa Lake. In Mesa Lake follow the west shore to the outlet of Gokachin Lakes; portage the outlet on the east side. In Gokachin Lake, follow to the northernmost inlet (outlet from unnamed lake); portage the outlet on the northeast side. Paddle to a creek at the south end of the unnamed lake and from here portage through the saddle to Basin Lake, 0.75 mile southwest of the unnamed lake, following the east shore of the creek in muskeg much of the time. Cross Basin Lake to the north of the northernmost island and begin to portage from the north bank of the outlet (there are two outlets from Basin Lake; the portage outlet is not shown on the 1949 U.S. Geological Survey map). Go west through muskeg to Big Lake, then paddle to its outlet. Portage the Low Lake trail for the return to Thorne Arm, about 2.1 miles. Low Lake trail is partially boardwalk and is well brushed. A Forest Service cabin is available at Low Lake, 0.6 mile from Thorne Arm. Allow 5–6 days for the complete trip.

Wolf Lake trail*

Sixteen air miles north of Ketchikan. Access by floatplane or boat. Trail begins in Moser Bay and is 2.6 miles long. Poor trail, possibly hard to follow, ends at a three-sided CCC shelter at the outlet of Wolf Lake.

Long Lake trail*

Forty-two air miles north of Ketchikan; trail starts from south shore of Behm Narrows (North Behm Canal) south of Bell Island. Access is by floatplane or boat. Trail needs improvement and some portions are difficult to locate. It ends 1.3 miles from tidewater at a three-sided CCC shelter on the west side of Long Lake.

Grace Lake trail*

Thirty-six air miles northeast of Ketchikan. Trail is 2.3 miles long, starting from the west shore of East Behm Canal, and is in poor condition. Access is by floatplane or boat.

Manzanita Lake trail*

Trail starts from Manzanita Bay, 5 miles south of Grace Lake trail, runs 3 miles southwest to Manzanita Lake; it is in very poor condition. Access by floatplane or boat.

Ella Lake trail*

Trail, 2.8 miles long from tidewater to Ella Lake, starts from Ella Bay, 7 miles south of Manzanita Bay. It has been brushed but may be difficult to locate through muskeg areas. Soda springs in Ella Bay are ringed with CCC concrete foundations. Access by floatplane or boat.

KETCHIKAN: NORTH BEHM CANAL (mainland)

Bell Island

Forty-three air miles, 50 nautical miles north of Ketchikan. Access by floatplane or boat to Bell Island hot springs and resort. A good trail, partly boardwalk, goes 1 mile through forest to lower Bell Lake. Saltwater fishing is excellent.

Short Bay*

Six air miles, 10 nautical miles north of Bell Island hot springs. Trail, which runs 1.9 miles from Short Bay to Reflection Lake, is brushed to Reflection Lake cabin 0.5 mile from the lake outflow.

Yes Bay*

Eight air miles, 10 nautical miles west-southwest of Bell Island hot springs. A primitive trail heavily used by Yes Bay Lodge visitors extends 1.5 miles from Yes Bay, up Wolverine Creek, to Lake McDonald. A Forest Service cabin is available at the lake.

Bailey Bay

Five nautical miles north-northwest of Bell Island hot springs. The 2.3-mile trail starts from the west shore of Bailey Bay and wends a muddy course to Shelokum Hot Springs on Lake Shelokum. Trail badly needs restoration; the boardwalk at the far end is disintegrating and is dangerous, and the trail itself, which was used by the early settlers, is in poor condition. The collapsed three-sided CCC shelter at the hot springs needs rebuilding.

KETCHIKAN: EAST BEHM CANAL (mainland)

Rudyerd Bay and Walker Cove are within a U.S. Forest Service Granite Fjords Wilderness Proposal. A much larger Misty Fjords joint wilderness proposal of Tongass Conservation Society and SEAMA includes magnificent, unspoiled fjord country bounded by the Leduc River drainage in the north and Boca de Quadra to the south. The latter proposal also includes protection from logging and other unsightly developments on the west shore of East Behm Canal.

Nooya Lake

Forty-two air miles, 63 nautical miles east-northeast of Ketchikan. Trail begins on the west bank of the Nooya Lake outlet and penetrates deep forest to the lake, 1 mile from Rudyerd Bay west shoreline. The trail is brushed and ascends gradually at first then steeply to the lake, 700 feet above sea level. Typical of the general area, Nooya Lake scenery is vertical, the lake enclosed within granite walls of wild splendor. Fishing is good in the lake; a three-sided CCC shelter stands near the lake outlet.

Punchbowl Lake trail

Thirty-six air miles, 59 nautical miles east-northeast of Ketchikan. The trail leaves from Punchbowl Cove close to the entrance of Rudyerd Bay and goes 1.5 miles from the southern end of the cove to Punchbowl Lake. An extensive slide obliterates about 100 feet of trail; the Forest Service does not presently plan to repair this section because of cost. The vertical sweep of granite walls from tidewater and Punchbowl Lake to 4000 feet is breathtaking; the lake offers camping in a superb setting.

Checats Cove trail*

Five nautical miles south of the entrance into Rudyerd Bay. The trail travels 1.1 miles from tidewater to Lower Checats Lake, is in good condition, and follow the outlet to the lake. Prime use is fishing.

Winstanley Creek trail*

Eleven nautical miles south of the entrance into Rudyerd Bay. Trail starts from tidewater behind Winstanley Island on the east shore of East Behm Canal and follows Winstanley Creek 2.3 miles to Winstanley Lake. Trail is fairly easy to locate through muskeg and scrub and has been brushed. It gives access to fishing in Winstanley Lake and to a three-sided CCC shelter by the lake outflow.

Bakewell Arm trail*

Forty air miles, 47 nautical miles east of Ketchikan. The 1.3-mile trail leaves the southern shore of Bakewell Arm within Smeaton Bay, and follows an old road for the first 0.5 mile, then traverses muskeg and scrub to a cabin by Bakewell Arm Lake. Native log bridges are used for stream crossings and should be traversed only by experienced hikers; trail may be difficult to follow in places.

KETCHIKAN: BOCA DE QUADRA

Boca de Quadra is suggested for kayak or canoe exploration; minimum length of time, 6 days.

Hugh Smith Lake trail*

Forty-one air miles, 46 nautical miles east-southeast of Ketchikan. Situated almost halfway in Boca de Quadra, between Marten Arm and Mink Bay, Hugh Smith Lake lies within 0.25 mile of the beach. The trail is brushed but has mud holes; its main use is access for fishermen. A Forest Service skiff is provided at the trail terminus on Hugh Smith Lake; visitors are requested to return the skiff to the trail terminus. There is a cabin 2.5 miles up the lake on the south shore. Those canoeing within Boca de Quadra may be interested in portaging the trail.

Humpback Creek trail*

Five miles south of Hugh Smith Lake trail, at the southeastern extremity of Mink Bay, a 3-mile trail follows Humpback Creek to Humpback Lake and a three-sided CCC shelter. The trail follows the creek for about 1.5 miles before climbing a steep ridge for 0.5 mile; it traverses muskeg and beaver sloughs with wet footing. Trail is brushed and provides access for fishermen.

KETCHIKAN: PRINCE OF WALES ISLAND

Karta River

Forty air miles, 42 nautical miles west-northwest of Ketchikan. Trail starts from tidewater in Karta Bay at the head of Kasaan Bay, east coast of Prince of Wales Island. It is 6.6 miles to the Forest Service cabin at the west end of Salmon Lake and 3.1 miles to the Forest Service cabin on Karta Lake. A similar cabin is located close to tidewater at the trailhead. The trail is in good condition with boardwalk and some corduroy; the Karta River affords some of the finest steelhead fishing in the United States. Karta River drainage is within a 50-year pulp sale to Ketchikan Pulp Company. Already there is danger of logging within the watershed; some beach logging has taken place. Proposed for protection from logging by Tongass Conservation Society.

Kegan Lake

Thirty air miles, 33 nautical miles southwest of Ketchikan; trail is located within Moira Sound and travels from the north shoreline up Kegan Creek to Kegan Lake, 0.5 mile. Forest Service cabins are available at both ends of trail, which is in good condition with boardwalk in sections. Good fishing. A skiff is available on Kegan Lake for cabin users. Moira Sound and Kegan Lake are recommended for canoe wilderness travel. Kegan Lake and Mount Eudora are within a Tongass Conservation Society wilderness proposal.

Totem Park*

Thirty-four air miles, 36 nautical miles west-northwest of Ketchikan on west shoreline of Kasaan Peninsula. Trail starts from village of Kasaan and goes 0.8 mile to the totem park over flat ground; partly gravel or earth tread or boardwalk. Access is to totem poles; the land is subject to Native Land Claims Selection.

Honker Divide canoe portage

Seventy air miles northwest of Ketchikan to Sweetwater Lake on the east coast, northern section of Prince of Wales Island. The southern terminus is Thorne Bay, 44 air miles northwest of Ketchikan. Route length is about 34 miles. There are two cabins at the northern end, at Barnes Lake and Sweetwater Lake, and another on the east shore of Lake Galea. The route starts with a portage from Sweetwater Lake up Hatchery Creek to Hatchery Lake (no trail), and thence by canoe to Lake Galea. A 1.25-mile portage over a brushed trail with puncheon in the wet areas traverses a low watershed to the Thorne River drainage. Difficulties with beaver dams may be encountered in Thorne Lake and an unnamed lake, then log jams, falls, and rocks on Thorne River downstream. Trail ends close to the Thorne Bay logging camp. Many days are needed for the portage. The area is within a 50-year timber sale to Ketchikan Pulp Company. These superb low-level virgin forest lands are in danger of logging within a quarter of a mile of the lakes; a Forest Service logging road is planned to cross Hatchery Creek. The entire drainage is recommended as a canoe wilderness area by Tongass Conservation Society.

Sunnahee Mountain trail*

Fifty-eight air miles west of Ketchikan on the west coast of Prince of Wales Island. Commercial amphibious airlines connect Ketchikan with Craig and Klawock. The trail begins 1 mile north of Craig on the Craig-Klawock road and is 5 miles long to the summit of Sunnahee Mountain and a Forest Service cabin on Table Mountain. Trail is fair; difficult to find on higher slopes. Area subject to Native Land Claims Selection.

WRANGELL

Pat's Creek

Eleven road miles south of Wrangell. Quarter to a half-mile of good trail from campgrounds to Pat's Lake. Area spoiled by logging road and logging.

SITKA

Mount Edgecumbe

Trail starts on eastern shoreline of Kruzof Island 10 miles west of Sitka. Access by small boat or plane. Anchorage by Freds Creek not recommended; landings limited by weather and prevailing winds. Trail to summit of Mount Edgecumbe is fair to good. Cabins available. Overnight stay recommended.

Silver Bay to Redoubt Lake

Ten miles southeast of Sitka to trail beginning at southern extremity of Silver Bay. Access by boat or plane. Cabin available on Redoubt Lake. Canoes can be portaged from Redoubt Bay into Redoubt Lake; there is a trail between Goddard Hot Springs and Redoubt Lake. None but the most experienced kayaker should attempt to round Cape Burunof from Sitka without help. From Goddard Hot Springs south, kayakers will find mostly sheltered waters to Crawfish Inlet.

ADMIRALTY ISLAND (Juneau vicinity)

Admiralty Cove

Ten air miles, 20 sea miles west of Juneau on the east shoreline of Admiralty Island, east end of Young Bay. Access by boat or plane. Trail runs 4 miles to Young Lake, which is close to beautiful alpine peaks. Cabins available.

Oliver Inlet Tram

Thirteen air miles south of Juneau, north end of Glass Peninsula. Access by boat or plane. Cabin available. A short and useful portage between Oliver Inlet and Seymour Canal.

Windfall Harbor to Hasselborg Lake and Thayer Lake

See Admiralty Island Canoe Traverse, page 234. Trail badly in need of rehabilitation.

JUNEAU

Salmon Creek

Access by bus, bicycle, or car, 2.8 miles north of Juneau. Trail goes up old tramway to a dam 3 miles from road. Considered dangerous by the State because of rotten trestles. Trail requires repair or relocation.

Echo Cove

For access see J19. Formerly the Yankee Basin trail, continues through to Echo Cove. About 11 miles long.

Bessie Creek

About 34 road miles north of Juneau. This trail connects with the Echo Cove complex.

HAINES

Dalton Trail

Sadly neglected and now almost totally obliterated, this trail extended from the south side of Chilkat Flats, Haines to Dawson, approximately 400 miles north. Jack Dalton herded cattle over the route he discovered at the height of the gold rush.

GLACIER BAY

Bartlett Lake Trail

Recently relocated by the National Park Service, this trail now starts at the end of the Bartlett River trail (GB1). About 3 miles long, it goes through spruce forests to Bartlett Lake.

Wood Lake

Twenty-five air miles, 35 nautical miles west-northwest of Bartlett Cove. A short, maintained fishing trail of about 1.5 miles to Wood Lake. Starts on the south shoreline, close to the head of Geikie Inlet.

Dundas Bay

Twenty-two nautical miles to the entrance of Dundas Bay, west of Bartlett Cove. Highly recommended for canoe travel. Tidal waters are shallow, contain prolific wildlife. It is included as tidal wilderness in the National Park proposal.

RECOMMENDED READING

MOUNTAINEERING AND BACKPACKING

Ferber, Peggy, ed. *Mountaineering: The Freedom of the Hills.* Seattle: The Mountaineers, 1974.

Manning, Harvey. *Backpacking: One Step at a Time.* Seattle: REI Press, 1972.

Mitchell, Dick. *Mountaineering First Aid.* Seattle: The Mountaineers, 1972.

CANOEING

McNair, Robert E. *Basic River Canoeing.* Martinsville, Indiana: American Camping Association, Inc., 1968.

Urban, John T. *A White Water Handbook for Canoe and Kayak.* Boston: Appalachian Mountain Club, 1970.

U.S. Department of Commerce. *U.S. Coast Pilot, Pacific Coast; Dixon Entrance to Cape Spencer.* U.S. Government Printing Office, 1969 edition.

FLORA AND FAUNA

Dufresne, Frank. *Alaska's Animals and Fishes.* New York: A. S. Barnes and Co., 1946.

Heller, Christine. *Wild Flowers of Alaska.* Portland, Oregon: Graphic Arts Center, 1966.

Ricketts, Edward F., and Jack Calvin. *Between Pacific Tides.* Stanford, California: Stanford University Press, 1952.

Sharples, Ada White. *Alaska Wild Flowers.* Stanford, California: Stanford University Press, 1938.

Sudworth, George. *Forest Trees of the Pacific Slope.* U.S. Forest Service, U.S. Government Printing Office, 1908.

HISTORY

Andrews, C. L. *Story of Alaska.* Caldwell, Idaho: Caxton Printer, Ltd., 1943.

Burton, Pierre. *Klondike Fever.* New York: Alfred Knopf, 1958.

Chevigny, Hector. *Lord of Alaska.* Portland, Oregon: Binfords & Mort, 1951.

Colby, Merle. *A Guide to Alaska — Last Frontier.* Federal Writer's Project. New York: The Macmillan Co., 1942.

DeArmond, R. N. *Some Names Around Juneau.* Sitka, Alaska: Sitka Printing Co., 1957.

Morgan, Murray. *One Man's Gold Rush.* Seattle: University of Washington Press, 1967.

CONSERVATION

Bohn, Dave, *Glacier Bay, The Land and the Silence.* San Francisco: Sierra Club, 1967.

Cooley, Richard A. *Alaska, A Challenge in Conservation.* Madison: University of Wisconsin Press, 1967.

McClosky, Maxine. *Wilderness, The Edge of Knowledge.* San Francisco: Sierra Club, 1970.

Radford, George. *Alaska, The Embattled Frontier.* New York: Audubon Society with Houghton Mifflin, 1971.

GENERAL

Dufresne, Frank. *No Room for Bears.* New York: Holt, Rinehart and Winston, 1965.

Muir, John. *Travels in Alaska.* New York: Houghton Mifflin Co., 1915 (out of print).

Williams, Howel. *Landscapes of Alaska: Their Geologic Evolution.* Berkeley: University of California Press, 1958.

There are many other personal accounts of life in Southeast Alaska, too numerous to list here.

OTHER BOOKS FROM THE MOUNTAINEERS

Mountaineering: The Freedom of the Hills

Textbook for the Mountaineers Climbing Course, the new Third Edition carries on the tradition of being the standard in its field. Technical rock and ice climbing techniques and equipment updated, as well as first aid, rescue, and information on camping and hiking. Profusely illustrated with line drawings and photographs. 478 pages, 6″ × 9″, hardbound.

The Alpine Lakes

Superb, full-color presentation on the wilderness heart of Washington's Cascade Mountains. Ed Cooper and Bob Gunning, in 95 outstanding color photos, portray the area's mountains, forest trails, tarns, snowfields, granite cliffs. Text describes personal experiences in exploring the Alpine Lakes. 128 pages, 10″ × 13½″, hardbound.

Cascade Alpine Guide

Climbing and High Routes: Columbia River to Stevens Pass. First completely detailed climbing guide to the south Cascades; prepared by Fred Beckey. Includes extensive route coverage, plus approach-route material, data on Cascade geology, weather, and natural history. Over 100 pages of maps, sketches; photos with routes overprinted in red. 354 pages, 7″ × 8½″, flexible binding.

Climber's Guide to the Olympic Mountains

Covers every climbing and approach route on the Olympic peaks; also high alpine traverses, ski and snowshoe tours. Prepared by Olympic Mountain Rescue. 240 pages, 9 maps, 17 peak sketches with routes; flexible binding.

Routes and Rocks

Hiker's Guide to the North Cascades from Glacier Peak to Lake Chelan. Detailed descriptions of trails, off-trail high routes; with point-to-point mileages, elevations, campsites, notes on geology. By D. F. Crowder and R. W. Tabor, U.S.G.S. Plus four modified U.S.G.S. quad maps with overprint for routes, 240 pages, hardbound.

The Challenge of Rainier

Dee Molenaar's complete documentation of the climbing history of Mount Rainier, from the discovery years and the pioneering efforts to today's climbing parties. Personal anecdotes and word-portraits of guides through the various eras. Sketches, more than 100 photos, 7″ × 10″, hardbound.

Challenge of the North Cascades

Famed climber Fred Beckey, one of the first and more persistent explorers of the North Cascades, chronicles 30 years of adventures and climbs in a personal, highly readable style. 280 pages, 46 photos, 12 maps; hardbound.

Wildflowers of Mount Rainier and the Cascades

More than 100 full-color photos by Bob and Ira Spring of wildflowers, common and rare; authoritative text by Mary Fries. 220 pages, 7″ × 8½″, paperbound or hardbound.

Medicine for Mountaineering

Handbook for treating accidents, illnesses in remote areas. Compiled by climber-physicians, includes treatment of traumatic, environmental injuries; emphasizes high-altitude illnesses. 350 pages, 100 drawings, hardbound.

Mountaineering First Aid

A guide to accident response and first aid care; helpful for dealing with remote-area accidents, and preventing them. Excellent added text for outdoor safety, first aid classes. 96 pages, paperbound.

In the Hikes Series:

All detailed guides to trail or road-and-trail hikes, with complete descriptions, sketch maps, and scenic photos for each. Volumes are 7″ × 8½″, paperbound, approximately 200 pages each.

101 Hikes in the North Cascades
102 Hikes in the Alpine Lakes, South Cascades and Olympics
50 Hikes in Mount Rainier National Park
Trips and Trails, 1: Camps, Short Hikes and Viewpoints in the North Cascades and Olympics
Trips and Trails, 2: Family Camps, Short Hikes and View Roads in the South Cascades and Mt. Rainier
Footloose Around Puget Sound: 100 Walks on Beaches, Lowlands and Foothills
55 Ways to the Wilderness in Southcentral Alaska
103 Hikes in Southwestern British Columbia
Snowshoe Hikes in the Cascades and Olympics
Bicycling the Backroads Around Puget Sound

INDEX

SHORT TRAILS CLOSE TO FERRY, TOUR SHIP (OR AIRPORT IN JUNEAU), FOR THOSE WITH LIMITED TIME:

FULL DAY HIKE FROM TOUR SHIP, FERRY OR TOWN WITHOUT OTHER TRANSPORTATION:

TRAILS REQUIRING EXTRA TRANSPORTATION FROM TOWN, FERRY, TOUR SHIP, ETC.:

CANOE WILDERNESS:

WINTER TRAILS

TRAILS TO BE AVOIDED IN THE WINTER & EARLY SPRING

All trails classified as 'alpine' unless experienced in winter mountaineering.

OVERNIGHT TRAILS — OR LONGER

HISTORICAL TRAILS

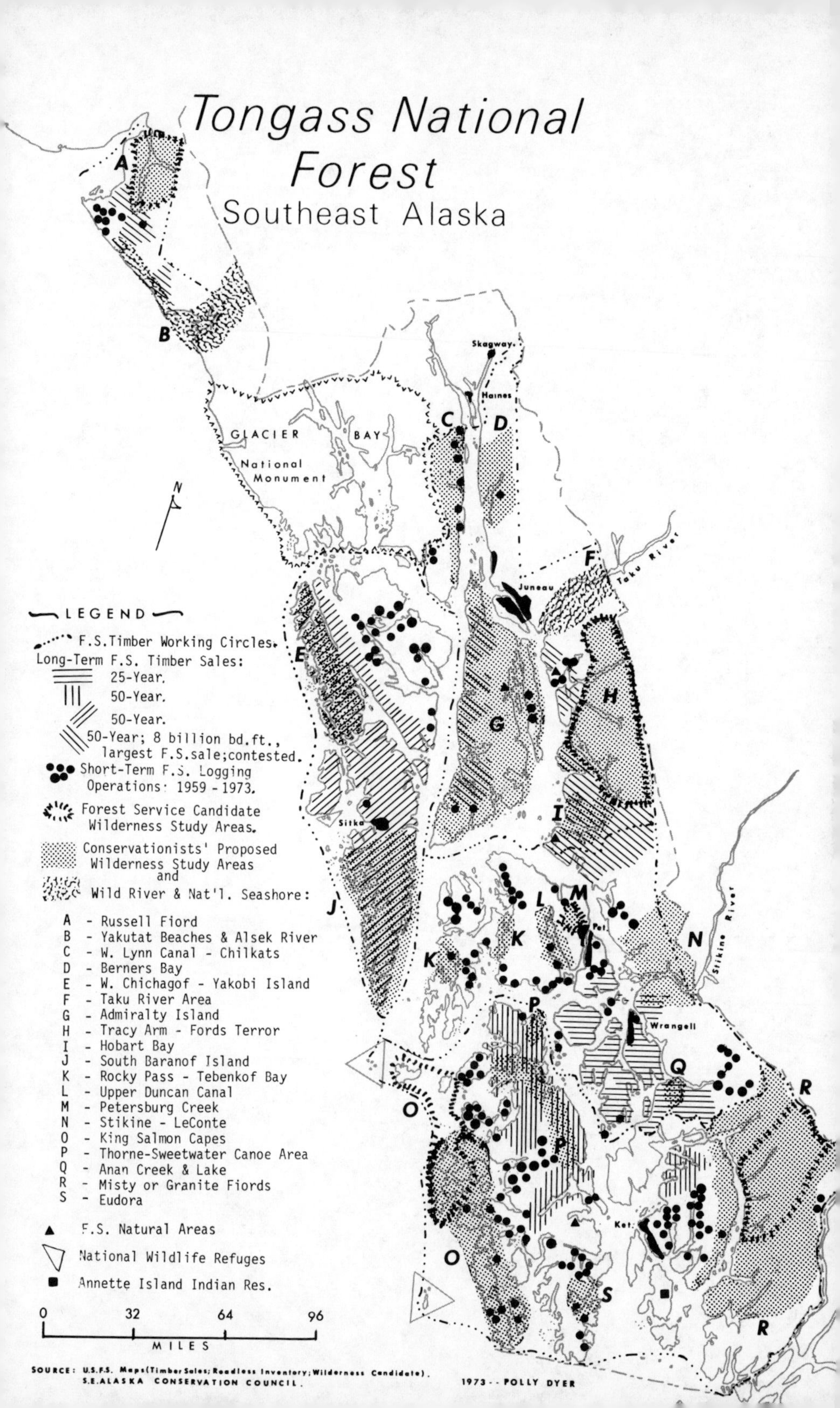
Tongass National Forest
Southeast Alaska
Skagway
Haines
GLACIER BAY
National Monument
Juneau
Taku River
Sitka
Pet.
Wrangell
Stikine River
Ket.
LEGEND
F.S.Timber Working Circles.
Long-Term F.S. Timber Sales:
25-Year.
50-Year.
50-Year.
50-Year; 8 billion bd.ft., largest F.S.sale;contested.
Short-Term F.S. Logging Operations: 1959 - 1973.
Forest Service Candidate Wilderness Study Areas.
Conservationists' Proposed Wilderness Study Areas and
Wild River & Nat'l. Seashore:
A - Russell Fiord
B - Yakutat Beaches & Alsek River
C - W. Lynn Canal - Chilkats
D - Berners Bay
E - W. Chichagof - Yakobi Island
F - Taku River Area
G - Admiralty Island
H - Tracy Arm - Fords Terror
I - Hobart Bay
J - South Baranof Island
K - Rocky Pass - Tebenkof Bay
L - Upper Duncan Canal
M - Petersburg Creek
N - Stikine - LeConte
O - King Salmon Capes
P - Thorne-Sweetwater Canoe Area
Q - Anan Creek & Lake
R - Misty or Granite Fiords
S - Eudora
F.S. Natural Areas
National Wildlife Refuges
Annette Island Indian Res.
0 32 64 96
MILES
SOURCE: U.S.F.S. Maps(Timber Sales; Roadless Inventory; Wilderness Candidate).
S.E.ALASKA CONSERVATION COUNCIL.
1973 - - POLLY DYER